The Chartered Institute of Marketing

Professional Certificate in Marketing

STUDY TEXT

Marketing Essentials

2010 edition

Second edition August 2010
First edition July 2008

ISBN 9780 7517 8935 5
(Previous ISBN 9780 7517 4862 8)
e-ISBN 9780 7517 9143 3

British Library Cataloguing-in-Publication Data
A catalogue record for this book
is available from the British Library

Published by

BPP Learning Media Ltd
Aldine House, Aldine Place
London W12 8AA

www.bpp.com/learningmedia

Printed in the United Kingdom

We are grateful to the Chartered Institute of Marketing for
permission to reproduce in this text the syllabus, tutor's
guidance notes and past examination questions..

Author: Kate Machattie
Photography: Terence O'Loughlin

Your learning materials, published by BPP Learning Media Ltd,
are printed on paper sourced from sustainable, managed
forests.

Contents

Introduction

• Aim of the Study Text • Studying for CIM qualifications • The Professional Certificate Syllabus • The CIM's Magic Formula • A guide to the features of the Study Text • A note on Pronouns • Additional resources • Your personal study plan v

Chapters

⑩ 1   Marketing and market orientation 1

⑨ 2   Relationships with customers and the community ....23 ✓

③ 3   The marketing planning process ....43 ✓

⑧ 4   The marketing audit ....59 ✓

① 5   Product planning ....77 ✓

② 6   Pricing ....103 ✓

④ 7   Channel decisions ....119 ✓

⑥ 8   Marketing communications ....137 ✓

⑤ 9   Services marketing ....165 ✓

⑦ 10 Measuring marketing effectiveness ....181 ✓

Key concepts   203

Index   205

Review form & free prize draw

1 Aim of the Study Text

This book has been deliberately referred to as a 'Study Text' rather than text book, because it is designed to help you though your specific CIM Professional Certificate studies. It covers Unit 1 Marketing Essentials.

So, why is it similar to but not actually a text book? Well, the CIM have identified key texts that you should become familiar with. The purpose of this workbook is not to replace these texts but to pick out the important parts that you will definitely need to know in order to pass, simplify these elements and, to suggest a few areas within the texts that will provide good additional reading but that are not absolutely essential. We will also suggest a few other sources and useful press and CIM publications which are worth reading.

We know some of you will prefer to read text books from cover to cover whilst others amongst you will prefer to pick out relevant parts or dip in and out of the various topics. This text will help you to ensure that if you are a 'cover to cover' type, then you will not miss the emphasis of the syllabus. If you are a 'dip in and out' type, then we will make sure that you find the parts which are essential for you to know. Unlike a standard text book which will have been written to be used across a range of alternative qualifications, this Study Text has been specifically written for your CIM course, so if a topic appears in this book then it is part of the syllabus and therefore will be a subject the examiners could potentially test. Throughout the study text you will find real examples of marketing in practice as well as key concepts highlighted.

2 Studying for CIM qualifications

There are a few key points to remember as you study for your CIM qualification:

(a)   You are studying for a **professional** qualification. This means that you are required to use professional language and adopt a business approach in your work.

(b)   You are expected to show that you have 'read widely'. Make sure that you read the quality press (and don't skip the business pages), read Marketing, The Marketer, Research and Marketing Week avidly.

(c)   Become aware of the marketing initiatives you come across on a daily basis, for example, when you go shopping look around and think about why the store layout is as it is, consider the messages, channel choice and timings of ads when you are watching TV. It is surprising how much you will learn just by taking an interest in the marketing world around you.

(d)   Get to know the way CIM write their exam papers and assignments. They use a specific approach called the Magic Formula to ensure a consistent approach when designing assessment materials. Make sure you are fully aware of this as it will help you interpret what the examiner is looking for (a full description of the Magic Formula appears later and is heavily featured within the chapters).

(e)   Learn how to use Harvard referencing. This is explained in detail in our CIM Professional Certificate Assessment Workbook.

(f)   Ensure that you read very carefully all assessment details sent to you from CIM. They are very strict with regard to deadlines, completing the correct paperwork to accompany any assignment or project and making sure you have your CIM membership card with you at the exam. Failing to meet any assessment entry deadlines or completing written work on time will mean that you will have to wait for the next round of assessment dates and will need to pay the relevant assessment fees again.

3 The Professional Certificate Syllabus

The Professional Certificate in Marketing is aimed at anyone who is employed in supporting marketing role such as Marketing Co-ordinator or Executive. You may also be a manager with a senior role within in a small or medium sized company where marketing only forms part of a wider work remit. Or you may be looking to move into your first marketing role or to specialise.

The aim of the qualification is to provide a strong foundation of marketing knowledge. You will develop the breadth of knowledge of marketing theory but also appreciate issues faced within the organisation as CIM qualifications concentrate on applied marketing within real work-places.

The complete qualification is made from four units:

- Unit 1 Marketing Essentials
- Unit 2 Assessing the Marketing Environment
- Unit 3 Marketing Information and Research
- Unit 4 Stakeholder Marketing

CIM stipulate that each module should take 40 guided learning hours to complete. Guided learning hours refer to time in class, using distance learning materials and completing any work set by your tutor. Guided learning hours do not include the time it will take you to complete the necessary reading for your studies.

The syllabus as provided by CIM can be found below with reference to our coverage within this Study Text.

Unit characteristics

The aim of this unit is to provide a detailed explanation of the key theories and practice behind marketing as an exchange process and a business function, but also as a means of creating customer value in the short to medium term. This unit introduces individuals to the importance of the marketing planning process and the role of marketing across the organisation.

The unit also aims to provide knowledge of the key marketing tools to support an innovative range of marketing activities. Students will be taught the nature and implications of the use of marketing tools as both independent tools and tools that are often integrated to maximise the impact of the marketing proposition.

On completion, students should be able to explain how to utilise all elements of the marketing mix and how they can be co-ordinated to create a value proposition that reflects the organisation's objectives.

Overarching learning outcomes

By the end of this unit, students should be able to:

- Explain how marketing has evolved and the importance of market orientation in creating customer value

- Assess the importance of marketing, its cross-functional role and the contribution it makes to the organisation and society

- Identify and explain the stages in the marketing planning process

- Assess the key elements of the internal and external marketing environment that impact upon the organisation, its objectives and its activities

- Identify and describe the characteristics and applications of each element of the marketing mix (7Ps)

SECTION 1 – The nature and scope of marketing (weighting 25%)

		Covered in chapter(s)
1.1	Explain the evolution of market orientation: • Product orientation • Production orientation • Sales orientation • Market versus marketing orientation	1
1.2	Assess the contribution of marketing as a means of: • Creating customer value • Creating and responding to competition	1
1.3	Appreciate the different characteristics of a market-oriented approach to business: • An exchange process • A philosophy of business • A managerial function • A dynamic operation, requiring analysis, planning and action • A catalyst for change	1
1.4	Identify and evaluate the factors that may make market orientation difficult to achieve within the organisation: • Lack of committed leadership and vision • Lack of customer knowledge • Lack of infrastructure eg, technology • Autocratic leadership • Conflict between marketing and other functions • Preference for production or sales focus • Transactional approach to business	1
1.5	Explain the cross-functional role of marketing and its importance to organisational performance: • The importance of internal relationships and information sharing • The setting and achievement of common and realistic goals • Establishing common information and control systems • Establishing clear company policies in relation to products, branding, production, etc • The role of marketing as an internal service provider for other business departments • Contribution of marketing to the development of the business strategy	1
1.6	Evaluate the impact of marketing actions on consumers, society and the environment, and the need for marketers to act in an ethical and socially responsible manner: • Ethical codes of practice for marketers (CIM Code of Practice) • Corporate Social Responsibility as a cultural value • Corporate citizenship – upholding the law and behaving responsibly • Social awareness of key marketing issues relating to social causes • Societal marketing	2

		Covered in chapter(s)
1.7	Explain the significance of buyer-seller relationships in marketing and comprehend the role of relationship marketing in facilitating the attraction and retention of customers: • Benefits of customer retention • Drawbacks of customer defection • Relationship management in B2B and B2C • The link between degrees of customer loyalty and long-term organisational stability and growth • The role of technology in enhancing or undermining relationships and thereby affecting retention	2

SECTION 2 – Planning within the marketing context (weighting 25%)

		Covered in chapter(s)
2.1	Explain the importance of objectives, the processes for setting them and the influences upon them: • Objectives as a basis for determining future direction, consistency, motivation and measurement • Objectives as a basis for determining achievement • SMART Objectives (Specific, Measurable, Achievable, Realistic, Timebound) • Internal and external influences on setting objectives	3
2.2	Identify the different types of organisational objectives: • Profit • Sales/Revenue • Marketing • Growth e.g. market share • Technical – technology innovation • Survival • Ethically and socially responsible	3
2.3	Evaluate the importance of the marketing planning process to the market oriented organisation. Using a marketing plan as a means of: • Delivering strategies and achieving objectives • Implementing a marketing project • Monitoring of timeline progress against schedule • Managing implementation • Resource management (human and physical) • Financial management • Measurement of successful implementation	3
2.4	Explain the different stages of the marketing planning process: • Corporate objectives/business mission • Marketing audit • Setting business and marketing objectives • Marketing strategies • Marketing tactics/mix decisions • Implementation • Monitoring and control	3

2.5	Explain the concept of the marketing audit as an appraisal of:	4
	• The internal and external environment	
	• Organisational strengths, weaknesses, opportunities and threats	
	• Organisational competencies and capabilities	
	• Organisational resource versus an organisation's capacity to deliver	
	• Competitor analysis	

SECTION 3 – The marketing mix (weighting 50%)

		Covered in chapter(s)
3.1	Explain and illustrate the principles of product and planning:	5
	• Branding	
	• Product lines/ranges (depth and breadth)	
	• Packaging eg, sustainability, design eg, re-cyclying	
	• Service support	
3.2	Explain the concept of the Product Life Cycle, (PLC) and its limitations as a tool for assessing the life of the product/services:	5
	• Development	
	• Introduction	
	• Growth	
	• Maturity	
	• Decline	
	• Obsolescence	
	• Limitations including failure of the product to succeed/no measurable outcome	
3.3	Explain the importance of new products and services into the market:	5
	• Changing customer needs	
	• Digital revolution	
	• Long-term business strategies	
3.4	Explain the different stages of the process of New Product Development:	5
	• Idea generation	
	• Screening new ideas	
	• Concept testing	
	• Business analysis	
	• Product development	
	• Test marketing	
	• Commercialisation and launch	
3.5	Explain the importance of price as an element of the marketing mix:	6
	• Brings together the marketing mix elements to fulfill customer needs	
	• Income, revenue and profit generation	
	• Contributing to the organisation's business and financial objectives	
	• Limitations of price as a competitive tool	

3.6	Identify and illustrate a range of different pricing approaches that are adopted by organisations as effective means of competition:	6

- Absorption costing
- Cost base and marginal costing
- Cost Plus
- Price skimming
- Penetration pricing
- Loss-leader
- Promotional pricing

3.7	Define the different channels of distribution, and the role they play in a coordinated marketing mix:	7

- Wholesaling
- Retailing
- Direct marketing
- Internet marketing
- Vending
- Telephone selling
- Franchising
- Digital/e-channels

3.8	Explain the factors that influence channel decisions and the selection of alternative distribution channels:	7

- Multiple channels
- Location of customers
- Compatibility
- Nature of the goods/services
- Geographic/environmental/terrain
- Storage and distribution costs
- Import/export costs

3.9	Evaluate a range of marketing communications tools that comprise the marketing communications mix and consider their impact in different contexts:	8

- Direct Response Advertising
- Personal selling
- Sponsorship
- Public relations
- Direct marketing
- Sales promotions
- Digital technologies
- Website

3.10	Evaluate the range of marketing communications media and consider their impact in different contexts: • TV • Cinema • Bill Boards • Press • Magazine • Web-advertising • Sales promotions	8
3.11	Explain the importance of a coordinated services marketing mix, its characteristics and implications for the marketing of service products: • Coordinated approach to people, physical evidence and process • Characteristics/implications: inseparability, intangibility, variability, perishability and non-ownership	9
3.12	Explain the different methods used for measuring the success of marketing activities: • Budget measurement • Objectives attained • Sales/revenue, profit/loss • Efficiency/effectiveness • Zero defects/returns • Customer service complaints • Increased awareness and changing attitudes • Repeat purchase and loyalty	10
3.13	Explain the process of product and service adoption explaining the characteristics of customers at each stage of adoption: • Innovators • Early Adopters • Early majority • Late majority • Laggards	5
3.14	Explain the concept of developing a coordinated approach to the marketing mix, as a means to satisfying customers' requirements and competing effectively: • Designing a mix which is compatible and co-ordinated effectively • Being mindful of the target market, their needs and expectations • Being mindful of tactical competitive activities • Being mindful of the impact of other elements of the marketing mix	10

The unit covered by this Study Text (Unit 1 Marketing Essentials) is assessed in a three hour formal examination. In order to help you revise and prepare for the exam we have also written a Professional Certificate in Marketing Assessment Workbook which is available either through your usual book retailer or our website www.bpp.com/learningmedia.

4 The Magic Formula

The Magic Formula is a tool used by CIM to help both examiners write exam and assignment questions and you to more easily interpret what you are being asked to write about. It is useful for helping you to check that you are using an appropriate balance between theory and practice for your particular level of qualification.

Contrary to the title, there is nothing mystical about the Magic Formula and simply by knowing it (or even mentioning it in an assessment) will not automatically secure a pass. What it does do however is to help you to check that you are presenting your answers in an appropriate format, including enough marketing theory and applying it to a real marketing context or issue. After passing the Professional Certificate in Marketing, if you continue to study for higher level CIM qualifications, you would be expected to evaluate more and apply a more demanding range of marketing decisions. As such the Magic Formula is weighted with an even greater emphasis on evaluation and application as you move to the Professional Diploma and Postgraduate CIM levels.

Graphically, the Magic Formula for the Professional Certificate in Marketing is shown below:

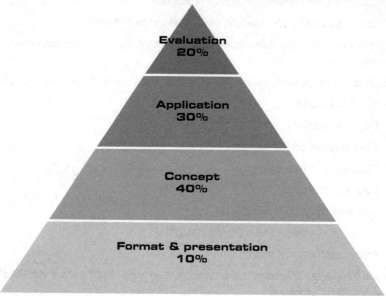

Figure 1 The Magic Formula for the Professional Certificate in Marketing

You can see from the pyramid that for the Professional Certificate marks are awarded in the following proportions:

- ## Presentation and format – 10%

  Remember you are expected to present your work professionally which means that it should ALWAYS be typed and attention should be paid to making it look as visually appealing as possible even in an exam situation. It also means that CIM will stipulate the format that you should present your work in. The assessment formats you will be given will be varied and can include things like reports to write, slides to prepare, emails, memos, formal letters, press releases, discussion documents, briefing papers, agendas, and newsletters.

- ## Concept – 40%

  Concept refers to your ability to state, recall and describe marketing theory. The definition of marketing is a core CIM syllabus topic. If we take this as an example, you would be expected to recognise, recall, and write this definition to a word perfect standard to gain the full marks for concept. Understanding marketing concepts is clearly the main area where marks will be given within your assessment.

- ## Application – 30%

  Application based marks are given for your ability to apply marketing theories to real life marketing situations. For example, you may be asked to discuss the definition of marketing, and how it is applied within your own organisation. Within this sort of question 40% of the marks would have been awarded within the 'concept' aspect of the Magic Formula. You will gain the rest of the marks through your ability to evaluate to what extent the concept is applied within your own organisation. Here you are not only using the definition but are applying it in order to consider the market orientation of the company.

- ## Evaluation – 20%

  Evaluation is the ability to asses the value or worth of something sometimes through careful consideration of related advantages and disadvantages or weighing up of alternatives. Results from your evaluation should enable you to discuss the importance of an issue using evidence to support your opinions.

  Using the example of you being asked whether or not your organisation adopts a marketing approach. If you were asked to 'evaluate' this, you should provide reasons and specific examples of why you think they might take this approach as well as considering why they may not take this approach before coming to a final conclusion.

5 A guide to the features of the Study Text

Each of the chapter features (see below) will help you to break down the content into manageable chunks and ensure that you are developing the skills required for a professional qualification.

Chapter feature	Relevance and how you should use it	Corresponding icon
Chapter topic list	Study the list: each numbered topic denotes a numbered section in the chapter	–
Introduction	Shows why topics need to be studied and is a route guide through the chapter	–
Syllabus linked Learning Objectives	Outlines what you should learn within the chapter based on what is required within the syllabus	–
Format & Presentation	Outlines a key marketing presentation format with reference to the Magic Formula	10%
Concept	A key concept to learn with reference to the Magic Formula	40%
Application	An example of applied marketing with reference to the Magic Formula	30%
Evaluation	An example of evaluation with reference to the Magic Formula	20%
Activity	An application based activity for you to complete	✏
Key text links	Emphasises key parts to read in a range of other texts and other learning resources	📚
Marketing at work	A short case study to illustrate marketing practice	NEWS
Exam tip	Key advice based on the assessment	✓
Quick quiz	Use this to check your learning	
Objective check	Use this to review what you have learnt	

6 A note on Pronouns

On occasions in this Study Text, 'he' is used for 'he or she', 'him' for 'him or her' and so forth. Whilst we try to avoid this practice it is sometimes necessary for reasons of style. No prejudice or stereotyping according to sex is intended or assumed.

7 Additional resources

7.1 CIM's supplementary reading list

We have already mentioned that CIM requires you to demonstrate your ability to 'read widely'. CIM issue an extensive reading list for each unit. For this unit they recommend supplementary reading. Within the Study Text we have highlighted in the wider reading links to specific topics where these resources will help. CIM's supplementary reading list for this unit is:

Blythe, J. (2005) Essentials of marketing communications. 3rd edition. Harlow, Prentice Hall.

Fill, C. (2006) Simply marketing communications. Harlow, FT/Prentice Hall.

Jobber, D. (2006) Principles and practice of marketing. 5th edition. Maidenhead, McGraw-Hill.

McDonald, M. (2007) Malcolm McDonald on marketing planning. London, Kogan Page.

Palmer, A. (2008) Principles of services marketing. 5th edition. Maidenhead, McGraw-Hill.

Smith, P. and Taylor, T. (2004) Marketing communications: an integrated approach.
4th edition. London, Kogan Page.

Worthington, I. and Britton, C. (2006) Business environment. 5th edition. Harlow, FT/Prentice Hall.

7.2 Assessment preparation materials from BPP Learning Media

To help you pass the entire Professional Certificate in Marketing we have created a complete study package. The **Professional Certificate Assessment Workbook** covers all four units for the Professional Certificate level. Practice question and answers, tips on tackling assignments and work-based projects are included to help you succeed in your assessments.

Our A6 set of spiral bound **Passcards** are handy revision cards, ideal to reinforce key topics for the Marketing Essentials and Assessing the Marketing Environment exams.

8 Your personal study plan

Preparing a Study Plan (and sticking to it) is one of the key elements to learning success.

CIM have stipulated that there should be a minimum of 40 guided learning hours spent on each unit. Guided learning hours will include time spent in lessons, working on fully prepared distance learning materials, formal workshops and work set by your tutor. We also know that to be successful, students should spend *at least* an additional 40 hours conducting self study. This means that for the entire qualification with four units you should spend 160 hours working in a tutor guided manner and at least an additional 160 hours completing recommended reading, working on assignments, and revising for exams. This study text will help you to organise this 40 hour portion of self study time.

Now think about the exact amount of time you have (don't forget you will still need some leisure time!) and complete the following tables to help you keep to a schedule.

	Date	Duration in weeks
Course start		
Course finish		Total weeks of course:
Examination date	Revision to commence	Total weeks to complete revision:

Content chapter coverage plan

Chapter	To be completed by	Revised ?
1 Marketing and market orientation		
2 Relationships with customers and the community		
3 The marketing planning process		
4 The marketing audit		
5 Product planning		
6 Pricing		
7 Channel decisions		
8 Marketing communications		
9 Services marketing		
10 Measuring marketing effectiveness		

Chapter 1

Marketing and market orientation

Topic list

1   The development of marketing
2   The contribution of marketing
3   Market orientation: a philosophy
4   Marketing as a managerial function

Introduction

This chapter introduces the concept of marketing and defines marketing as an exchange process. 'Market'-ing, quite obviously, is to do with markets. Originally a market was a physical place, where buyers and sellers met up and exchanged things, so that they both got what they needed: a sheep in exchange for three bags of corn, say.

A market today is not really much different, except that buyers and sellers do not necessarily need to meet in person (or even live on the same continent), and it is easier to carry money around than bags of corn or sheep.

However, this simple chore of going to market to satisfy basic needs and exchange wares has evolved into a marketing concept that many would argue dictates all the actions and the philosophy of a modern business organisation. We will focus upon the CIM's definition of marketing and what it implies for the organisation, its customers and suppliers.

This chapter examines the development and contribution of marketing as both a philosophy of business and a managerial function. When properly analysed and planned, marketing should involve cross functional activities to ensure that the organisation is working to meet overall business aims and promote customer satisfaction. This requires good working relationships between the marketing function and other key departments.

Syllabus linked learning objectives

By the end of the chapter you will be able to:

Learning objectives	Syllabus link
1 Explain the evolution of market orientation	1.1
2 Assess the contribution of marketing	1.2
3 Appreciate the different characteristics of a market-oriented approach to business	1.3
4 Identify and evaluate the factors that may make market orientation difficult to achieve within the organisation	1.4
5 Explain the cross-functional role of marketing and its importance to organisational performance	1.5

1 The development of marketing

1.1 Definitions

"For some people, marketing is about managing exchange. For others, it is about meeting customer needs at a profit (or in ways which lead to other organisational objectives). For others, marketing is everything that businesses do, and for yet others marketing is what marketers do. All these definitions have some degree of truth in them." Blythe, J. (2009) Principles and Practice of Marketing, . Try to look through a variety of different basic marketing texts in your local library. You will see a range of alternatives. ■

To begin, here are some formal definitions of modern marketing.

KEY CONCEPT   Concept

'**Marketing** is the management process responsible for identifying, anticipating and satisfying customer requirements profitably.' (CIM: www.cim.co.uk)

'Marketing is the process of planning and executing the conception, pricing, promotion, and distribution of ideas, goods, and services to create exchanges that satisfy individual and organisational objectives.' (American Marketing Association: www.marketingpower.com)

'Marketing consists of individual and organisational activities that facilitate and expedite satisfying exchange relationships in a dynamic environment through the creation, distribution, promotion and pricing of goods, services and ideas.' (Dibb, Simkin, Pride and Ferrell, 2005).

These definitions have several key points in common.

- They make it clear that there has to be some motivation for the selling organisation such as **'profit'** or, more broadly, satisfied **'organisational objectives'**.
- They stress the importance of **customer satisfaction**, making marketing a **'mutual exchange'** between buyer and seller.
- They see marketing as a process that is **planned and managed**.

There are also some subtle differences, most notably the reference to 'enhancing long-term customer relationships' in the third definition: this is of great importance in the latest ideas about relationship marketing.

ACTIVITY 1   Application

The CIM definition of marketing has been criticised because it focuses heavily upon 'profit' as the key outcome of marketing, and for treating customers as passive participants in the process of promoting and purchasing goods and services. Is such criticism justified?

1.2 The development of marketing

Marketing grew out of **exchange** (in other words, 'markets').

- In early societies trade is by **barter**: exchanging goods for other goods.
- When a society becomes capable of producing more than is necessary for individual survival (a **surplus**), the extra can be **traded** for other goods and services.
- And as societies develop, trade takes place using an agreed medium of exchange, usually **money**.

The production of goods before the industrial revolution was usually small-scale and aimed at local customers. Buyers and sellers had **direct contact**, which made it easy for sellers to find their buyers' needs and wants. There was no real need for marketing in the modern sense.

This began to change due to a number of factors: Figure 1.1.

Figure 1.1: Factors in the growth of marketing

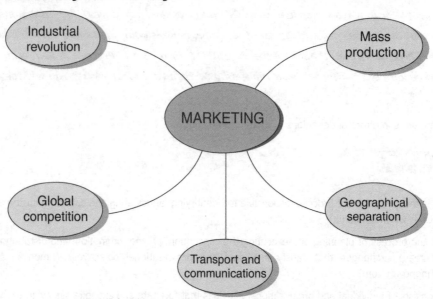

During the **industrial revolution** (18th and 19th centuries), production became organised into larger units. As towns grew bigger, producers and the people they sold to began to be geographically separated. However, until the early 20th century the primary consideration was to **produce enough** of a product to satisfy strong demand. Thinking about 'customer needs' was secondary.

Mass production techniques have increased the volume and range of goods on the market. For most products and services the ability now exists to produce much more than is demanded. Meanwhile developments in transportation and communications have made it possible to reach buyers in any part of the world.

Simple **mass marketing techniques** were first used in the 1950s for fast-moving consumer goods (FMCG) such as washing powder and groceries. The focus switched from 'how to produce and supply enough' to 'how to increase demand'. Marketing techniques, and marketing as a **managerial function**, grew out of this switch.

MARKETING AT WORK

 Application

Topping the list in a book of 'The 100 Most Influential People Who Never Lived' is the Marlboro Man – a 1950s marketing creation to increase demand and boost cigarette sales. Only characters that have helped to 'shape society, change our behaviour and set the course of history' made the list.

http//news.bbc.co.uk (accessed 27 April 2008)

Marketing techniques – and marketing departments – have grown in importance as **competition** (that is, consumer choice) and **geographical separation** have increased. From concentrating on advertising and sales, marketing methods have become wide-ranging, complex and scientific.

Modern marketing is about identifying ever-changing customer needs in a global market and continually creating products that satisfy those needs.

Many organisations have adopted this as the philosophy that drives all of their business functions.

1.3 The nature of exchange

For a **profit-making organisation**, the exchange of mutual benefits will be an exchange of products/services (supplied to customers) for money (supplied by customers in payment) and other resources (such as customer feedback information). This is not the only type of exchange.

Government units, charities, churches and other **voluntary/not-for-profit** organisations are also now seen as engaging in marketing. In such organisations, the nature of the exchange is different. Services, advocacy, membership and other features such as information are supplied to a variety of 'customers' (or **stakeholders**) in exchange for a range of returns: allegiance, volunteer labour, donations, information and other benefits.

So it can be seen that the concept of 'exchange' exists where something of value (a product or service) is obtained from another party, by offering something else of value – this could be money or another product or service in a barter agreement.

1.4 Models of marketing

There are four key models of marketing.

Sales support

The emphasis in this role is essentially reactive: marketing supports the direct sales force. It may include activities such as telesales or telemarketing, responding to inquiries, co-ordinating diaries, customer database management, organising exhibitions or other sales promotions, and administering sales agents. These activities normally come under a sales and marketing manager. This form of marketing is common in small or medium size enterprises (SMEs) and some organisations operating in a B2B context.

Marketing communications

The emphasis in this role is more proactive: marketing promotes the organisation and its product or service at a tactical level, either to customers ('pull') or to distributors ('push'). It typically includes activities such as providing brochures and catalogues to support the sales force. Some B2C organisations may use marketing to perform the selling role using direct marketing techniques, and to manage campaigns aimed at raising awareness, generating leads and taking orders. In B2B markets, larger organisations may have marketing communications departments and specialists to make efficient use of marketing expenditures and to co-ordinate communications between business units.

Operational marketing

The primary role of operational marketing is to support the organisation's business or corporate objectives and strategies. Marketers at this level may influence the culture of the organisation to ensure that it has a strong customer focus.

The emphasis in this role is for marketing to support and guide the policies of the organisation with a co-ordinated range of marketing activities including marketing research, brand management, product development and management, corporate and marketing communications and customer relationship management. Planning is also usually performed in this role, making decisions about resource utilisation and the selection of the most appropriate marketing tools – brands, innovation, customer service, alliances, distribution channels and price.

Strategic marketing

The emphasis in this role is on marketing being a contributor to the creation of business strategy. As such, it is practised in customer-focused and larger organisations. In a large or diversified organisation, it may also be responsible for the co-ordination of the activities of several specialist marketing departments (research, communications etc).

The models of marketing described above can all be linked in some way to its 'cross functional' role – take note of the syllabus where it lists the following.

- The importance of internal relationships and information sharing

- The setting and achievement of common and realistic goals

- Establishing common information and control systems

- Establishing clear company policies in relation to products, branding, production, etc

- The role of marketing as an internal service provider for other business departments

- Contribution of marketing to the development of the business strategy

2 The contribution of marketing

 "The philosophical idea underlying all marketing thought is that corporate success comes from satisfying customer needs. The idea of placing customers at the centre of everything the company does is basic to marketing thought: this idea of customer centrality is the key concept in marketing."
Blythe, J. (2009).

2.1 Creating customer value

In order to make profits businesses obtain inputs (resources) from the environment and transform them into outputs to the environment. The diagram below illustrates this process.

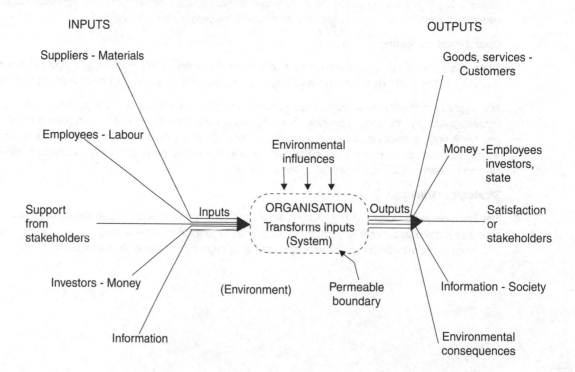

Inputs

- Materials, components and sub-components
- Labour
- Money
- Information and ideas
- Tangible property

Transformation processes

- Using people and machinery to make goods such as cars
- The provision of services (eg transport)
- The creation of knowledge to be more efficient

Outputs

- Goods and/or services
- Money (dividends, interest, wages)
- Information
- Environmental consequences of its activities (eg pollution, increased traffic)
- Social consequences of its activities

Sometimes this is known as the process of adding value. In other words the process of transformation ensures that the outputs are worth more in the customers' estimation than the inputs.

There are two points to note here.

(a) Customers **purchase value**, which they measure by comparing a firm's products and services with similar offerings by competitors.

(b) The business **creates value** by carrying out its activities either more efficiently than other businesses, or combined in such a way as to provide a unique product or service.

Marketing aims to make sure that the customer **values** an organisation and what it has to offer. How does it do this? It makes sure that the customer knows that the organisation produces the products or services the customer wants to buy, at a price they are prepared to pay, in a place that is mutually convenient.

Marketing also **adds value** to the customer's **experience** of the organisation's offering: giving them products that satisfy their needs better; enhancing sales and after-sales service; helping them make better buying decisions and making purchasing easier and more enjoyable.

 MARKETING AT WORK Application

Creating value for the customer, making his experience easier and more enjoyable, is vitally important – in the words of Sam Walton, founder of WalMart stores: 'There is only one boss – the customer. And he can fire everybody in the company from the chairman on down, simply by spending his money somewhere else.'

2.1.1 The four Ps

Marketing mix variables are traditionally expressed in a highly memorable form called **'the Four Ps'**: Product, Price, Place and Promotion.

These four variables are at the heart of all aspects of marketing. They have been supplemented by three extra service marketing variables: People, Process and Physical Evidence, to make up the 7Ps referred to in the overarching learning outcomes.

The complete ('extended') marketing mix can be illustrated as follows: Figure 1.2

Figure 1.2: The extended marketing mix

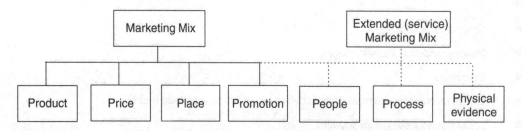

The ways in which marketing **adds value** – both for the **marketing organisation** and for the **customer** – through the 4Ps can be summarised as follows. They are examined in greater detail in Chapters 5 to 8 of this Text.

Four Ps	How marketing creates value
Product (Chapter 5)	Marketing undertakes various kinds of product and market research about customers' needs and wants. This generates ideas for **product improvements** and **new products**, either extending the existing product range, or meeting a previously unrecognised need. This adds value to the *business* (by enhancing its offering) and adds value for *customers* (by meeting their needs and preferences).
Price (Chapter 6)	Some products are valued because they are cheap (low-cost phone calls), some because they are expensive (designer-label clothes). Marketing adds value for the *business* by researching how buyers **perceive prices** for different goods and enabling the organisation to **target** its goods or services appropriately. Price decisions add value for *customers* by offering value for money, rewards for bulk or repeat purchases and esteem value.
Place (Chapter 7)	This is more usually called **distribution** or **logistics**. Marketing adds value for the *business* by getting goods and services to market reliably and efficiently. It adds value for *customers* by creating a comfortable and convenient place to buy, in the case of a supermarket or restaurant. Or it invents new ways of displaying goods and getting them into people's homes, in the case of e-commerce sites such as Amazon.com.
Promotion (Chapter 8)	Also called **marketing communications**, this includes a vast array of techniques, from media advertising to personal selling (the sales force) to direct mail to public relations. Promotion adds value to the *business* by securing demand for its offering, building customer loyalty, promoting a positive image (for its brands and for the organisation as an employer). It adds value for *customers* by making sure that they can make well-informed **buying decisions**, are rewarded for their loyalty and are able to feel good about their purchases.

Why do you think the term 'mix' is used, when talking about these 'marketing mix variables'?

2.2 Marketing as a form of competition

Marketing must also aim to make sure that customers value an organisation and what it has to offer *more highly* than they value the other organisations who are after their money too. This means 'doing your Ps' better than anyone else!

Four Ps	Marketing as a form of competition
Product	Marketing keeps a close eye on the products of competitors, finds out why customers prefer (or do not prefer) them, and aims to produce better quality, better targeted or more highly differentiated products.
Price	The competitive element is highly important in setting price. If your product is regarded as the same in all respects as a competitor's but is cheaper, then the chances are yours will be preferred – in theory! However, you may also compete on the basis of perceived *quality*, in which case your offering may be 'reassuringly expensive'.
Place	An organisation may aim to deliver goods faster than its competitors or give a cast-iron guarantee to deliver within a specific time, or deliver in a more convenient way (eg purchase online or by phone), or in a more pleasant environment. Competition can actually be a *determinant* of place. For instance, several different car dealers often set up showrooms in the same street, because that means that customers are more likely to come to that street to look at cars in the first place.
Promotion	Marketing communications have a key role in *informing* customers about the competitive features of products and services. They also compete themselves: more effective advertisements, more highly skilled sales people, more attractive free gifts, better press coverage, more effective website or sponsorship of a more prominent sports event.

3 Market orientation: a philosophy

"The marketing concept did not arrive fully formed. It is popularly supposed to have developed through a series of business orientations." Blythe, J. (2009).

We saw earlier that the historical trend has been for organisations to move from a focus on producing as much as possible to a focus on producing what the market *wants*. In other words, organisations have become increasingly **market oriented**. The stages of development – production orientation, product orientation, sales orientation and marketing orientation – are described in this section.

3.1 Different ways of doing business

The **marketing concept** holds that 'achieving organisational goals depends on determining the needs and wants of target markets and delivering the desired satisfactions more effectively and efficiently than competitors' (Kotler, 2008).

This concept can be contrasted with other concepts (or 'orientations') by which organisations conceive, conduct and co-ordinate their marketing activities.

Concept	Focus	Means	Aims
Marketing orientation	Customer needs and wants; long-term customer relationships	Integrated marketing activities	Profitability through customer satisfaction
Selling orientation	Existing products made by the firm; creating sales transactions	Energetic selling and promoting	Profitability through sales volume
Production orientation	Assumed customer demand for product availability and affordability	Improving production and distribution efficiency	Profitability through efficiency
Product orientation	Assumed customer demand for product quality, performance and features	Continuous product improvements	Profitability through product quality

The activities and philosophy of **market oriented** companies contrast sharply with **production oriented** and **sales oriented** organisations.

 KEY CONCEPT    Concept

An organisation that follows a **marketing orientation** is one which implements the marketing concept - first of all by determining what customers want, and then setting about providing those goods or services which meet customers' wants and needs (at the right price, at the right time, at the right place) and communicating effectively with these customers. The organisation will do this in a way consistent with achieving its own objectives, but always with the customer at the forefront.

Figure 1.3: Market orientation compared to other orientations

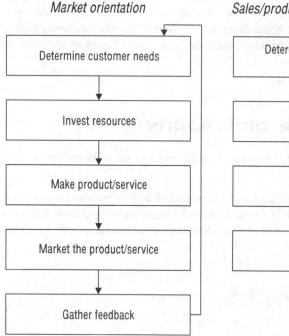

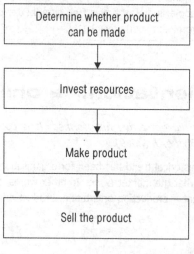

3.1.1 Production orientation

KEY CONCEPT

The emphasis with a **production orientation** is upon making products that are affordable and available – efficiency of production processes is the key.

This usually prevails in conditions where demand exceeds supply.

MARKETING AT WORK

The production orientation is epitomised by the famous comment attributed to Henry Ford about his Model T car, which customers could buy in 'any colour, so long as it's black'. In order to keep the production process as fast as possible, all cars needed to be the same colour – and black was the fastest-drying paint.

Whether or not Ford really made the comment, the point remains that it was inconvenient for his company's production process to make cars in colours other than black. The customer's wishes were unimportant because there was no competition and the customers had no choice.

Of course, at any particular point in time all organisations still offer their customers only what they are capable of producing (at a profit). But in the modern world, if Organisation A cannot quickly learn to produce the equivalent of a Model T in pink (because that is what customers want to buy) then Organisation B will come along, with better knowledge and/or better technology, and take their place.

3.1.2 Product orientation

KEY CONCEPT

A **product orientation** is found in a 'product-led' organisation which concentrates on the product itself and tends to de-emphasise other elements of the marketing mix. It takes the view that if the product is right it will sell itself.

There are also still many companies that have a product orientation, based on the illusion that because an idea looks good to the producer it will satisfy the customer. To an extent this is understandable. The producers are usually people who have a deep love of the product and an in-depth understanding of its qualities, and the effort it takes to make it: who better, in theory, to judge?

It is all too easy, however, to become blinkered by the beauty of your own product. Most people who buy electric drills do not really want an electric drill at all: what they want is holes! If there were some easier, safer way of making holes than by using an electric drill, the electric drill market would disappear.

ACTIVITY 3

Did you buy this book because you wanted something to read? Or was it because you want to pass your *Marketing Essentials* exam? What did you really want?

3.1.3 Sales orientation

KEY CONCEPT

A **sales orientation** is found in a 'sales-led' organisation is one where the selling function is dominant. It is typically found where capacity exceeds demand and where the organisational aim is to sell what it makes rather than what the market wants.

Sales oriented organisations make the product first, and then try to sell it. Underlying this philosophy is a belief that a good sales force can sell just about anything to anybody, and that sales 'transactions' rather than customer 'relationships' are the key to business success.

3.2 Market orientation

A market oriented organisation avoids the problems of short-term sales-focused relationships with potentially indifferent or resistant customers.

- It **focuses** on meeting the needs of customers, which have been clearly identified and fully understood.

- Its **structure** and **processes** are designed to meet the needs of customers.

- All activities are **co-ordinated** around the needs of the customer.

Underlying all of this is the belief that a market orientation is fundamental to the **continuation** and **competitiveness** of the organisation. When customers' needs change, as they surely will, or whenever better solutions emerge that more closely meet customers' needs, the organisation **adapts and responds**. Otherwise the organisation does not survive.

The marketing concept, as the basic philosophy that underpins modern corporate strategy, is now widely accepted. How far it is actually put into practice in different organisations still depends very much on the power and interests of different stakeholders in the organisation. Stakeholder relationships are examined in more detail in Unit 4 *Stakeholder Marketing*.

Referring back to the models of marketing outlined in section 1, the strategic and operational marketing models are likely to be found in organisations with a strong market orientation. In organisations with a weak marketing orientation (typically a production, sales or product orientation), the role of marketing is likely to be manifested in terms of sales support or marketing communications.

ACTIVITY 4

Application

Quality Goods makes a variety of widgets. Its Chairman, in the annual report, boasts of the firm's 'passion for the customer'. 'The customer wants quality goods, and if they don't get them they'll complain. We are doing as much as we can for them!'

Is this a marketing oriented firm?

3.3 Measuring market orientation

Marketing orientation is not confined to the marketing department: it is a **culture** that needs to permeate the whole organisation. How can you tell if this is happening?

An organisation wishing to **assess its market orientation** might look at:

- Self-appraisal or feedback from managers and employees in different organisational functions

- Formal attitude surveys of managers and staff

- Evidence in the organisation's business definition, mission statement, value statements and strategies

- Formal marketing audit results (specifically asking questions about the customer focus of different structures and processes)

- Evidence in the extent of organisation-wide communication on customer needs; willingness to gather and use customer feedback; co-ordination between functions in the interest of meeting customer needs

- Customer feedback and research: are customer needs truly being met (regardless of perceived 'orientation')?

3.4 Fostering market orientation – a catalyst for change

For a product or sales-oriented organisation to *become* market oriented represents a major, possibly transformational change. It may require a **programme of change** including the following measures.

- Review and change of the **organisation structure**:

    - To remove 'vertical' barriers (between different functions) which get in the way of people co-operating to meet customer needs. 'Horizontal' structures (such as customer account or product teams) match customers' essentially horizontal experiences of the organisation (needing to flow smoothly from sales information to transaction processing to after-sales service, say – without needing to know that these are three different departments!)

    - To enhance the influence of the marketing function (as discussed later in the chapter), in order to set a customer focused strategic direction

- Review and align **business processes**. 'Process alignment' refers to the exercise of ensuring that all business systems and processes (work and information flows) contribute to the satisfaction of customer needs. Customer needs are satisfied not just by the product, but by all the processes associated with designing, creating, delivering and consuming it.

- Engage in **internal marketing**. The marketing function, supported by senior management, needs to promote the business needs for marketing orientation and the values associated with it. An extensive programme of employee education and communication may be necessary to introduce customer focus.

- Implement relevant customer research, customer care, quality and service **policies** and programmes.

- Create and reinforce **cultural values** based on customer focus. This may be done by:

    (a) Expression and modelling of the desired values by management (from the top down)

    (b) Expression of values in corporate mottos, slogans, team-building

    (c) Use of customer service values as recruitment and selection criteria

    (d) Reinforcing values through other HR systems: education, training, coaching and employee development programmes; incentives, pay and bonuses (or non-financial awards such as 'employee of the month' schemes); performance appraisal and management

    (e) Management style: celebrating and praising customer focused behaviour; encouraging initiative and learning in the interests of customer service

- **Benchmarking** the organisation's processes and performance against best practice

 ACTIVITY 5

Application

Think about applying the marketing orientation to different areas of business. How would a market-based approach be characterised in a bank?

The point of a marketing orientation for not-for-profit organisations (NFPs) appeared on the March 2009 paper. Although NFPs do not have the pursuit of profit as their motive, they still need to appeal to 'customers' such as potential members (to increase their income from donations) or even the general public in order to raise their profile, for example.

3.5 Problems in introducing a market orientation

The organisation should understand what a market orientation actually means, and that major **organisational**, **structural** and **cultural changes** will be required.

The organisation will have to consider **the four Ps** with the customers' needs as the priority. Thorough knowledge of customer needs is required – if this is absent, a market orientation is difficult to achieve.

Problems may arise within the **structure** of the company. Sales and product oriented firms do not require the same degree of 'working together' as a marketing oriented company. Conflict between various functions will also inhibit the ability to work effectively together. Blythe (2008) gives the example of a legal department stating "We have no legal obligation to do more than return people's money if things go wrong. Why go to the expense of sending somebody round to apologise?" The marketer would respond that a company cannot afford to upset any customers – without them, there is no business.

When progressing to marketing orientation, **effective communication** is vital to prevent confusion and provide reassurance.

Problems will arise if senior managers do not commit to a marketing philosophy and build it into their systems and **culture**. Commitment and vision from management will feed down to other staff. Without total **organisation-wide** dedication – and reinforcement by the staff recruitment, training, appraisal and reward systems – changing to a market oriented organisation is not possible. The necessary infrastructure needs to be in place.

Without care, a marketing orientation itself can have **adverse consequences**.

- Organisations may develop a **bias** that favours marketing activities at the expense of production and technical improvements which could offer a more appealing product.

- Focusing new product development on satisfying immediate customer perceptions of what is needed can **stifle innovation.** Organisations should devote at least some of their expertise to *future* customer requirements.

It is worth noting, too, that the total marketing concept itself may or may not represent a real shift in philosophy.

- Perhaps it simply reflects the fact that the **business environment** is now much more sophisticated. For instance, it just makes sense to use advanced information management techniques and technologies in advertising and market research. Those techniques weren't used before simply because they weren't available.

- Perhaps today's **consumers** are more sophisticated, with more information, better education and greater expectations of influence. So-called 'modern marketing techniques' are really just the same old process of persuasion, more cleverly disguised.

In the syllabus, element 1.4 lists those factors that may make a marketing orientation difficult to achieve:

- Lack of committed leadership and vision
- Lack of customer knowledge
- Lack of infrastructure eg, technology
- Autocratic leadership
- Conflict between marketing and other functions
- Preference for production or sales focus
- Transactional approach to business

ACTIVITY 6

Application

A customer contacts your company and asks whether it can make a completely silent washing machine. This is not possible with current technology. What is your reaction?

4 Marketing as a managerial function

"Marketing orientation ... implies that customer needs are the driving force throughout the organisation. This means that everyone in the organisation, from the salespeople through to the factory workers, needs to consider customer needs at every stage.

"Quality control in the factory, accurate information given by telephonists and receptionists, and courteous deliveries by drivers all play a part in delivering customer value." Blythe, J. (2009)
Principles and Practice of Marketing, ▮

The role and relationships of the marketing function within any business depend upon a variety of practical factors particular to that business. These factors may include the corporate culture, the size of the business, the nature of the industry, the position of its products and services in relation to the product life cycle (see Chapter 5), the nature of the product or service and the expectations of customers and potential customers.

This section examines how marketing fits in with the **management structure** of the organisation as a whole.

Some businesses are fragmented, and the functions operate independently. Other businesses are more integrated and operations have a high degree of co-ordination. In order to implement the marketing concept, market-orientated companies need proper **co-ordination** between market needs, production decisions and financial well-being. That requires good cross functional **communication** between marketing and people responsible for development, design and manufacturing, and finance.

However, that does not mean that the marketing department can impose its will upon all other departments. Relationships with other departments should be developed and managed to ensure all departments are working towards the **same overall goal**.

4.1 The scope of marketing activities

The table below shows the types of decision typically taken by a marketing department. However, bear in mind that in the truly market-oriented organisation, marketing is not an activity that can be pigeon-holed as the responsibility of the marketing department. *All* of the company's activities must be co-ordinated around the needs of the customer, and policies enforced. Marketing is therefore to be seen as a dynamic process requiring plenty of planning and analysis. Chapter 3 discusses the marketing planning process.

Product planning	Product lines to be offered – qualities, design, detailed contents
	Markets - to whom, where, when and how much
	New product policy – research and development programme
Branding	Selection of trade marks and names
	Brand policy – individual or family brand
	Sale under private brand or unbranded
Pricing	The level of premiums to adopt
	The margins to adopt – for the trade, for direct sales
Channels of distribution	The channels to use between company and consumer
	The degree of selectivity amongst intermediaries
	Efforts to gain co-operation of the trade
Selling	The burden to be placed on personal selling
	The methods to be employed (1) within the organisation and (2) in selling to intermediaries and the final consumer
Marketing communications (promotions)	The amount to spend – the burden to be placed on advertising
	The platform to adopt – product image, corporate image
	The mix of tools used – to the trade, to consumers
Service and customer relationships	Providing after-sales service to intermediaries and to final consumers (such as direct mail offers)
	Creating points of contact with customers in an integrated way

4.2 Relationships with other departments

Although every organisation is different, common patterns appear in the structure of organisations.

- Marketing departments have often **evolved from sales departments**. In traditional sales or production orientated organisations, marketplace issues were the responsibility of a **sales director** reporting to senior management.

- When the need for a market orientated approach became apparent, a **marketing director** appeared in parallel to the sales director, but each had **separate functional departments**.

- With fuller recognition of the marketing approach to business, sales and marketing may become a **single department**, with **sales as a sub-group** within marketing (as opposed to marketing being a sub-group within sales).

Marketing managers have to take responsibility for planning, resource allocation, monitoring and controlling the marketing effort, but it can also be claimed that marketing involves every facet of the organisation's operations. If the philosophy of a market orientation is regarded as a prerequisite for success, the marketing department naturally becomes the main **co-ordinator**, maintaining relationships and ensuring that all relevant information is shared with whoever else in the organisation might legitimately need it.

4.2.1 Conflicts with other departments

Nevertheless, care should be taken not to understate the role of finance, production, personnel and other business functions, as this may cause resentment and lack of co-operation. To reduce the potential for conflict, senior management should ensure that departmental heads have clear instructions as to the organisation's goals.

ACTIVITY 7

Application

Conflict is often reported between the marketing and research and development (R&D) departments. What possible causes of conflict exist between R&D and marketing? Why is it essential, in a marketing orientated organisation, for R&D and marketing to have a close relationship?

The following table illustrates areas of business that need to be co-ordinated, and information shared, to ensure that some compromise acceptable to both parties is found and that overall business strategy can be developed.

Other departments	Their emphasis	Emphasis of marketing
Engineering	Long design lead time	Short design lead time
	Functional features	Sales features
	Few models with standard components	Many models with custom components
Purchasing	Standard parts	Non-standard parts
	Price of material	Quality of material
	Economic lot sizes	Large lot sizes to avoid stockouts
	Purchasing at infrequent intervals	Immediate purchasing for customer needs
Production	Long order lead times and inflexible production schedules	Short order lead times and flexible schedules to meet emergency orders
	Long runs with few models	Short runs with many models
	No model changes	Frequent model changes
	Standard orders	Custom orders
	Ease of fabrication	Aesthetic appearance
	Average quality control	Tight quality control
Inventory management	Narrow product line	Broad product line
	Economic levels of stock	Large levels of stock
Finance	Strict rationales for spending	Intuitive arguments for spending
	Hard and fast budgets	Flexible budgets to meet changing needs
	Pricing to cover costs	Pricing to further market development
Accounting	Standard transactions	Special terms and discounts
	Few reports	Many reports
Credit control	Full financial disclosures by customers	Minimum credit examination of customers
	Lower credit risks	Medium credit risks
	Tough credit terms	Easy credit terms
	Tough collection procedures	Easy collection procedures

A company sells electrical equipment such as fridges, washing machines, stoves and televisions. It has 50 stores spread over the country working from local retail parks.

Purchasing is done on a centralised basis and a large proportion of the goods are sourced from countries such as China, Korea, Germany and Italy. Each store or outlet places an internal orders for supplies.

There is a centralised HR department which develops recruitment practices and training standards and programmes. However, actual recruitment and training is done locally at each outlet.

The company also believes in developing innovative financing arrangements to help customers to buy its products. A popular arrangement is hire purchase schemes with 0% finance for the first six months.

The marketing function needs to work closely with other functions to ensure that the customer experiences a seamless offering. In practice, this may require significant discussion and internal negotiation until the needs of each function can be mutually met.

- *Finance*

    The company must have enough working capital to carry its customers through the interest free period. The paperwork must be easy to deal with so that the customer does not feel intimidated by entering into a contract to buy a piece of equipment.

    The marketing function might like 0% financing to be an ongoing sales offer, whereas the finance function might prefer a limited period. Marketing must liaise with finance to develop a business solution that satisfies the needs of the customer and the company.

- *Purchasing*

    The systems must be sufficiently sophisticated and efficient to ensure that stock-outs do not arise and also that customers receive their deliveries within the promised period.

    Marketing might prefer a delivery time of three days, but purchasing might be more comfortable with a delivery period of 7 days

    Again, marketing and purchasing must discuss and agree on a viable and sustainable policy.

- *Human resources*

    Marketing also needs to liaise with HR on person and pay specifications so that the company hires the appropriate sorts of employees at the appropriate pay rates.

    Marketing needs to clarify the types of skills staff should have such as selling, customer care and effective communication.

EXAM TIP

Application

The topics covered in this chapter are very important within the syllabus, and consequently in the exam. Do not be tempted to view it as introductory, scene-setting material. On the specimen paper for this Unit, four out of the 10 questions in Part A (worth 16 marks) were concerned with issues of marketing orientation and the role of marketing in the organisation.

Jobber (2009) Principles and Practice of Marketing (6th Edition) has an excellent first chapter which covers the broad overviews of the marketing concept. ■

Learning objectives	Covered
1 Explain the evolution of market orientation	☑ Product orientation
	☑ Production orientation
	☑ Sales orientation
	☑ Market versus marketing orientation
2 Assess the contribution of marketing as a means of	☑ Creating customer value
	☑ Creating and responding to competition
3 Appreciate the different characteristics of a market-oriented approach to business	☑ An exchange process
	☑ A philosophy of business
	☑ A managerial function
	☑ A dynamic operation, requiring analysis, planning and action
	☑ A catalyst for change
4 Identify and evaluate the factors that may make market orientation difficult to achieve within the organisation	☑ Lack of committed leadership and vision
	☑ Lack of customer knowledge
	☑ Lack of infrastructure eg technology
	☑ Autocratic leadership
	☑ Conflict between marketing and other functions
	☑ Preference for production or sales focus
	☑ Transactional approach to business
5 Explain the cross-functional role of marketing and its importance to organisational performance	☑ The importance of internal relationships and information sharing
	☑ The setting and achieving of common and realistic goals
	☑ Establishing common information and control systems
	☑ Establishing clear company policies in relation to products, branding, production etc
	☑ The role of marketing as an internal service provider for other business departments
	☑ Contribution of marketing to the development of the business strategy

Quick quiz

1 Give a definition of marketing that takes into account relationship marketing.

2 State four factors that contributed towards the growth of marketing.

3 How does marketing 'add value' to the customer experience?

4 How can an organisation improve on the 'place' element of the mix that is offered by competitors?

5 Give three characteristics of a market oriented organisation.

6 Fill in the blanks in the statements below, using the words in the box.

Market oriented companies need proper (1).......................... . This requires good (2)................. between departments.

Production departments favour (3).................... while marketing departments prefer (4) ....

Marketing departments favour (5) .... while credit controllers prefer (6) ....

No model changes	Tough credit terms	Communication
Easy credit terms	Co-ordination	Frequent model changes

7   Contrast a 'product' and a 'production' orientation.

8   How can internal marketing assist in promoting a marketing orientation?

9   Contrast some possible emphases of the finance department with those of the marketing department.

10   How can potential conflict between organisational departments be reduced?

1   The criticism could be justified because marketing techniques can be equally well applied by organisations where profit is not the primary motive (and often not a motive at all), such as charities and government departments. Consumers are not just passive players in the market – they take decisions for themselves and can shape marketing campaigns. Marketing takes place within the wider social environment and is subject to its forces and influences.

2   The clue is in the question. The four Ps are 'variables' because they are of varying importance to the marketing effort as a whole, depending what it is you are marketing and what you are trying to achieve. They can be 'mixed' together in a huge number of different ways (and sometimes you have to add in other ingredients), just like flour, water and eggs may make pasta or they may make a Victoria sponge. The marketer's job is to find the right mix.

3   Perhaps what you want is promotion, or a new job, or a larger salary, none of which you will get simply by possessing this book. Hopefully, though, you also want more knowledge: read on!

4   No. A mere absence of complaints is not the same as the identification of customer needs. The firm, if anything, has a product orientation.

5   In the case of banking, a market-based approach would be characterised by managers with responsibility for personal markets, large corporates and small corporates.

6   First, establish the demand for completely silent washing machines. If demand is sufficiently widespread it is worth trying to address the problem. However, you must find out, by talking to customers, what the real problem is – perhaps that the sound travels to other rooms and wakes the baby or annoys the neighbours. There may well be product modifications, or add-on products, that can minimise this problem.

7   Part of the problem might be cultural. To the marketing department, the R&D department is filled with scatty boffins; to the R&D department, the marketing department is full of intellectually vacuous wideboys. Furthermore the R&D department may have an 'academic' or university atmosphere, not a commercial one.

Part of the problem is organisational. If R&D consumes substantial resources, it would seem quite logical to exploit economies of scale by having it centralised.

Marketing work and R&D work differ in many important respects. R&D work is likely to be more open-ended than marketing work.

Two good reasons why R&D should be more closely co-ordinated with marketing.

- With the marketing concept, the 'identification of customer needs' should be a vital input to new product developments.

- The R&D department might identify changes to product specifications, so that a variety of marketing mixes can be applied.

1   'Marketing is to establish, maintain and enhance long-term customer relationships at a profit, so that the objectives of the parties involved are met. This is done by mutual exchange and fulfilment of promises.' (Grönroos)

2   Four from: industrial revolution; mass production; geographical separation; transport and communications and global competition. These factors contributed towards a developing ability to sell more and more goods to people, who did necessarily live near where the goods were being produced.

3   Marketing enables organisations to improve the organisation's offering – giving people products that satisfy their needs better; enhancing the quality of customer service; helping customers make better (ie more informed) buying decisions and making the purchasing experience more enjoyable.

4   Faster delivery; give guarantees on delivery times; deliver in a more convenient way (via online for example) or in a more pleasant environment.

5
- It focuses on meeting the needs of customers, which have been clearly identified and fully understood.
- Its entire structure and all of its processes are designed to meet the needs of customers.
- All activities are co-ordinated around the needs of the customer.

6   (1) Co-ordination   (2) Communication   (3) No model changes   (4) Frequent model changes
(5) Easy credit terms   (6) Tough credit terms.

7   A product orientation concentrates upon the product itself, because if the product is right it will 'sell itself'. A production orientation is subtly different because it focuses upon production processes and trying to make them as efficient as possible to ensure that products are affordable and available.

8   The marketing function can promote the benefits of marketing orientation to the whole organisation. This may involve employee training and regular communication to emphasise that customer needs are satisfied by the whole organisation working together (design, creation, selling, delivery).

9

Finance	Marketing
Strict rationales for spending	Intuitive arguments for spending
Hard and fast budgets	Flexible budgets to meet changing needs
Pricing to cover costs	Pricing to further market development

10   It needs to be recognised that all organisational departments have their part to play in realising the overall business strategy and that particular roles must not be understated. All departments need to have a clear understanding of policies and goals. Information must be shared.

References

Blythe, J (2009) <u>Principles and Practice of Marketing</u>, 2nd edition, South-Western/Cengage Learning.

Blythe, J (2008) <u>Essentials of Marketing</u>,4th edition, FT Prentice Hall.

Brassington, F and Pettitt, S (2006) <u>Principles of Marketing</u>, 4th edition, FT Prentice Hall.

Dibb S, Simkin L, Pride WM, Ferrell OC (2005) <u>Marketing: Concepts and Strategies</u>, 5th edition, Houghton Mifflin.

Jobber (2009) <u>Principles and Practice of Marketing</u>.6th edition, McGraw Hill Higher Education

Kotler, P (2008) <u>Principles of Marketing</u>, 5th edition, FT Prentice Hall.

Chapter 2
Relationships with customers and the community

Topic list

1   Marketing and society
2   Relationship marketing

Introduction

This chapter looks at the impact of marketing activities on the wider world. Consumers, society and the environment all feel the impact of business activity (and therefore the actions of marketers) and it is important for marketers to act in a responsible way towards these stakeholders. Section 1 looks at responsibilities towards the community as a whole (customers, community, environment, employees, suppliers and competitors) – this brings in considerations of social responsibility and ethics.

Section 2 is an introductory session on the importance of relationship marketing. The attraction and retention of customers will hopefully lead to long-term relationships with them. Relationship marketing is concerned with the lifetime value of a customer - "selling products that don't come back to customers that do" (Blythe, 2005). The classic context for marketing is of course the FMCG market, where most of the tools and techniques of marketing were originally developed. Business-to-business (B2B) marketing is concerned with goods and services specifically designed for business use (as well as with ordinary consumer items used in business). Such goods may be of a different standard to consumer goods. Relationship marketing is applicable to both of these markets.

Syllabus linked learning objectives

By the end of the chapter you will be able to:

Learning objectives	Syllabus link
1 Evaluate the impact of marketing actions on consumers, society and the environment, and the need for marketers to act in an ethical and socially responsible manner	1.6
2 Explain the significance of buyer-seller relationships in marketing and comprehend the role of relationship marketing in facilitating the attraction and retention of customers	1.7

1 Marketing and society

"The view that companies should exercise a responsible approach and consider their relationships with society at large is part of the societal marketing philosophy, but is also an important part of maintaining public relations." *Blythe, J. (2009)* ▌

1.1 Societal marketing and social responsibility

Critics of the marketing concept which was described in Chapter 1 suggest that marketing is so powerful that it can make people want things they don't really need, or worse, create a desire for products and services that are against the long-term interests of consumers and of society as a whole. Current examples include cigarettes; non-nutritious 'junk' or convenience food products; and gambling products like instant-win scratch cards which appeal most to the poorest members of society.

A number of writers have suggested that a **societal marketing concept** should replace the marketing concept as a philosophy for the future.

 KEY CONCEPTS

Concept

The **societal marketing concept** is a management orientation that holds that the key task of the organisation is to determine the needs and wants of target markets and to adapt the organisation to delivering the desired satisfactions more effectively and efficiently than its competitors in a way that preserves or enhances the consumers' and society's well-being. Activities need to be carried out in a sustainable way if customers' needs are to be met in the longer term.

Social responsibility is accepting ethical responsibilities to the various publics of an organisation which go beyond contractual or legal requirements. It recognises that organisational activities may have adverse impacts on external stakeholders, and that these should be minimised.

Marketing should aim to maximise **business performance** through **customer satisfaction**, but within the constraints that all firms have a responsibility to **society** as a whole and to the **environment**. For example:

(a)   Some products which consume energy (eg motor cars) should perhaps make more efficient use of the energy they consume.

(b)   It may be possible to extend the useful life of certain products, rather than encouraging obsolescence for repeat or updating purchases.

(c)   Other products might be made smaller, so that they make use of fewer materials (eg products made using microtechnology).

(d)   The organisation should exercise fair, safe and sustainable business and employment practices. (This is currently a major issue for firms employing off-shore low cost labour for manufacturing.)

(e)   The organisation should arguably resist the temptation to persuade people to consume excessively (creating debt, disposal issues etc).

(f)   The organisation may seek to 'put something back' into the communities or societies on which it depends.

 MARKETING AT WORK

Application

Furniture giant IKEA has rapidly expanded world-wide to more than 250 stores in 35 countries; most of them in Europe, and in the United States, Canada, China, Japan and Australia. Human rights and environmental campaigners say that IKEA's self-proclaimed ethics are being squeezed in favour of profits.

The company has made the astonishing admission that some of its suppliers in the developing world use exploitative child labour and others are involved in illegal logging which destroys protected forests.

Anders Dahlvig, the multi-national's Chief Executive Officer, made the candid revelations after investigations by the *Washington Post* and the BBC. He said: 'If you know how production takes place in the world you cannot guarantee that, for instance, there is no child labour or that some wood doesn't comes from illegal (logging at protected) forests ... If you produce rugs in India and countries like this and if you have been there then you will know that many of these rugs are produced in the homes of individuals. So, how can anyone guarantee that at any given time a child is not sitting behind a loom in their homes?'.

'Of course [to manufacture in low or no wage countries like India] has a business case. But we also want to be able to change or influence the places where we are ... I think all multi-national companies going to developing countries and producing could make a difference from an environmental and social perspective. Because if we are there we can influence and change how people produce and how things get done and through that we speed up the development.'

Dahlvig said IKEA was not being hypocritical with the slogan that its products had a 'low price but not at any price'. The company website asserts that all products must be manufactured in a responsible manner with as little effect on the environment as possible.

www.the-latest.com – accessed 1 May 2008

 ACTIVITY 1

Application

Does your own organisation do anything that indicates to you that it takes a responsible attitude towards society and the environment? Think through each of the four Ps as a framework for your answer: how might your organisation be responsible in each of the four areas?

 MARKETING AT WORK

Application

80 DHL employees clean up beaches for DHL Volunteer Day in Australia – September 4, 2009

"As part of the annual Volunteer Day, 80 DHL employees are volunteering their time to help clean up beaches in Sydney, Melbourne, Perth and Brisbane in preparation for the busy summer season. And with South Maroubra SLC marking its 50th anniversary this weekend, DHL employees will be helping to clean up the clubhouse in preparation for the celebrations.

DHL are also pleased to announce that they have renewed their sponsorship with Surf Life Saving Australia (SLSA), which will see them continuing to invest in keeping Australian beaches safe and contributing to the invaluable work done ever year by SLSA. The partnership, which began in September 2003, continues to be the largest corporate sponsorship ever received by SLSA, which relies on the funds for ongoing training and assessing, and the supply of uniforms, rescue gear and equipment to its surf clubs, branches and state centres around Australia.

"DHL welcomes the opportunity to continue to work alongside SLSA to keep our beaches safe. The partnership with SLSA is one that we are extremely proud of," said Gary Edstein, Senior Vice President Oceania, DHL

"We are also extremely happy that our staff in Sydney, and indeed across the country, can help prepare Australian *beaches for the summer, creating a tremendously positive impact on local communities", added Terry Ryan, Senior Vice President, DHL Supply Chain, South Pacific*

DHL Volunteer Day gains momentum and expands beyond Asia Pacific

Following the success of the program in Asia Pacific last year, DHL has extended the footprint of the activity to include Africa, Europe and Latin America this year. As part of DHL Volunteer Day activities this year, which runs from 1 to 6 September, more than 15,000 employees, customers and business partners in over 40 countries across Asia Pacific, Africa, Europe and Latin America undertook over 70 community projects that support various local causes. These programs deliver to the company's corporate social responsibility pillars - Education, Environment and Disaster Management."

www.dhl.com.au – accessed 2 June 2010

1.2 Why be socially responsible?

 KEY CONCEPT   Concept

Corporate social responsibility suggests that organisations consider not just their customers and profits, but the good of the wider community. Marketing within a CSR context attempts to act responsibly and in a way that assists the well-being of society.

Institutions like hospitals and schools exist because health care and education are seen to be *desirable* **social objectives** by government and the public at large. Where does this leave *businesses*? How far is it reasonable, or even appropriate, for businesses to exercise 'social responsibility' by giving to charities, voluntarily imposing strict environmental objectives on themselves, offering the same conditions of work to all workers, and other 'desirables'?

 EXAM TIP   Evaluation

Social responsibility and the related issue of business ethics are highly topical, so be clear about their meaning and the arguments for and against. You need to be able to identify specific ethical and social responsibility issues facing a given organisation, or more generally facing marketers in recent times – and within your own national culture and the global marketplace. Asking the 'added value' question of any given marketing decision should highlight areas in which the organisation's interests potentially conflict with those of other stakeholders in its activity ... Think through the news headlines: what corporate social responsibility issues have faced Nike, McDonalds and Oxfam?

Managers need to take into account the effect of organisational outputs into the market and the wider **social community**, for several reasons.

(a)   The modern **marketing concept** says that in order to survive and succeed, organisations must satisfy the needs, wants and values of customers and potential customers. Communication and education have made people much more aware of issues such as the environment, the exploitation of workers, product safety and consumer rights. Therefore an organisation may have to be seen to be responsible in these areas in order to retain public support for its products.

(b)   There are skill shortages in the labour pool and employers must compete to attract and retain high quality employees. If the organisation holds a reputation as a socially responsible employer it will find it easier to do this, than if it has a poor **'employer brand'**.

(c)   Organisations **rely** on the society and local community of which they are a part, for access to facilities, business relationships, media coverage, labour, supplies and customers. Organisations which acknowledge their responsibilities as part of the community may find that many areas of their operation are facilitated.

(d)   'Corporate citizenship' (upholding the law and behaving responsibly) is very important. Law, regulation and Codes of Practice **impose** certain social responsibilities on organisations, in areas such as employment protection, equal opportunities, environmental care, health and safety, product labelling and consumer rights. There are financial and operational **penalties** for organisations which fail to uphold the law and behave responsibly.

It can be argued that the social responsibility of business is **profit maximisation**. The responsibility of a business organisation – as opposed to a public sector one – is to maximise wealth for its owners and investors. This does not mean that the business will not be socially responsible, but it will be so out of 'enlightened self interest': protecting its corporate image, ability to retain staff, consumer rights, product safety and other areas.

1.3 Responsibilities to customers

To some extent these responsibilities coincide with the organisation's marketing objectives. As we saw in the previous chapter, the evolution of marketing as a discipline saw the consumer with more buying, and therefore influencing, power.

Some organisations have realised that they need to shift from being 'P-focused' to becoming 'C-focused' (that is, customer-focused). A marketing model (called the '7Cs') could look like this:

From	To
Product	**C**ustomer solution or value
Price	**C**ost to the customer or user of the product / service
Promotion	**C**ommunication
Place	**C**onvenience
People	**C**onsideration
Process	**C**o-ordination
Physical evidence	**C**onfirmation

A successful marketer will take into account all of the elements of the marketing mix for the marketing plan and, where necessary, will combine Ps and Cs according to the product or service on offer. Often, products are combined with services, such as after-sales service on a large or expensive item (cars, white goods and so on).

So the importance of customer care has been acknowledged as a result of the growth of **consumerism**. In the UK, a number of consumer rights have been recognised in law.

•   The right to be **informed of the true facts** of the buyer-seller relationship (eg truth in advertising) and the content of products (eg in food labelling).

•   The right to be **protected** from unfair exploitation or invasion of privacy (eg in the use of personal information or the sale of mailing lists).

•   The right to **safety and health protection**: safe products, health warnings, product labelling.

 KEY CONCEPT   Concept

Consumerism is a term used to describe the increased importance and power of consumers. It includes the increasingly organised consumer groups, and the recognition by producers that consumer satisfaction is the key to long-term profitability.

Marketers are increasingly responsive to consumer pressures to maintain a responsible image and reputation. This may deter aggressive marketing tactics, as the need to consider the best interests of customers should be paramount in a marketing strategy. This approach should bring long-term benefits, rather than attempting to maximise short-term profits.

1.4 Responsibilities towards the community

A business only succeeds because it is part of a wider community. It should demonstrate its social awareness by:

- Upholding the social and ethical **values** of the community.

- Contributing towards the **well-being** of the community, eg by sponsoring local events and charities, or providing facilities for the community to use (eg sports fields), or (more fundamentally) by producing safe products, pricing essential products for affordability and maintaining a local employment market.

- Responding constructively to **complaints** from local residents or politicians (eg about problems for local traffic caused by the organisation's delivery vehicles).

- Maintaining a **sustainable** presence in the community, in terms of the exploitation of labour and business relationships, impacts on the environment and use of resources.

Artistic sponsorships, charitable donations and the like are, of course, also a useful medium of **public relations** and can reflect well on the business.

1.5 Responsibilities to employees

Responsible policies should address matters such as:

- Fair pay and conditions

- Safe and healthy working conditions

- Learning/development opportunities: consultation and participation in decisions which affect the workforce

- Commitment to equal opportunity, non-discrimination and wider diversity

- Fair and humane management of disciplinary situations, dismissals and redundancies and so on

- Support for employee welfare (benefits, counselling and so on, where required)

1.6 Responsibilities to suppliers and competitors

The responsibilities of an organisation towards its **suppliers** come down mainly to maintaining trading relationships.

- The organisation's size could give it considerable **buying power**. It should not use its power unscrupulously (eg to force the supplier to lower his prices under threat of withdrawing business).

- The organisation should not delay **payments** to suppliers beyond the agreed credit period. Suppliers (especially small businesses) might rely on getting prompt payment in accordance with the terms of trade negotiated with its customers.

- All **information** obtained from suppliers and potential suppliers should be kept confidential, particularly where competing tenders or offers are being considered.

- All suppliers should be **treated fairly**, including:

    - Giving potential new suppliers a chance to win some business

    - Maintaining long-standing relationships that have been built up over the years.

Some responsibilities should also exist towards **competitors**. Responsibilities regarding competitors are by no means solely directed by social conscience or ethics, however: there is also a great deal of law surrounding the conduct of fair trading, monopolies, mergers, anti-competitive practices, abuses of a dominant market position and restrictive trade practices. Companies may compete aggressively (as in the case of Coke and Pepsi), but they may not compete unfairly (as, for example, Microsoft has been accused of doing).

1.7 Business ethics

 KEY CONCEPT

Concept

Questions of **ethics**, at the most simple level, are about deciding between right and wrong.

An organisation may have **values** covering non-discrimination, fairness and integrity. It is very important that managers understand:

- The importance of **ethical behaviour**, and
- The differences in what is considered ethical behaviour in **different cultures**.

Business ethics in a **global market place** are, however, far from clear cut. If you are working outside the UK, you will need to develop – in line with whatever policies your organisation may have in place – a kind of 'situational' ethic to cover various issues.

- **Gifts** may be construed as bribes in Western business circles, but are indispensable in others.
- Attitudes to **women** in business vary according to ethnic traditions and religious values.
- The use of **cheap labour** in very poor countries may be perceived as 'development' – or as 'exploitation'.
- The expression and nature of **agreements** varies according to cultural norms.

Assuming a firm wishes to act ethically, it can embed ethical values in its decision processes in the following ways.

- Include **value statements** in corporate culture, policy and codes of practice
- Ensure that **incentive systems** are designed to support ethical behaviour
- Identify ethical objectives in the **mission statement**, as a public declaration of what the organisation stands for
- Encourage **communication** about ethical dilemmas and issues (eg in employee forums, ethics committees)

 MARKETING AT WORK

Application

Blythe (2008) states: "In most cases marketers do not become enmeshed in the deeper recesses of philosophy, but instead rely on the moral rules which are part of the corporate culture".

He gives the following examples from the context of the marketing mix:

- Products should be honestly made and described
- Promotions need to be 'legal, decent, honest and truthful'
- Pricing raises all kinds of ethical issues – price fixing, predatory pricing, or not disclosing the full costs of purchase
- Distribution should not involve abuse of power – large retailers often have significant power over smaller manufacturers who supply them

 KEY CONCEPT

Concept

Predatory pricing is the pricing of products so far below those of competitors that those competitors cannot hope to match it without being driven out of business.

1.8 The CIM and ethics

The CIM has issued a Code of Professional Standards, Ethics and Disciplinary Procedures. The main points are listed below.

MARKETING AT WORK

Application

1 A member shall at all times conduct himself with integrity in such a way as to bring credit to the profession of marketing and The Chartered Institute of Marketing.

2 A member shall not by unfair or unprofessional practice injure the business, reputation or interest of any other member of the Institute.

3 Members shall, at all times, act honestly in their professional dealings with customers and clients (actual and potential), employers and employees.

4 A member shall not, knowingly or recklessly, disseminate any false or misleading information, either on his own behalf or on behalf of anyone else.

5 A member shall keep abreast of current marketing practice and act competently and diligently and be encouraged to register for the Institute's scheme of Continuing Professional Development.

6 A member shall, at all times, seek to avoid conflicts of interest and shall make prior voluntary and full disclosure to all parties concerned of all matters that may arise during any such conflict. Where a conflict arises a member must withdraw prior to the work commencing.

7 A member shall keep business information confidential except: from those persons entitled to receive it, where it breaches this code and where it is illegal to do so.

8 A member shall promote and seek business in a professional and ethical manner.

9 A member shall observe the requirements of all other codes of practice which may from time to time have any relevance to the practice of marketing insofar as such requirements do not conflict with any provisions of this code, or the Institute's Royal Charter and Bye-laws; a list of such codes being obtainable from the Institute's head office.

10 Members shall not hold themselves out as having the Institute's endorsement in connection with an activity unless the Institute's prior written approval has been obtained first.

11 A member shall not use any funds derived from the Institute for any purpose which does not fall within the powers and obligations contained in the Branch or Group handbook, and which does not fully comply with this code.

12 A member shall have due regard for, and comply with, all the relevant laws of the country in which they are operating.

13 A member who knowingly causes or permits any other person or organisation to be in substantial breach of this code or who is a party to such a breach shall himself be guilty of such breach.

14 A member shall observe this Code of Professional Standards as it may be expanded and annotated and published from time to time by the Ethics Committee in the manner provided for.

2 Relationship marketing

"Customer retention has become increasingly recognised as the key to long-term survival. In the past, most companies have operated on a 'leaky bucket' basis, seeking to refill the bucket with new customers while ignoring the ones leaking away through the bottom...a one percent improvement in customer retention will lead to a five percent improvement in the firm's value." Blythe, J. (2009)

Since the mid–1990s the concept of relationship marketing has been gaining steady ground.

KEY CONCEPT

Concept

Relationship marketing is the process of creating, building up and managing long-term relationships with customers, distributors and suppliers. It aims to change the focus from attracting customers to retaining customers.

Transaction marketing is a business approach that concentrates on the transactions between a firm and its customers.

2.1 Types and levels of relationship

The type of relationship between a buyer and a seller may be of two types.

(a) In a **transaction**, a supplier gives the customer a good or service in exchange for money. The marketer, in offering the good or service, is looking for a response. Transaction-based marketing is based on individual transactions and little else, such as when you buy a bar of chocolate.

(b) In a **relationship approach**, a sale is not the end of a process but the start of an organisation's relationship with a customer.

So building up customer relationships requires a change of focus from the transaction-based approach to the relationship approach. The contrast is summarised in the table below.

TRANSACTION MARKETING (*mainly one-way communication*)	RELATIONSHIP MARKETING (*mainly two-way communication*)
• Focus on single sale	• Focus on customer retention
• Orientation on product features	• Orientation on product benefits
• Short timescale	• Long timescale
• Little customer service	• High customer service
• Limited customer commitment	• High customer commitment
• Moderate customer contact	• High customer contact
• Quality is the concern of production	• Quality is the concern of all

There are five different levels of customer relationship, reflecting varying degrees of customer loyalty.

(a) **Basic**

The organisation sells the product/service without initiating or inviting any further contact with the customer.

(b) **Reactive**

The customer is invited to contact the organisation if there are any problems.

(c) **Accountable**

The organisation follows up the sale, contacting the customer to see if there are any problems and inviting feedback for future improvements.

(d) **Proactive**

The organisation contacts the customer on a regular basis, for a range of purposes (additional offerings, incentives, updates, loyalty rewards, feedback seeking).

(e) **Partnership**

Organisation and customer exchange information and work together to achieve customer savings and added value. Commercial buyers often work closely with a supplier to ensure that all aspects of the deal suit the needs of both parties, not just for *this* deal, but those that can be expected in the future.

Broadly speaking, the greater the number of customers and the smaller the profit per unit sold, the greater the likelihood that the type of marketing will be basic. At the other extreme, where a firm has few customers, but where profits are high, the partnership approach is most likely. Many firms, however, have begun to move towards proactive relationships – even in consumer markets – in order to build customers' loyalty to the brand, open feedback channels and cross-sell related products.

  EXAM TIP   Application

We saw in Chapter 1 that a 'transactional' approach to marketing can form a barrier to the development of a marketing orientation within the organisation. This is also explicitly noted in syllabus reference 1.4. the adoption of relationship marketing represents a reinforcement of the marketing orientation for many businesses, particularly in the B2B context (see paragraph 2.5).

2.2 Benefits of relationship marketing

The lifetime value of a customer to a company can be measured in terms of revenue and profits. Existing, loyal customers are valuable because:

- They do not have to be acquired, or cost less to acquire

- They buy a broader range of products

- They cost less to service as they are familiar with the company's ways of doing business

- They become less sensitive to price over time

- They can recommend by word of mouth to others

Customers who defect may be lost forever. At the very least, they will be expensive to lure back.

Jobber (2009) identifies six benefits for organisations in developing and maintaining strong customer relationships.

1. **Increased purchases**. Customers tend to spend more each year with a relationship partner, as that relationship develops. Loyal customers generate more revenue, for more years.

2. **Lower cost of retaining** (as opposed to recruiting) customers

3. **Lifetime value of a customer** (profit made on a customer's purchases over the lifetime of that customer)

4. **Sustainable competitive advantage**. The intangible benefits of a loyal relationship are not easily copied by the competition: trust, friendship etc

5. **Word of mouth** from loyal customers leads to new customers

6. **Employee satisfaction and retention** – employees are more satisfied at work and can spend time improving relationships rather than constantly seeking out new ones

Studies have demonstrated that profits rise when customer defection rates decrease.

The process of retaining customers for a lifetime is an important one – and one in which **integrated marketing communications** have an important role to play. Instead of one-way communication aimed solely at gaining a sale, it is necessary to develop an effective two-way communication process to turn a prospect into a lifetime advocate. This is shown in the ladder of customer loyalty.

Figure 2.1: Ladder of customer loyalty

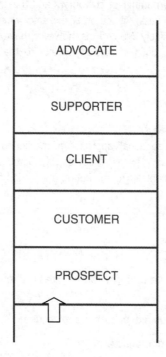

The main justification for relationship marketing comes from the need to **retain customers**. It has been estimated that the cost of attracting a new customer may be five times the cost of keeping an existing customer.

In terms of competitive forces, relationship marketing attempts to make it harder, or less desirable, for a buyer to **switch** to another seller. It raises switching costs (emotional, if not financial).

Relationship marketing also opens **channels of communication** for marketers to **cross-sell** related products, solicit **feedback** for further marketing planning and even make special offers (to boost sales or increase customer loyalty). It is clear that the more loyal customers that a business has, the better its prospects for survival and growth.

2.3 Characteristics of relationship marketing

Relationship marketing in business-to-consumer (B2C) markets tends to operate in three main ways.

(a)   Borrowing the idea of **customer/supplier partnerships** from industry (that is, B2B markets). By sharing information and supporting each other's shared objectives, marketers and their customers can create real mutual benefits.

(b)   Recreating the **personal feel** that characterised the old-fashioned corner store. Make customers feel **recognised and valued as individuals** as business take care to demonstrate that their **consumers' needs** are recognised and met. (This has been made more feasible through new technologies such as the Internet, databases and computer-integrated telephone systems.)

(c)   **Continually deepening and improving** the relationship. Making sure that every customer experience satisfies – and even **delights** – through reliable product quality, customer care and value-adding contacts.

In summary, the distinguishing characteristics of relationship marketing are as follows.

(a)   A focus on **customer retention** rather than attraction

(b)   The development of an **on-going relationship** as opposed to a one-off transaction

(c)   Emphasis upon the **benefits** of the product or service to the customer

(d)   A **long timescale** rather than short timescale

(e)   **Direct and regular** customer contact rather than impersonal, discrete sales

(f)   **Multiple employee/customer contacts,** hence the increased importance of all-staff customer care awareness

(g)   Quality and customer satisfaction being the concern of **all employees** rather than just those who work in the marketing department

(h)   Emphasis on **key account** relationship management, **service quality** and buyer (partner) behaviour rather than the marketing mix

(i)   Importance of **trust** and **keeping promises** rather than making the sale: to have an ongoing relationship, both parties need to trust each other and keep the promises they make. (Marketing moves from one-off potentially manipulative exchanges towards co-operative relationships built on financial, social and structural benefits.)

(j)   Multiple exchanges with a number of parties: **network relationships**, rather than a single focus on customers. Customer relationships are important, but so too are the relationships with other **stakeholders** such as suppliers, distributors, professional bodies, banks, trade associations etc.

 EXAM TIP Application

This is a core topic, because it is so tied up with 'marketing orientation', so make sure you've got to grips with the principles – and look out for examples! The benefits of relationship marketing are examined on the specimen paper.

 MARKETING AT WORK Application

Some firms are therefore trying to convert a 'basic' transaction based approach into relationship marketing. Many car dealerships, for example, seek to generate additional profits by servicing the cars they sell, and by keeping in touch with their customers so that they can earn repeat business. Other strategies for relationship marketing include **loyalty schemes** such as club cards, and **special privileges** such as hospitality at sporting events.

2.4 Customer relationship management (CRM)

 KEY CONCEPT Concept

Customer relationship management (CRM) describes the methodologies and ICT systems that help an enterprise manage customer relationships.

CRM consists of systems which:

• Help an enterprise to identify and target their **most profitable customers** and generate quality leads

• Assist the organisation to improve telesales, account, and sales management by optimising **information sharing**, and **streamlining** existing processes (for example, taking orders using mobile devices)

• Provide employees with **information** to **integrate all communications** with customers: facilitating the 'recognition' of customers and consistent and up-to-date account/product/ delivery information.

Each time a customer contacts a company with an effective CRM system – whether by telephone, in a retail outlet or online – the customer should be recognised and should receive appropriate information and attention. CRM software provides advanced personalisation and customised solutions to customer demands, giving customer care staff a range of key information about each customer which can be applied to the transaction.

Basically, CRM involves a single **comprehensive database** that can be accessed from any of the points of contact with the customer. Traditional 'vertical' organisation structures have tended to create stand-alone systems developed for distinct functions or departments, which were responsible for the four main types of interaction with the customer: marketing, sales, fulfilment and after-sales. These systems need to be integrated into (or replaced by) a central customer database, with facilities for data to be **accessed from** and **fed into** the central system from other departments and applications (including the website), so that all customer information can be kept up-to-date and shared.

ACTIVITY 2

Application

Can you think of other ways in which information and communications technology (ICT) can be used to develop and maintain long-term customer relationships?

2.5 The business-to-business (B2B) context

"Relationship marketing has been most apparent in business-to-business marketing, possibly because businesses need to ensure consistency of supply, whereas consumers are able to source products from many outlets and do not lose out as badly if a product is not immediately available from their usual supplier. For example, a car manufacturer who runs out of vital components might conceivably need to shut down production; the same is not true of a consumer who runs out of cornflakes." Blythe, J. (2008)

We have tended to concentrate so far upon relationship marketing in the context of business marketing to consumers (B2C), but building relationships with customers has long been practised in B2B marketing, and is in fact more widespread than in consumer marketing. A marketing orientation is just as valid within the business-to-business sector as it is in the consumer goods sector. Business customers seek answers to their problems. Business products must be full of customer benefits, providing answers to customers' problems rather than simply being 'good products'.

KEY CONCEPT

Concept

Business-to-business marketing (often abbreviated as B2B) is concerned with industrial goods and services, which are bought by manufacturers, distributors and other private and publicly owned institutions, such as schools and hospitals, to be used as part of their own activities.

In addition, of course, many of the products involved in business-to-business markets are the same as those bought within the ordinary consumer markets, for example, company cars, computers and mobile phones.

Blythe cites the examples of IBM and Microsoft, who forged a close working relationship in the 1980s and 1990s while the home computing market was experiencing massive growth. Companies such as Bose, Compaq and Motorola sent staff to liaise with key common suppliers on new product development at a similar time.

2.5.1 B2B markets and products

B2B market categories can be classified as follows.

- **Capital goods** include such items as buildings, machinery and motor vehicles.

- **Components and materials** include raw, partly and wholly processed materials or goods which are incorporated into the products sold by the company.

- **Supplies** are goods which assist production and distribution. This would include small but important items such as machine oil, computer disks and stationery, and cleaning products.

- **Business services** are services used by businesses, for instance employer's liability insurance.

When bought in a business-to-business context, products are distinct from consumer goods in several ways. All of them contribute to the high importance of establishing close relationships between buyer and seller.

- **Conformity with standards**. Industrial products are often bound by legal or quality standards, and as a consequence, products within a particular group are often similar. However, buyers often lay down their own specifications to which manufacturers must adhere.

- **Technical sophistication**. Many products in this area require levels of complexity and sophistication which are unheard of in consumer products.

- **High order values**. As a consequence of (a) and (b), many business goods, particularly capital equipment, are very often extremely costly items. Even in the case of supplies, where the single unit value of components and materials may be comparatively low, the quantity required frequently means that orders have a very high value.

- **Irregularity of purchase**. Machinery used to produce consumer goods is not bought regularly. Materials used to produce the goods certainly are, but components and materials are often bought on a contract or preferred supplier basis, so that the opportunity to get new business may not arise very often.

According to Brassington and Pettitt (2006): "*The links have to be forged carefully, and relationships managed over time to minimise the potential problems or to diagnose them early enough for action to be taken*".

2.5.2 The importance of personal selling in B2B markets

The main difference between B2C and B2B is in the importance of **personal selling** in business-to-business markets.

- Some business products are complex and **need to be explained** in a flexible way to non-technical people involved in the buying process. Exhibitions and demonstrations are also used extensively for this reason.

- Buying in business-to-business marketing is often a group activity and, equally, selling can be a **team effort**. Salespeople are expected to follow-up to ensure that the products are working properly and that the business buyer is perfectly satisfied.

- Where a business equipment manufacturer markets through an industrial dealer, the manufacturer's salesforce may be required to **train** the dealer's salesforce in product knowledge.

- A **partnership** approach to relationship marketing is present to a much greater degree in business-to-business selling, where the buyer needs information and services and the seller is seeking repeat business in the long term.

2.6 Issues in relationship marketing

Having said all of the above, you should note that not all customers *want* multiple, multi-source communications from organisations – even those from whom they have purchased products or services in the past!

- **Permission marketing** is an important concept, based on the belief that people should be given the choice of whether to receive further marketing communications or not – and that customers are likely to respond more positively to contacts that they have requested (or given permission for), than to unsolicited approaches. This was a major issue for 'junk mail' promotions, and is equally important in regard to Internet/email marketing: spam (unsolicited online direct mailings) are a major source of resistance to e-marketing.

- Many countries have **legislated** against unsolicited and intrusive marketing, and the sharing of personal data given to one organisation with other organisations. For some years, organisations have clearly stated their privacy polices and offered 'opt out' clauses ('if you do not wish to receive other offers, tick this box'). Many countries are now legislating for 'opt in' clauses ('if you wish to receive other offers, tick this box').

    - The UK **Data Protection Act 1998** requires data users to be registered with the Data Protection Registrar; to limit their use of personal data to registered users; and not to disclose data to third parties (even as email addresses sent in a 'cc' reference) without permission.

    - The UK **Privacy & Electronic Communications Regulations 2003** update existing UK legislation covering unsolicited email, phone calls, faxes and the Internet. It covers matters such as: explaining to customers the purpose of cookies (programs which personalise customer contacts with the website) and describing how to block them; obtaining permission for email/SMS/txt advertising to individuals; telephone marketing subject to 'opt out' ('Do not call') requests; and fax marketing to individuals by 'opt in' (request) only.

 MARKETING AT WORK   Application

Consistently high customer retention stemming from winning customer loyalty creates tremendous competitive advantage, boosts employee morale, produces fundamental bonuses in productivity and growth, and even reduces the cost of capital.

Organisations such as the AA, Citroen, Nationwide, Saga and Virgin Atlantic consistently succeed in making customers feel 'special' about being customers and that they are part of a 'club'. In some cases the organisation can promote and exploit the notion of membership to boost loyalty levels even higher, but the organisation has to do this with a degree of sincerity.

Conversely, organisations from which customers persistently defect because they are convinced they offer inferior value will find that these defecting customers soon outnumber loyal advocates and may even dominate the marketplace. If this happens, no amount of advertising, public relations or clever marketing will be likely to save the organisation's reputation.

www.capeconsulting.com

Learning objectives		Covered
1	Evaluate the impact of marketing actions on consumers, society and the environment, and the need for marketers to act in an ethical and socially responsible manner	☑ Ethical codes of practice for marketers (CIM Code of Practice)
		☑ Corporate Social Responsibility as a cultural value
		☑ Corporate citizenship – upholding the law and behaving responsibly
		☑ Social awareness of key marketing issues relating to social causes
		☑ Societal marketing
2	Explain the significance of buyer-seller relationships in marketing and comprehend the role of relationship marketing in facilitating the attraction and retention of customers	☑ Benefits of customer retention
		☑ Drawbacks of customer defection
		☑ Relationship management in B2B and B2C
		☑ The link between degrees of customer loyalty and long-term organisational stability and growth
		☑ The role of technology in enhancing or undermining relationships and thereby affecting retention

1   What is the 'societal marketing' concept?

2   What consumer rights have been recognised in UK law?

3   Is it correct to say that marketers have no responsibility towards competitors, except in the business sense that they should try to 'beat' them? If not, why not?

4   How can questions of ethics be applied to the four Ps?

5   There are five different levels of customer relationship. You could remember these using the acronym BRAPP. What does BRAPP stand for?

6   Customer relationship management describes the (1)...................... and (2)..................... systems that help an enterprise manage customer relationships.

7   What are the five rungs of the 'loyalty ladder'?

8   Why is personal selling so important in B2B markets?

1   There may be policies about recycling toner cartridges or other office waste, special deals for disadvantaged groups, a favourite charity, a payroll giving scheme, and so on. Find out, if you don't know what your organisation does: it may well promote it's ethics and socially responsible activities in its published accounts.

2   ICT applications in relationship marketing and maintenance include the following:

- The use of databases, to improve marketing planning, personalisation of customer contacts and provision of 'real-time' account/product/delivery details to customers (in conjunction with systems such as computer-telephony integration and sales force automation).

- The use of multiple communication channels for contact, including e-mail, website, mobile phone SMS messaging and so on.

- The use of websites to increase voluntary contact by customers: providing value-adding features (eg communities, database searches, special offers) and changing content to stimulate repeat 'visits'.

- The use of database, web and computer technology to personalise customer contacts: from personally addressed letters and postcards (using basic word processing 'merging' of databased details) to customer 'recognition' by customer service staff (using computer-telephony integration) to customised web experience (using cookies to 'remember' user preferences).

- The use of ICT to improve the quality of customer contacts and service: e-mail speeding up responses to queries; FAQs on websites allowing 'self-service' information; automated voice systems allowing telephone self-service (eg for routing of calls, bill payments by credit card, cinema ticket bookings and so on); e-commerce empowering customers (online shopping, Internet banking and so on).

- The use of online monitoring and feedback forms to gather customer preference data, enabling further contacts and offerings to be better tailored to customer needs.

- Creative applications aimed at customer 'delight' – eg sending birthday cards/e-mails to loyal customers.

- Using ICT tools for loyalty schemes: swipe card points systems, online vouchers and so on.

- Creating customer communities, as an incentive to identify with the organisation or brand (eg 'membership clubs', or online discussion boards).

1   Societal marketing is a management orientation that says that the key task of an organisation is to establish what customers want, and deliver this in a way that promotes the well-being of society.

2   The right to be informed of the true facts

The right to be protected from unfair exploitation

The right to a particular quality of life

3   No. There are many legal restrictions controlling actions with regard to competitors and it does not come down to social conscience or ethics alone: there is law surrounding fair trading, monopolies, mergers, anti-competitive practices and abuse of dominant market position.

4   Products should be honestly made and described

Promotions, such as TV advertisements, need to be 'legal, decent, honest and truthful'

Prices should be fairly derived and applied

Distribution should not involve any abuse of power

5   Basic, Reactive, Accountable, Proactive, Partnership.

6   (1) Methodologies (2) ICT

7   Prospect, customer, client, supporter, advocate

8   Some business products are complex and need to be explained. Salespeople are expected to follow-up to ensure that the products are working properly and that the business buyer is perfectly satisfied, and the manufacturer's salesforce may be required to train the buyer's staff. All in all, a partnership approach to relationship marketing is present to a much greater degree.

References

Blythe, J (2006) <u>Principles and Practice of Marketing</u>, Thomson Learning.

Blythe, J (2005) <u>Essentials of Marketing</u>, 3rd edition, FT Prentice Hall.

Brassington, F and Pettitt, S (2006) <u>Principles of Marketing</u>, 4th edition, FT Prentice Hall.

Anon (2007) "*Ikea slammed over child labour and green issues*", 22 May 2007, available online at: www.the-latest.com [accessed 1 May 2008]

Chapter 3
The marketing planning process

Topic list

1   Marketing planning in context
2   Types of organisational objective
3   Setting objectives
4   The marketing planning process

Introduction

"From an overall strategic perspective marketers need to decide on the following issues, and formulate strategies for coping with them:

- *Which market should the firm be in?*
- *What strengths and weaknesses is the firm bringing to the marketplace?*
- *Where does the firm intend to be in 5 to 30 years' time?*
- *What will the firm's competitors do in response to the market?*
- *Does the firm have sufficient resources to achieve the objectives decided upon?"*

Blythe, J. (2008)

Proper marketing planning will help to answer these questions and is a source of competitive advantage – it can help to put a company in the strongest possible position to take advantage of opportunities as they present themselves and meet the challenges posed by competitors.

A marketing plan must be created to meet clear objectives. Objectives can be related to market share, sales goals, reaching the target audience and creating awareness. Long-term objectives are broken down into shorter-term measurable targets, which can be used as milestones along the way.

Once marketing objectives are set the next stage is to define how they will be achieved. The marketing strategy is the statement of how objectives will be delivered. It explains what marketing actions and resources will be used and how they will work together. Results can be analysed regularly to see whether objectives are being met.

This is an important chapter because it places the planning of marketing activities (as discussed in Part C of the Text covering the marketing mix) firmly within the context of the overall strategy of the firm (section 1). Sections 2 and 3 cover the importance of objective setting, and the planning process is summarised in section 4.

The marketing audit, a key component of the marketing planning process, is described in the next chapter.

Syllabus linked learning objectives

By the end of the chapter you will be able to:

Learning objectives	Syllabus link
1 Explain the importance of objectives, the processes for setting them and the influences upon them	2.1
2 Identify the different types of organisational objectives	2.2
3 Evaluate the importance of the marketing planning process to the market oriented organisation	2.3
4 Explain the different stages of the marketing planning process	2.4

1 Marketing planning in context

1.1 What is a marketing plan?

A plan is a way of achieving something. The shopping list you take to the supermarket is a simple example: it aims to achieve a well-stocked fridge and larder.

But imagine you are writing a shopping list so that someone less familiar with your habits can do your food shopping for you. This is much closer to planning in an organisational sense.

- You will set out where the most convenient supermarket is for your house, and what brands you prefer.
- You will have to be flexible, giving the other person options if, for example, the brand specified on your list is out of stock.
- You will have to negotiate to ensure that doing your shopping to meet your timescale is in with the person's plans.
- You will need to set a limit on how much to spend.

A marketing plan is similar: as **detailed** as it needs to be; **adaptable** if necessary; **compatible** with the organisation's strategic level goals; properly **budgeted** and **controlled**.

 KEY CONCEPT   Concept

A **marketing plan** is a specification of all aspects of an organisation's marketing intentions and activities. It is a summary document, providing a framework that permits managers and specialists to undertake the detailed work of marketing in a co-ordinated and effective fashion.

The creation of a good marketing plan is likely to be a time-consuming exercise, since it should deal with both current circumstances and plans for the future.

- It should be based on **detailed knowledge** of both the **target market** and the company involved.
- It should give sufficient detail of intentions to support the design and operation of all **marketing-related activities**.

Planning enables organisations to be effective, not just efficient. Information is gathered and used to develop a corporate plan which acts as a framework within which specific functions such as marketing can develop their own objectives and plans.

 EXAM TIP   Application

Take good note of the following terms: you need to be familiar with them to be able to place marketing activities within the context of business activity, and you will encounter them whenever you are reading about any aspect of marketing or business as a whole.

 KEY CONCEPTS   Concept

Planning involves:

- setting objectives, quantifying targets for achievement and communicating these targets to others
- selecting strategies, tactics, policies, programmes and procedures for achieving the objective

Goals: what you are trying to achieve; the intention behind any action.

Objectives: a goal which often can be quantified. Example: increase profits by 30% over the next 12 months. They might not always be expressed in financial terms however. Example: customer satisfaction or loyalty measures may be used.

Strategy: the method chosen to achieve goals or objectives. Example: 'we will achieve our objective of increasing profits by growing market share in existing markets'.

A suggested format for a full market plan is given below. However, there is no standard template or list of contents for a marketing plan. Different organisations find it appropriate to consider different factors depending on where they are in their development and the industry that they are in. One possible approach is offered as an example.

Depending on the context, and the information available, some of the steps may change, or change in priority. For example, if you are working with a very constrained budget the constraints item may need to be stated early in the plan. Which models may be used to determine strategy will depend on the outcomes of the marketing audit and SWOT analysis (as we will see in the next chapter).

Marketing plan

1	**Executive summary**	A short high-level summary of the major points of the plan.
2	**Mission statement and corporate objectives**	The internal context of the plan: at the organisation is trying to achieve, and what its key guiding values.
3	**Situation analysis /marketing audit**	
	• Macro environment audit	Eg PEST factor analysis
	• Micro environment audit	Eg Internal systems/culture/skills audit
		Competitor analysis
		Customer analysis
		Market/product/price research
4	**SWOT analysis**	Appraisal of internal strengths and weaknesses, and external opportunities and threats
5	**Marketing objectives**	What the marketing plan is intended to achieve (in the light of elements 2-4)
6	**Marketing strategies**	How marketing objectives will be achieved
	• Matching or conversion?	Suggested by SWOT analysis
	• Competitive strategies?	Suggested by competitor/market/product analysis
	• Growth strategies?	Suggested by product/market analysis
	• Market segmentation/targeting?	Identifying targetable sub-sections of the market or customer population
	• Product/brand positioning?	Determining how product/brand should be perceived by the relevant target market/segment
7	**Marketing tactics**	Action plans for each of the elements of the (extended) marketing mix, to implement marketing strategies
	• Product plans	
	• Pricing plans	
	• Distribution plans	
	• Promotion plans	
8	**Marketing budget**	Quantified monetary plans: sales/revenue forecasts, costs/expenditure budgets, forecast profit and loss statement. Also covered here is the allocation of other resources such as time, staff and assets
9	**Timetable**	Detailed timescales for implementation of plans
10	**Monitoring and control**	How progress and results will be monitored, reviewed and measured against objectives/budget
11	**Summary/conclusion**	If required. There may also be an appendix with supporting documents and figures which are too detailed to include in the body of the plan

Syllabus reference 2.3 lists the uses to which a marketing plan will be put. The outline of the marketing planning document which is shown above can be directly matched to this list to show how it applies in the overall context of the marketing planning process.

Syllabus item	Where covered by marketing plan
Delivering strategies and achieving objectives	Points 2-5, 6 and 10
Implementing a marketing project	Point 7
Monitoring of timeline progress against schedule	Point 9
Managing implementation	Point 7
Resource management (human/physical/financial)	Point 8
Measurement of successful implementation	Point 10

MARKETING AT WORK

Application

There is a US company called Mplans that sells templates for marketing plans and you can look at some free samples if you visit the website: **www.mplans.com**. The CIM Learning Zone also contains an online marketing planning tool: **www.cim.co.uk**.

1.2 Corporate strategic plans

An organisation's overall development is guided by **corporate strategic plans**.

KEY CONCEPT

Concept

Corporate strategy is concerned with the overall purpose and scope of the organisation in meeting the expectations of owners or major stakeholders and adding value to the different parts of the enterprise.

Strategic planning is a sequence of analytical and evaluative procedures to formulate an intended strategy, and **tactics** are the detailed means of implementing it.

It is important to remember how the marketing plan fits into overall corporate strategy. Students are often confused by the appearance of environmental analysis in the marketing planning process and assume that this means that the marketing plan is the same thing as the overall corporate strategic plan. This may be true in some highly marketing-oriented organisations, but it is not **necessarily** so.

The marketing plan and the corporate strategic plan are not the same thing. The difference is largely one of **scope:** the corporate plan has to consider **all aspects** of the organisation's business, while a marketing plan is principally about **marketing activities**. The marketing plan is aligned with the corporate plan and **supports** it.

Marketing plans and strategies will be developed within an overall strategic framework and will be very closely linked with plans for other functions of the organisation. This approach ensures that marketing efforts are consistent with organisational goals and that the resources available within the organisation are used as effectively as possible.

This can be depicted as follows as 'Planning hierarchy'.

Figure 3.1: The hierarchy of planning

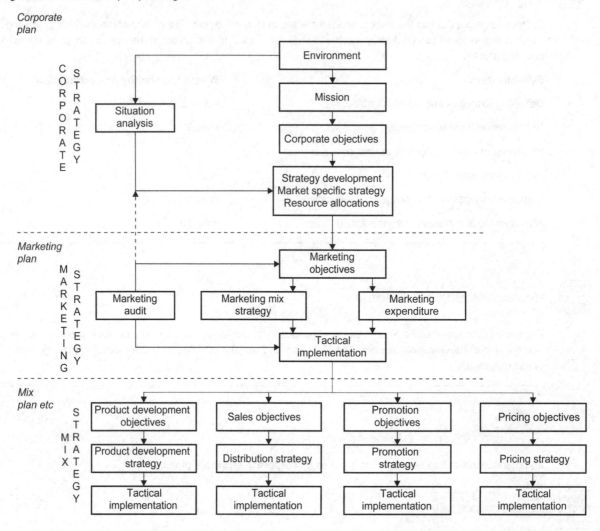

We will now look at the key elements within this hierarchy: the mission statement, situation analysis, strategy development, specific marketing plans, tactical implementation and finally (not shown on this diagram but critically important!) monitoring and control.

1.2.1 Mission statement

 KEY CONCEPT   Concept

The **mission statement** says what an organisation is aiming to achieve through the conduct of its business. The purpose is to provide the organisation with focus and direction.

The corporate mission depends on a variety of factors. Mission statements may change or evolve over time. They should be regarded as a **dynamic tool**. **Corporate history** will often influence the markets and customer groups served. A market-led business will be influenced by changing market conditions and customer tastes and behaviour.

An approach to the corporate mission is to consider the **company's product and market scope**. The mission statement then rests on customer groups, needs served and technology employed.

A mission statement should not be too defining; it should indicate the scope of future developments. It would be insufficient for a bank to identify its mission as being 'banking' – it would be more appropriate to identify that mission as being, for example, 'meeting consumer needs for financial transactions'.

A good mission statement should be concise. It should clearly answer the classic question, 'what business are we in?' or 'what satisfactions do we aim to provide for our customers?'

A contemporary approach to writing mission statements is to cover various key areas such as:

- Proper treatment of staff
- Customer service and satisfaction
- Environmental consciousness and social responsibility
- Product quality and innovation
- Profitability and shareholder value

 ACTIVITY 1 Application

Try to devise a mission statement about yourself as if you were a company. State what you aim to achieve, what your focus and direction is, according to the criteria given above.

1.2.2 Situation analysis

 KEY CONCEPT Concept

Situation analysis involves a thorough study of the broad trends within the economy and society, and a comprehensive analysis of markets, consumers, competitors and the company itself.

Environmental factors will affect the mission statement and the identification of objectives, but once strategic objectives are established, a much more comprehensive analysis is necessary. This detailed environmental analysis is considered further in the next chapter.

1.2.3 Strategy development

The process of strategy development links corporate level plans and market level plans. In developing strategy, most large organisations will be required to make important **resource allocation** decisions. This process of resource allocation is a key component of corporate strategy and it indicates the direction in which specific markets or products are expected to develop. It therefore provides direction for the development of **market level plans**. As we have already noted, the marketing plan is very important for resource management.

An **internal appraisal** can assess the company's resources and ability to compete. Corporate resources are sometimes described as the **five Ms**.

- Men: its human resources and organisation
- Money: its financial health
- Materials: supply sources and products
- Machines: the production facilities, fixed assets, capacity
- Markets: its reputation, position and market prospects

1.2.4 Specific marketing plans

Market specific plans express the organisation's intentions concerning **particular markets and products**. The **marketing audit** (examined in more detail in the next chapter) influences objectives and the tactics by which they can be achieved. Such analysis can provide information on patterns of competition, consumer behaviour and market segmentation, as an input to the development of marketing objectives and market specific strategies

Market specific variables, typically under the control of the marketing department, constitute the **marketing mix**: **product, price, promotion and place**, developed in more detail in Part C of this Text. The development of the marketing mix aims to ensure that the product is appropriate to the market in terms of its features, its image, its perceived value and its availability.

Marketing expenditure will depend on resource allocation decisions at corporate level, but any marketing plan will include, as a matter of course, a statement of the budget required and the way it is to be spent.

1.2.5 Tactical implementation

Implementation consists of identifying the specific tasks of the marketing mix strategy that are to be performed, the allocation of those tasks to individuals and putting in place a system of control. The implementation procedure may also include some elements of contingency planning. The market is always evolving so even the most well formed marketing plan will need to be changed and certain planned activities may turn out to be inappropriate or ineffective.

1.3 Monitoring and control

  KEY CONCEPT Concept

Once the marketing plan is implemented, the task of management is to monitor and control what happens. **Monitoring** means checking that everything is going to plan. **Control** means taking corrective action as early as possible if things are not going to plan.

Monitoring and control is accomplished in the following ways.

*   Regular comparison of actual sales and marketing costs against budget

*   Analysis of the performance of individual products, individual distribution outlets, individual salespeople and so on. Information collected by the accounting system and other management systems can be used to calculate a huge variety of financial and non-financial performance measures, as regularly as is felt necessary

*   Collection of feedback from customers and other stakeholders

*   Analysis of media coverage, for instance reviews of new products in the trade press

*   Continual observation of the environment. Have competitors unexpectedly launched a new product? Is the economy going into recession?

2 Types of organisational objective

 "Corporate objectives are the strategic statements of where the company wants to be." Blythe, J. (2008) ∎

Objectives can be quantitative (financial). Most commercial organisations will express their **primary** objective in financial terms.

*   Profitability
*   Sales/Revenue
*   Marketing
*   Growth eg market share (as a general rule, most firms want to grow)
*   Return on capital employed (ROCE) / return on investment (ROI)
*   Growth in shareholder value
*   Earnings per share (EPS)
*   Cash flow

Although a company must make profits, profit on its own is not satisfactory as an overall long-term corporate objective because it fails to allow for the size of the capital investment required to make that profit. Shareholders should be interested in maximising profits over time, and that means incurring costs today so that returns can be generated in the future.

 ACTIVITY 2 Application

What drawbacks can you identify to the use of profitability as a primary objective over the longer term?

 MARKETING AT WORK Application

Mercedes-Benz, along with many other companies, sees increased sales as one of its major quantifiable objectives. How can it achieve this?

It is launching a new campaign to make the marque more appealing to a younger generation of drivers. Concerned that it does not appeal to the under-50s market as much as Audi or BMW, Mercedes-Benz has recently appointed a new advertising agency to help drive its strategy to appeal to a younger and more aspirational market, using themes such as 'presence', 'attraction' and 'ambition'.

www.brandrepublic.com

Objectives may be more qualitative:

- Levels of technology and innovation achieved
- Survival
- Ethically and socially responsible aims
- Customer service and satisfaction levels
- Product quality
- Employee/HR practice

3 Setting objectives

Objective setting is a key part of marketing planning. Objectives should set out clearly what the organisation is aiming to achieve, both at the corporate level and at the marketing level.

Corporate objectives define specific goals for the organisation as a whole. As noted above, these may be expressed in terms of profitability, returns on investment, growth of asset base and earnings per share. They may also reflect non-financial goals: innovation, market share, corporate social responsibility, leading employer brand and so forth. Corporate objectives then need to be translated into market-specific marketing objectives.

3.1 Primary and subsidiary objectives

Whatever primary objectives are set, subsidiary objectives will be developed beneath them. The diagram below illustrates this process.

Figure 3.2: Hierarchy of objectives

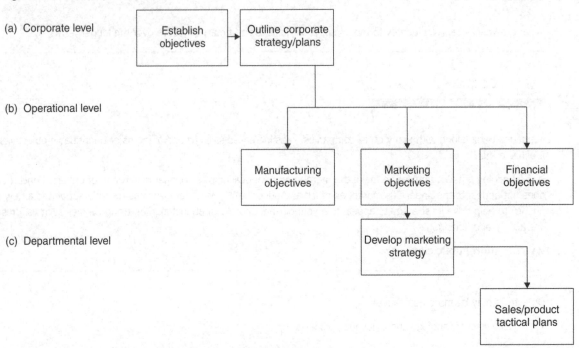

(a) Corporate level

(b) Operational level

(c) Departmental level

Unless an organisation is so small that it is a single unit, without functional departments, the overall objectives of the organisation must indicate different requirements for different functions. While some corporate goals cannot be stated in quantifiable terms, subsidiary objectives must be very clear cut, so that performance can be **measured**.

 MARKETING AT WORK   Application/Evaluation

For example, if a company sets itself an objective of growth in profits as its primary aim, it will then have to develop strategies by which this primary objective can be achieved. An objective must then be set for each individual strategy. Secondary objectives might then be concerned with sales growth, continual technological innovation, customer service, product quality, efficient resource management or reducing the company's reliance on loans as a source of finance.

British Airways publicly once indicated the following corporate goals.

- Safety and security
- Strong and consistent financial performance
- Global reach
- Superior services
- Good value for money
- Healthy working environment
- Good neighbourliness

What do you think of them? Which is most important? Will they have changed with such events as September 11 2001, the opening of Heathrow Terminal 5 or the recent strike action? Are there any other objectives that you would have expected to see listed?

Objectives in general should be evaluated for the following SMART criteria, in order to be effective for directing and controlling performance.

SMART	In what sense is an objective SMART?
Specific	Stating exactly what has to be achieved (although not how the job should be done).
Measurable	Quantified, so that that you can tell if the objective has been achieved. If you were aiming for a 10% market share and gained a 15% market share you can tell that you have exceeded your objective.
Achievable	The objective has to be realistic in the circumstances, given the resources that are available: people, equipment, materials, money, information and time.
Relevant	The objective must relate both to the roles of those who are to achieve the objective and to the wider objectives of the organisation.
Time bounded	There should be target deadlines and timeframes for achieving the objective.

3.2 The monitoring and revision of objectives

Successful planning requires a commitment to objectives, and so objectives should not be subject to frequent change. A planning review, in which objectives are reassessed and planning horizons reviewed, should however be held regularly, perhaps once a year.

3.3 Marketing objectives

Marketing objectives should be clear statements of where the organisation wants to be in marketing terms. They describe what the organisation expects to achieve as a result of its planned marketing actions. Using the SMART criteria, examples of marketing objectives might look like this:

- 'To increase market share from the current X% to Y% by 20X0.'
- 'To achieve a sales revenue of £X million at a cost of sales not exceeding 80% in 20X1.'

Objectives can be set for overall achievement as above, or for elements of the strategic plan. For example, if one of the strategies to achieve a profitable increase in sales revenue is to increase awareness of the product, then an advertising objective (a marketing sub-objective) might be: 'To increase product awareness in the target market from V% to W% in 20X1.'

When developing a strategy, a company is seeking a match with its operating environment. This usually means adjusting the company's strategy to fit into the existing market environment. Overall, the strategy must enable the company to meet the specific needs of its consumers and to do so more efficiently than its competitors.

3.3.1 Influences upon marketing objectives

As noted above, corporate objectives need to be translated into market-specific marketing objectives. These may involve targets for the size of the customer base, growth in the usage of certain facilities, gains in market share for a particular product type etc. Marketing objectives will be influenced by a range of factors including:

- The strategic **objectives** of the business as a whole (eg growth, innovation)

- The **resources** (skills, competences, finance, relationships) available

- **Marketing strategy** decisions, eg cost leadership (being the cheapest) or differentiation (having a unique product); how to place your product within the market (product/market strategy)

- Other **functional strategies** that need to be aligned with marketing (eg HR development to support marketing activity)

- The **competitive environment** in the industry or specific competitor activity; which may dictate specific competitive objectives (eg market share gains)

- **Environmental** (PEST) factors (eg presenting opportunities to exploit or constraints to be taken into account in setting realistic objectives)

If such factors are taken into account, objectives are more likely to be relevant (to the needs and challenges of the business) and realistic (given its constraints).

EXAM TIP

Application

Factors influencing the setting of objectives feature on the specimen exam paper. From the Mercedes-Benz example described in Section 2, such factors might include social issues (more young people can afford luxury cars) and the activities of competitors (who have successfully tapped into the under-50s market). Mercedes-Benz may have suffered in the past from an internal company culture that was too focused upon its older customers, and it is now trying to inject some 'new blood' with a new advertising agency and different ways of thinking.

4 The marketing planning process

KEY CONCEPT

Concept

'The **marketing planning process** combines the organisation's overall marketing strategy with fundamental analyses of trends in the marketing environment; company strengths, weaknesses, opportunities and threats, competitive strategies; and identification of target market segments. Ultimately the process leads to the formulation of marketing programmes or marketing mixes which facilitate the implementation of the organisation's strategies and plans'. Dibb, Simkin, Pride & Ferrell. (2005)

The marketing planning process includes the following stages. A large proportion of them are to be discussed in the following chapter where the marketing audit is examined in greater detail than this introductory chapter on marketing planning can allow.

- A general **overview**, setting the marketing function in context: a kind of 'marketing mission statement' , as we have already described, and
- The **definition of marketing objectives** as described in this chapter.
- The **marketing audit**   – external analysis (see Chapter 4)
  – competitor and customer analysis (see Chapter 4)
  – internal analysis (see Chapter 4)
  – SWOT analysis (see Chapter 4)
- **Segmentation** and **targeting** (see Chapter 4)
- **Evaluation** of strategic choices   (see Chapter 4)
- **Implementation** of the marketing mix (see Part C of this text – Chapter 5 to Chapter 9)
- **Control** and budgets (see Chapter 10)

A comprehensive plan provides for:

- **Analysis** of the situation/market/SWOT
- **Planning**: objective setting and strategy formulation
- **Implementation**: action plans and budgets to guide implementation
- **Control**: measuring progress/results against the plan

This is referred to as the **'APIC' framework** which is another way of describing the strategic planning process.

Planning requires good information. Give four examples of internally generated information that might be useful for a business when it is undertaking marketing planning.

In summary, the planning process can be expressed as shown in Figure 3.3. The process is continual and the plan could be reviewed and 'restarted' at any stage.

Figure 3.3: The marketing planning process

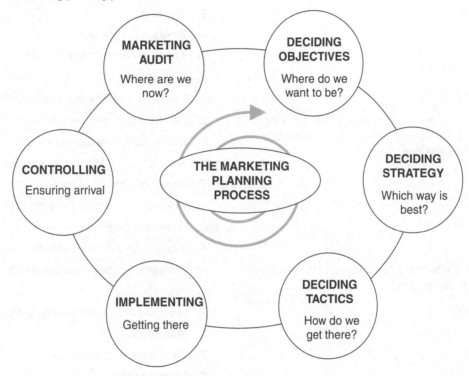

The importance of the marketing planning process (the subject of this whole chapter) features in a 20-mark question on the specimen paper. Meanwhile, remember a point that we made at the very beginning of this chapter (when we were delegating your weekly shop shopping). A marketing plan is not set in stone: it needs to be flexible. If market conditions have changed quite unpredictably there is no point in agonising over not meeting the original targets. It is time to draw up a new plan.

Marketing Planning guru Malcolm McDonald's (2007) text titled: Malcolm McDonald on Marketing Planning is very clear and readable. Chapter 1 and 3 in particular would be worth reading. Reading chapter 3 will be particularly useful for our next chapter – The Marketing Audit. ■

Learning objectives	Covered
1 Explain the importance of objectives, the processes for setting them and the influences upon them	☑ Objectives as a basis for determining future direction, consistency, motivation and measurement
	☑ Objectives as a basis for determining achievement
	☑ SMART objectives (Specific, Measurable, Achievable, Realistic, Timebound)
	☑ Internal and external influences on setting objectives
2 Identify the different types of organisational objectives	☑ Profit
	☑ Sales/Revenue
	☑ Marketing
	☑ Growth eg market share
	☑ Technical – technology innovation
	☑ Survival
	☑ Ethically and socially responsible
3 Evaluate the importance of the marketing planning process to the market oriented organisation	☑ Delivering strategies and achieving objectives
	☑ Implementing a marketing project
	☑ Monitoring of timeline progress against schedule
	☑ Managing implementation
	☑ Resource management (human and physical)
	☑ Financial management
	☑ Measurement of successful implementation
4 Explain the different stages of the marketing planning process	☑ Corporate objectives/business mission
	☑ Marketing audit
	☑ Setting business and marketing objectives
	☑ Marketing strategies
	☑ Marketing tactics/mix decisions
	☑ Implementation
	☑ Monitoring and control

1   What is a marketing plan?

2   What are the six stages in the marketing planning cycle?

3   What are the five Ms?

4   Why should objectives be 'measurable' and 'time-bounded'?

5   State three marketing objectives.

6   Why is profit on its own not necessarily a satisfactory objective?

7   Distinguish between 'monitoring' and 'control'

8   What is the APIC framework?

9   Give a definition of 'strategy'

10   What are some of the influences upon marketing objectives?

1　Everybody's statement will be individual to him or her. Here are some of the many aspects that could be considered.

- Levels of educational attainment
- Career or occupational aspirations
- Treatment of colleagues and other people
- Attitudes to material possessions and wealth accumulation
- Type of lifestyle
- Approach to health and recreational activities
- Activities on environmental issues
- Travel, leisure and entertainment
- Attitude to progress and stability
- Political outlook and participation
- International and local identity
- Approaches to modernity, progress and conservatism
- Works of charity
- Attitudes to law and order
- Honesty and ethical behaviour
- Family and friends
- Involvement in the community
- Fulfilment of emotional needs
- Pursuit of happiness

2　Typical examples of decisions which sacrifice longer-term objectives in the interest of short term profitability:

- Postponing or abandoning capital expenditure, which would eventually contribute to (longer-term) growth and profits, in order to protect short-term cash flow and profits

- Cutting R&D expenditure to save operating costs, and so reducing the prospects for future product development

- Reducing quality control, to save operating costs

- Reducing the level of customer service, to save operating costs

3　Examples of internally generated information.

- Sales records
- Customer records
- Marketing communications records

- Market research information
- Cost records
- Stock records

1　A specification of an organisation's marketing intentions and activities.

2　Marketing audit, deciding objectives, deciding strategy, deciding tactics, implementation and control.

3　Men (ie staff resources)

Money

Materials

Machines

Markets

4　They should be measurable so you can tell whether or not you have achieved them. They should be time-bounded because after a certain time it will be too late to achieve them.

5   •   Increasing sales

         •   Increasing market share

         •   Increasing product awareness

6   With the objective of maximising profits over time, costs will need to be incurred today (investment in assets, new product development etc) that will dent profits in the short term. If shareholders have a short-term view they may resist in investing in the future productive capacity of the company.

7   Monitoring means checking that everything is going to plan. Control means taking corrective action as early as possible if things are not going to plan

8   Analysis, planning, implementation and control

9   Strategy can be defined as 'the method chosen to achieve goals or objectives'.

10   •   The objectives of the business as a whole

         •   The resources available

         •   Marketing strategy decisions

         •   Other functional strategies that need to be aligned

         •   The state of competition in the industry

         •   Environmental (PEST) factors

References

Blythe, J (2006) Principles and Practice of Marketing, Thomson Learning.

Blythe, J (2005) Essentials of Marketing, 3rd edition, FT Prentice Hall.

Brassington, F and Pettitt, S (2006) Principles of Marketing, 4th edition, FT Prentice Hall.

Dibb S, Simkin L, Pride WM, Ferrell OC (2001) Marketing Concepts and Strategies, 4th edition, Houghton Miffin.

Brownsell, A (2008) "Mercedes-Benz targets younger drivers", Marketing. Available online from www.brandrepublic.com, [accessed 6 May 2008]

Chapter 4

The marketing audit

Topic list

1   Conducting a marketing audit

2   The micro environment

3   The macro environment

4   Competitors and customers

5   Internal appraisal – competences and resources

6   SWOT analysis

Introduction

Marketing management aims to ensure the company is pursuing effective policies to promote its products, markets and distribution channels. This involves exercising strategic control of marketing, and the means to apply strategic control is known as the **marketing audit**. Not only is the marketing audit an important aspect of marketing control, it can be used to provide much information and analysis for the corporate planning process by contributing to the corporate SWOT.

The marketing audit is really the 'launch pad' for the marketing plan (Brassington and Pettitt) and this chapter describes its elements in some detail, as important additional material to reinforce the previous chapter which looked at marketing planning as a whole.

The marketing environment (broadly categorised as either internal or external) is covered in sections 2 and 3. Customer and competitor analysis, important for the formulation of marketing strategy, is described in section 4. Section 5 covers the analysis of organisational resources and competences, and how this analysis can be applied to marketing planning. Finally, section 6 deals with SWOT analysis. By understanding strengths, weaknesses, opportunities and threats, an organisation can begin to put together plans for making the most of its market.

Once the marketing audit exercise has been completed, managers should have a clearer idea about what needs to be done to meet the firm's overall objectives.

Syllabus linked learning objective

By the end of the chapter you will be able to:

Learning objectives	Syllabus link
1 Explain the concept of the marketing audit	2.5

1 Conducting a marketing audit

"The marketing audit is a review of the firm's current objectives, strategies, organisation, performance and activities, and its primary purpose is to pick out the firm's strengths and weaknesses so that managers can improve on them in future". Blythe, J. (2008) ■

KEY CONCEPT

Concept

A **marketing audit** is a systematic and comprehensive review of a firm's current marketing activities and capacity, used in marketing planning.

In order to exercise proper strategic control a marketing audit should satisfy four requirements.

- It should take a **comprehensive** look at every product, market, distribution channel and ingredient in the marketing mix.

- It should not be **restricted** to areas of apparent ineffectiveness such as an unprofitable product or a troublesome distribution channel.

- It should be carried out according to a set of predetermined, **specified procedures**.

- It should be conducted **regularly,** usually on an annual basis.

A marketing audit will evaluate six aspects of marketing (see paragraph 2.1 for more detail on these points):

- Environment
- Strategy
- Organisation
- Systems
- Productivity
- Functions

The marketing audit should look at both the organisation's **micro environment** (see Section 2) and its **macro environment** (PEST factors – see Section 3).

1.1 Advantages of a marketing audit

- It should reduce the need for crisis management
- It should identify information needs
- A formal process forces people to think

EXAM TIP

Application

Past papers have asked about the potential *disadvantages* of a marketing audit. This does not appear in the syllabus but perhaps the resource requirements (such as time and manpower) could be cited as an example.

1.2 The auditing process as a control mechanism

A **marketing audit** performs a dual role in checking both where the company is, and where it has come from. It reinforces the idea of marketing planning (of which the marketing audit forms a part) as a cyclical process.

Figure 4.1: The marketing process

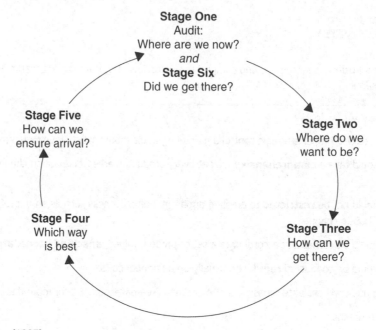

Wilson, Gilligan, Pearson (1997)

  EXAM TIP

Application

A question on the specimen paper asks how the marketing audit fits into the planning process. The short answer is that it kicks the whole thing off.

2 The micro environment

 KEY CONCEPTS

Concept

The **internal environment** is those cultural, social and economic factors that are contained within the organisation itself.

The **micro environment** (also known as the "task' environment) comprises the **market environment** (all aspects of a market which affect the company's relationship with its customers and the patterns of competition – Section 4) and also includes **internal operations and aspects of the organisation** (such as corporate culture), which may influence the development of a marketing strategy.

Figure 4.1 supports this definition.

BPP
LEARNING MEDIA

Figure 4.1: The micro environment

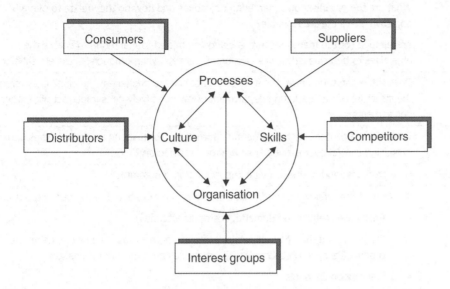

2.1 Areas to consider

An examination of the **micro** and **internal environments** would cover the following.

Micro environment	Audit issues
Suppliers	The availability of resources, selling policies
Distribution	Main distribution channels, their efficiency levels and potential for growth
Markets	Developments in major markets, market growth, and changes in turnover and profits. Performance of different market segments
Customers	Customer views on price quality and service given by organisation and its competitors. Decision processes of different types of customer
Competitors	Objectives and strategies, market share, and strengths and weaknesses. Developments in future competition.
Stakeholders/publics	Important groups and how they have been dealt with

 MARKETING AT WORK — — — — — — — — — — Application

Fortune magazine recently released its list of the world's most admired companies, which included a section covering airlines that have managed to boost their reputations in the past year. Singapore Airlines topped the list, ahead of Continental Airlines and Delta. The top ten also included the Lufthansa group, Cathay Pacific, British Airways and Qantas.

Fortune's list of the world's most admired companies across all industries was topped by Apple, with Google in second position and Berkshire Hathaway ranked third. Walt Disney took top place in the entertainment section, while BMW was named the most admired brand in the motor vehicles industry.

www.justtheflight.co.uk – accessed 3 June 2010

Internal environment	Audit issues
Marketing strategy	What are the organisation's marketing objectives and how do they relate to overall objectives? Are they reasonable?
	Are enough (or too many) resources being committed to marketing to enable the objectives to be achieved; is the division of costs between products, areas etc satisfactory?
Marketing organisation	Does the organisation have the structural capability to implement the plan? How effective is the structure of the marketing department? How effectively does it interact with other departments?
Marketing systems	What are the procedures for gathering information, formulating marketing plans and exercising control over these plans? Are they satisfactory?
Marketing productivity	How profitable and cost effective is the marketing programme?
Marketing functions	A review of the effectiveness of each element of the mix should be carried out, evaluating:
	• Price levels (effects on demand, customer attitudes)
	• Products (and their market 'health') and the product mix as a whole, using the product life cycle (PLC) and/or BCG matrix as a framework for analysis
	• Distribution channels
	• The promotion mix: personal selling, advertising, promotions

ACTIVITY 1

Application

What questions might a marketing auditor want answered about the sales force?

EXAM TIP

Application

You may have to explain the purpose, focus and components of a marketing audit. Show how it can be made relevant to the firm, how it can be conducted, and how the results might be used.

3 The macro environment

KEY CONCEPT

Concept

Marketing environment research is the gathering of information about the organisation's environment in terms of political, social/cultural, economic and technological threats and opportunities.

The wider macro (external) environment may be analysed using the PESTEL mnemonic.

- Political
- Economic
- Social
- Technological
- Environmental (green)
- Legal

3.1 The political environment

An organisation's freedom of action is constrained by what is politically acceptable. Note that this is not the same thing as 'legal'. Changes in society are reflected in the priorities of politicians and governments have many ways of bringing pressure to bear on business. They frequently use such levers as economic power, codes of conduct and statements of policy to set the ground rules for organisational life.

The government **controls** much of the economy, being the nation's largest supplier, employer, customer and investor. It also influences the **money supply**, controls the level of **interest rates** and sets **exchange rate** policy.

3.2 The economic environment

The general state of the economy influences prospects for all businesses. Generally, economic growth produces a benign environment with healthy demand for most goods and services.

Some **economic influences** relevant to marketers are listed below.

- The rate of inflation
- Unemployment and the availability of manpower
- Interest rates
- The level and type of taxation
- The availability of credit
- Exchange rates

  ACTIVITY 2 Application

Give examples of economic influences at an international level. Many of these are subject to the policies of national governments.

3.2.1 Economic trends – regional, national and international

The **local** economic environment affects wage rates, availability of labour, disposable income of local consumers, and the provision of business infrastructure and services.

National economic trends will affect prospects for growth, inflation, unemployment and taxation levels.

World trends have an important influence on the future of any company with plans to trade abroad, whether buying imports or selling as exporters.

3.3 The social environment

Social change involves changes in the nature, attitudes and habits of society.

(a) **Rising standards of living** may result in wider ownership of items like DVD players, dishwashers, microwave ovens, MP3 players and sailing boats.

(b) **Society's changing attitude to business** tends to increase companies' obligations and responsibilities with respect to environmental protection and ethical conduct.

(c) An increasing proportion of people are employed in clerical, supervisory or management jobs.

3.3.1 Cultural changes

Cultural variables are particularly significant for overseas marketing.

Language differences have clear marketing implications. For example, brand names have to be translated, often leading to entirely different meanings in the new language.

Cultural differences may affect marketing in a variety of ways.

- Design of goods
- Trading hours
- Distribution methods

3.3.2 Socio-economic groups

Members of particular groups have similar lifestyles, beliefs and values which affect their purchasing behaviour. Socio-economic classification involves taking factors such as occupation, education and income into account. Family background is also a very strong influence on purchasing behaviour. Family structure is changing in most of the developed world. There are more single person and single parent households due to the increased divorce rate and population ages. The traditional nuclear family represents a relatively small proportion of all families.

3.4 The technological environment

Developments in technology can affect the market in several ways.

(a) **Types of products and services**. Within consumer markets we have seen the emergence of home computers and Internet services. There are products and services available today that would not have been dreamed of even 10 years ago.

(b) **The way in which products are made**. Modern automated systems of design and manufacture have revolutionised manufacturing. Cuts in costs may afford the opportunity to reduce prices.

(c) **The way in which services are provided**. Call centres and Internet trading have expanded widely.

(d) **The way in which markets are identified and communicated with**. Database systems make it easier to analyse the market place. New types of marketing strategy, and new organisational structures, have been developed.

 MARKETING AT WORK

Application

Using technology to campaign and communicate

Social networking site Facebook launched a campaign to encourage its 23 million UK users to engage with the 2010 election campaign. Democracy UK asked questions and then aggregated opinion and debate.

Richard Allan, Facebook's director of European public policy said that "Facebook has as many users as voted for all of the three main parties in the last election - social networks will prove to be as central to political debate and the general election as the post, the phone and television have been in the past."

The most popular politician on Facebook is currently Mayor of London Boris Johnson, who has more than 36,000 fans; of the main parties, the Conservatives has 25,094 fans to Labour's 7,459 and the Liberal Democrats' 7,829

www.telegraph.co.uk

3.5 The ecological (green) environment

Public awareness of the connections between industrial production, mass consumption and environmental damage is higher than it has ever been, with information flooding out through the mass media and sometimes generating profound public reaction. Modern marketing practice needs to reflect awareness of these concerns, and is itself being changed by the issues that they raise.

3.5.1 Green concerns

The modern green movement is animated by concerns over pollution, overpopulation and the effects of massive growth on the finite resources of the earth. Green economists have tried to put together an economics based on alternative ideas.

- Monetary valuation of economic resources
- Promoting the quality of life
- Self reliance
- Mutual aid
- Personal growth
- Human rights

3.5.2 The impact of green issues on marketing practices

Environmental impacts on business

(a) **Direct**

    (i)   Changes affecting costs or resource availability

    (ii)   Impact on demand

    (iii) Effect on power balances between competitors in a market

(b) **Indirect**. Examples are pressure from concerned customers or staff and legislation affecting the business environment.

The green consumer is a driving force behind changes in marketing and business practices. There is extensive evidence of this, provided by:

- Surveys which indicate increased levels of environmental awareness and concern
- Increasing demand for, and availability of, information on environmental issues
- Value shifts from consumption to conservation
- Effective PR and marketing campaigns by environmental charities and causes

3.6 The legal environment

The legal system may be thought of as part of the political environment. It lays down the framework for business, with rules about business structure and ownership such as the Companies Act in the UK. It regulates business relationships with contract law and guarantees individual rights with employment law. There is a wide range of regulations dealing with general business activities such as health and safety regulations, rules about emissions into the environment and planning regulations.

4 Competitors and customers

"Frequently firms fail to recognise who their competitors are. It is not at all unusual for firms to define competition too narrowly, simply because they define their business too narrowly ... Marketing managers need to decide which competitors offer the closest substitutes in terms of meeting the consumers' needs." Blythe, J. (2008)

4.1 Competitor analysis

The nature of competition is a key element in the environment of commercial organisations. There are four main issues.

- Identifying the competitors
- The strength of the competition
- Characteristics of the market
- The likely strategies and responses of competitors to the organisation's strategies

Here are five key questions for the tactical assessment of competitors.

- **Who** are we competing against?
- What are their **objectives**?
- What **strategies** are they pursuing, with what success?
- What **strengths and weaknesses** do they possess?
- How are they likely to react to any actions of ours?

4.2 Customer analysis

 KEY CONCEPT Concept

Consumer behaviour can be defined as the behaviour that consumers display in searching for, purchasing, using, evaluating and disposing of products. It provides the underpinning knowledge which guides subsequent marketing strategy.

4.2.1 Factors affecting consumer behaviour

A number of factors influence the consumer buying process.

Fig. 4.3: Influences upon the consumer buying process

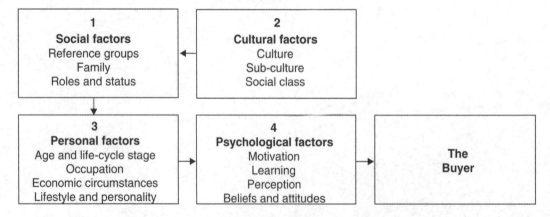

(a)   **Cultural factors** exert the broadest and deepest influence on consumer behaviour. The culture in which we live determines our **values, beliefs and perceptions**. **Buying behaviour** is also affected by **subculture** and **social class**. Different social classes also display distinct brand preferences in areas such as clothing, decorative products and cars.

(b) A consumer's behaviour is also influenced by **social factors**. People are influenced in their buying by the groups they are members of, called **associate groups**, and by the groups whose behaviour they reject, called **disassociate groups**. Marketers, in planning their target market strategy, should try to identify the groups and the key individuals whose behaviours and lifestyles are followed. For example, football stars are used in advertising to appeal to the male youth market.

(c) A buyer's decisions are also influenced by **personal factors**.

    (i) The **family life cycle model** proposes that as we move through different phases of our lives, we buy different products and services and change our priorities.

    (ii) **Occupation** also influences consumption patterns.

    (iii) A person's **lifestyle** also influences what is deemed important to purchase, where they search for information on those goods and how they make the purchase decision.

(d) Finally **psychological factors** such as motivation, learning, perception, beliefs and attitudes influence the consumer buying process.

 ACTIVITY 3   Application

It is critical to have a sound marketing information system covering the marketing environment. Summarise the information needed for an appraisal of the task environment.

5 Internal appraisal - competences and resources

 " [The marketing audit] encourages management to reflect systematically on the environment and the organisation's ability to respond, given its actual and planned capabilities." Brassington, F and Pettitt, S. (2006) ∎

 KEY CONCEPT   Concept

An **internal appraisal** assesses the company's resources and ability to compete.

5.1 Corporate resources

As we saw in the previous chapter, corporate resources are sometimes described as the **five Ms**. To recap:

- **Men**: its human resources and organisation
- **Money**: its financial health
- **Materials**: supply sources and products
- **Machines**: the production facilities, fixed assets, capacity
- **Markets**: its reputation, position and market prospects

In addition to this list it is also necessary to remember the less obvious intangibles like goodwill and brand names.

 ACTIVITY 4   Application

For each of the five Ms identified above, give examples of the types of question which you would wish to ask in order to obtain information for use in an internal analysis.

5.2 Measuring the gap

The organisation needs to measure any gap between what it *possesses* in terms of resources, and what it *needs* in order to deliver its products and/or services to customers. Typically, the analysis would use information from all areas of company activity. Here are some examples from a marketing viewpoint.

(a) **Marketing**

- Success rate of new product launches
- Advertising: evaluating advertising strategies and individual campaigns
- Market shares and sizes: is the organisation in a strong or weak position?
- Portfolio of business units: new, growth, mature and declining markets
- Sales force organisation and performance
- Service quality
- Customer care strategies: nature of markets targeted

(b) **Products**

- Sales by market, area, product groups, outlets
- Margins and contributions to profits from individual products
- Product quality
- Product portfolio: age and structure of markets
- Price elasticity of demand and price sensitivity of demand for products

(c) **Distribution**

- Delivery service standards – lead times for competitors and products
- Warehouse delivery fleet capacity
- Geographical availability of products

(d) **Research and development (R & D)**

- R & D projects in relation to marketing plans
- Evaluation of R & D in new products/variations on existing products
- Evaluation of R & D in comparison to what competitors are doing

(e) **Finance**

- Contribution of products to cash flow and return on investment
- Profitability of individual customers

(f) **Management and staff**

- Age profile
- Skills and attitudes
- State of morale and labour turnover
- Training and recruitment facilities
- Manpower utilisation
- Management team strengths and weaknesses

(g) **Organisation**

- Organisation structure in relation to the organisation's needs
- Appropriateness of management style and philosophy
- Communication and information systems

5.3 Growth strategies

The objective of most organisations that supply goods and services to customers is to grow. In this way they can continue to supply ever increasing numbers of customers. The capacity of an organisation to deliver this growth depends upon an analysis of its products and markets which will give rise to a selection of growth strategies.

The **Ansoff Product/Market matrix** is used to classify growth strategies. It offers four strategies: market penetration or development, product development and diversification.

Ansoff's Product/Market matrix (below) suggests that an organisation's attempts to grow its business depend upon whether it markets new or existing products in new or existing markets. This produces four possible options.

Figure 4.4: Ansoff's growth strategies

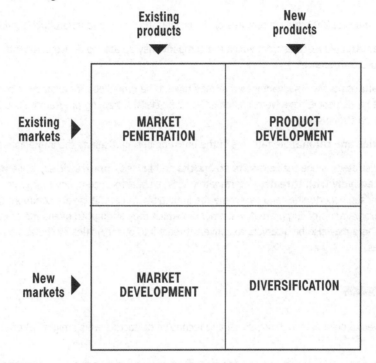

(a)   **Market penetration**

This involves selling more of the existing products in existing markets. Possible options are persuading existing users to use more; persuading non-users to use; or attracting consumers from competitors. This is only a viable strategy if the market is not already saturated with suppliers.

(b)   **Market development**

This involves expanding into new markets with existing products. These may be new markets geographically, new market segments or new uses for products. For example, a lawyer based in the north of a country may start to offer an online legal advice service, thereby opening up a much larger market nationwide, or even worldwide.

(c)   **Product development**

This approach requires the organisation to develop new products to appeal to existing markets. This may be done by tailoring the products more specifically to the needs of existing consumers, or by developing related products which will appeal to the customer base. An example might be a supermarket that extends its opening hours to 24 hours a day, and starts selling petrol or financial services on site.

(d)   **Diversification**

Diversification – new products into new markets – is a more risky strategy because the organisation is moving into areas in which it has little or no experience. Instances of pure diversification are rare and usually occur only when there are no other possible routes for growth available. Virgin is one example of a company that has diversified very successfully.

6 SWOT Analysis

KEY CONCEPT

Concept

SWOT analysis is a commonly used technique to assess the current situation of the business. Strengths and weaknesses are features of the organisation; opportunities and treats are features of the environment. Effective SWOT analysis does not simply require a categorisation of information, but also requires some assessment of the relative importance of the various factors.

Strengths and weaknesses are features of the organisation itself and its product/service range.

(a)   **Strengths** are features from which the company may be able to derive competitive advantage. They are also known as core competences.

(b)   **Weaknesses** are disadvantages that may have to be remedied. For example a company's growth is being hampered because its people have weak customer handling skills. A training programme could be introduced to help its people develop strong skills.

Opportunities and threats are features of the environment, particularly the immediate competitive or task environment.

A successful strategy is one that **exploits strengths** and **seizes opportunities**, while **remedying weaknesses** and **dealing effectively with threats**. Unfortunately, it is unusual for a company to possess all the strengths it needs to exploit its chosen opportunities and overcome the immediate threats. It is very common, therefore, for companies to undertake programmes of corporate development in which they attempt to overcome crucial weaknesses and build new strengths. There may also be attempts to convert threats into opportunities by the same process eg buying out a rival group of companies.

 ACTIVITY 5

Application

Give examples of political, economic, social and technological factors which might (a) offer opportunities or (b) be a source of threats.

SWOT analysis is sometimes presented using a grid, as in the diagram below. The goal is to match strengths with prevailing opportunities, and try to convert the 'negatives' (weaknesses and threats) into 'positives' (strengths and opportunities). This is easier said than done!

Figure 4.5: Swot analysis grid

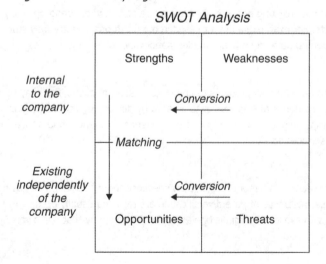

Learning objectives	Covered
1 Explain the concept of the marketing audit as an appraisal of	☑ The internal and external environment
	☑ Organisational strengths, weaknesses, opportunities and threats
	☑ Organisational competencies and capabilities
	☑ Organisational resource versus an organisation's capacity to deliver
	☑ Competitor analysis

Quick quiz

1 What is a marketing audit?

2 What is the business environment?

3 State four economic influences on business.

4 Summarise the effect of technological change on business.

5 State six areas of marketing activity that would be examined during an internal appraisal.

6 What is a SWOT analysis?

7 Name Ansoff's growth strategies.

8 What are the main factors affecting consumer buying behaviour?

9 What is the meaning of the term 'marketing productivity'?

10 Why are marketers interested in the analysis of socio-economic groups?

1   Here are some suggestions.

- What are the organisation's sales force objectives?

- Is the sales force large enough to accomplish the company's objectives?

- Is the sales force organised along the proper principle(s) of specialisation (territory, market, product?)

- Does the sales force show high morale, ability, and effort? Are they sufficiently trained and motivated?

- Are the procedures adequate for setting quotas and evaluating performance?

- How is the company's salesforce perceived in relation to competitors' sales teams?

2   Comparative growth rates, inflation rates, interest rates and wage rates in other countries

The extent of protectionist measures against imports

The nature and extent of exchange controls

The development of international economic communities such as the European Union and the prospects of international trade agreements between countries

The levels of corporate and personal taxation in different countries

3   (a)   *Markets*. What changes are occurring in market trends – sales, profits, geographic distribution? What changes are occurring in market segments and niches?

(b)   *Customers*. How do customers/potential customers rate us on aspects such as reputation, product quality, service, sales force, advertising/price etc, relative to our competitors? What sorts of customers do we have? Are they changing? What is our customers' buying behaviour? Is it changing? How well do we understand our customers and their buying motives?

(c)   *Competitors*. Who are our major competitors? What are their market shares? What are their strengths and weaknesses? Competitors' marketing strategies and likely responses to our marketing actions. Future changes in competition.

(d)   *Distributors*. What are the major distributive channels in our markets? What are the channels' efficiency levels and growth trends?

(e)   *Suppliers*. Outlooks for future supplies. Trends in patterns of buying/selling. Changes in power bases. Evaluations of suppliers against buying/ marketing criteria

(f)   *Agencies*. What are the costs/availability outlooks for transportation services, for warehousing facilities, for financial resources and so on? Just how effective are our advertising, PR and marketing research agencies?

(g)   *Publics*. What publics offer particular opportunities or problems for us? What steps have we taken to deal effectively with each public?

4   Gathering this information involves obtaining answers to the following sort of questions.

(a)   **Men and women**

(i)   Labour. What is the size of the labour force? What are their skills? How much are they paid? What are total labour costs? How efficient is the workforce? What is the rate of labour turnover? How good or bad are industrial relations?

(ii)   Management. What is the size of the management team? What are its specialist skills? What management development and career progression exists? How well has management performed in achieving targets in the past?

(b) **Money**

    (i)   Finance. What are the company's financial resources?

    (ii)   Working capital. How much working capital does the organisation use? What are the average turnover periods for stocks and debtors? What is the credit policy of the organisation? What credit is taken from suppliers? What is the level of bad debts? How is spare cash utilised by the treasury department? How are foreign exchange transactions dealt with? How profitable is our product portfolio?

(c) **Materials**

Where do they come from? Who supplies them? What percentage of the total cost of sales is accounted for by materials? What are wastage levels? Are new materials being developed for the market by suppliers?

(d) **Machines**

(ie fixed assets). What fixed assets does the organisation use? What is their current value? How old are the assets? Are they technologically advanced or out of date?

(e) **Markets**

Market share, reputation, level of competition, deals with distributors and the level of goodwill. Is the company customer oriented and how is the customer contact/service perceived?

5   Opportunities and threats may arise in the following areas.

(a) **Political**: legislation involving, for example, pollution control or a ban on certain products would be a threat to various industries, but also an opportunity for selling lead free petrol and suitable cars. Taxation incentives, rent free factory buildings, or investment grants might be available for exploitation. Government policy may be to increase expenditure on housing, defence, schools and hospitals or roads and transport and this gives opportunities to companies. Political upheaval might damage market and investment prospects, especially overseas.

(b) **Economic**: unemployment, the level of wages and salaries, total customer demand, the growth and decline of industries and suppliers, general investment levels etc. At an international level, world production and the volume of international trade, demand, recessions, import controls, exchange rates.

(c) **Social**: Social attitudes will have a significant effect on customer demand and employee attitudes. Social issues such as environmental pollution, women's roles, and the need to solve social problems offer opportunities for new products and services. Demographic change and population structure will provide continuing product opportunities. Unemployment will strongly affect the total spending power of consumers.

(d) **Technology**: new products appearing, or cheaper means of production or distribution will clearly have profound implications.

---

1   A detailed analysis of marketing capacity and practice, which enables plans to be made with the aim of improving company performance.

2   All the factors that act on the company's markets, including its suppliers, competitors and customers.

3   Examples include:

• Inflation rate	• Unemployment rate
• Interest rates	• Exchange rates
• Tax regime	• Availability of credit

You may think of others.

4
- New products and services
- New methods and processes
- New means of delivering services
- New ways to identify markets

5   Six from:

- Market specifics eg advertising and customer care
- Products
- Distribution
- R&D
- Finance
- Plant and equipment
- Management and staff
- Organisation
- Stocks

6   The analysis of the current situation into strengths, weaknesses, opportunities and threats.

7   Market penetration; market development; product development; diversification

8   Social, cultural, personal and psychological factors

9   How profitable and cost effective the marketing programme is

10   Members of particular groups have similar lifestyles, beliefs and values which affect their purchasing behaviour

References

Blythe, J (2009) Principles and Practice of Marketing, 2nd edition, South-Western/Cengage Learning

Blythe, J (2008) Essentials of Marketing, 4th edition, FT Prentice Hall.

Brassington, F and Pettitt, S (2006) Principles of Marketing, 4th edition, FT Prentice Hall.

Dibb S, Simkin L, Pride WM, Ferrell OC (2005) Marketing: Concepts and Strategies, 5th edition, Houghton Mifflin.

Matt Warman (2010) "General election campaign begins on Facebook", Telegraph online 23 March 2010 (http://www.telegraph.co.uk/technology/facebook) accessed 3 June 2010

Chapter 5
Product planning

Topic list

1   Features and benefits
2   Packaging
3   Services
4   The product life cycle
5   New product development
6   Product and service adoption

Introduction

This Text now begins its coverage of the marketing mix.

- The **product** (this chapter) can be a **service** such as an insurance policy, as well as a physical thing. Products have tangible benefits which can be measured, such as the top speed of a car, and intangible benefits that cannot be measured, such as the enjoyment the customer will get from owning and using the product. Marketing organisations need to put together a 'bundle' of the benefits that will be most valued by customers.

- **Price** is obviously very important (Chapter 6). If it is set too high, target customers may not be able to afford it; if it is set too low, customers may think there is something wrong with the product and better quality may be obtained if they pay more. More fundamentally, if the price is set too low, the company will not cover its costs and may go out of business! There are many different pricing strategies that companies can use to decide on a price.

- **Place** is more accurately called distribution or 'channel management' (Chapter 7). This is partly determined by the nature of the product (you wouldn't try to sell a cement mixer in a supermarket), but there is a wide variety of choices: selling direct to the customer, selling through a retailer or wholesaler or even delivery over the Internet.

- **Promotion** is more accurately called marketing communications (Chapter 8). There is no point in making a product, setting a price and putting the product on shelves unless you tell people you've done so! Promotion is used to inform people about the benefits of a product and persuade them to purchase it. Promotional methods include: advertising, public relations, direct selling, sales promotions (eg free gifts) and many other communication tools. The suite of tools chosen by the organisation is called the 'promotional mix' (not to be confused with the marketing mix).

In this chapter we'll start off by thinking about the essential characteristics of a product and the main types of product (section 1). This includes principles such as branding and packaging (section 2). Section 3 is an introduction to the essential characteristics of services.

Next we will consider the 'life' of a product (Section 4). As you will appreciate, the marketing implications for a product that has just been introduced to the market are different to the implications for a product that consumers already know and love – or one that has 'had its day' and been supplanted by the 'Next Big Thing'.

We'll think about product development in Section 5: where do ideas for new products come from, and how do they get onto the market? Finally in Section 6 we examine the process of product and service adoption.

Do not forget the impact of ICT (Information and Communication Technology) and the 'digital revolution'. Technological developments, especially the Internet, have had, and will continue to have, a significant influence on all aspects of the marketing mix and marketing management.

Syllabus linked learning objectives

By the end of the chapter you will be able to:

Learning objectives	Syllabus link
1 Explain and illustrate the principles of product and planning	3.1
2 Explain the concept of the Product Life Cycle, (PLC) and its limitations as a tool for assessing the life of the product/service	3.2
3 Explain the importance of new products and services into the market	3.3
4 Explain the different stages of the process of New Product Development	3.4
5 Explain the process of product and service adoption explaining the characteristics of customers at each stage of adoption	3.13

The exam may require you directly to recommend the appropriate marketing mix for a particular product, including suggestions for its price, product features, distribution and promotion, and their appropriateness for the chosen marketing strategy. Get used to thinking how each of the four Ps could be used to market any product or service you come across!

The four Ps would, however, also make a good framework to structure answers on questions such as: 'How can an organisation market ...?', 'How do PEST/environment factors affect the marketing of ...?'. When you see the phrase 'marketing', consider whether the four Ps would be a helpful structuring device. However, you need to watch out: if the question refers to the 'full marketing mix', you may need to address the 'extended' marketing mix: the additional three Ps of people, process and physical evidence.

1 Features and benefits

" ... the product is more than just the sum of its physical characteristics; it includes fringe elements such as the brand image, the way the product is packed and delivered, even the colour of the box it comes in." Blythe, J. (2008) ■

Those unfamiliar with marketing probably think of a 'product' as a physical object. However, in marketing the term must be understood in a broader sense.

1.1 What is a product?

A product is a bundle of benefits which satisfy a set of wants that customers have.

A product is a 'thing' with 'features', which offer a total package of benefits. Products have:

- A **physical aspect**, which relates to the components, materials and specifications (colour, size etc) of the product: for example, a size 12 pullover made of 100% pure wool in a natural colour.

- A **functional aspect**, which describes how a product performs and for what purpose it is likely to be bought: for example, a pullover which gives warmth and comfort and lasts well through washing.

- A **symbolic aspect**, which represents the qualities the product suggests to, or offers, the buyer: the '100% pure wool' label may represent quality, status or eco-friendliness.

1.1.1 Product attributes

For the marketer, the total benefit package will include:

- **Tangible attributes**

    - Availability and delivery
    - Performance (usefulness, effectiveness, efficiency)
    - Price
    - Design (appearance, feel etc)
    - Packaging (durability, convenient size, information given)
    - The range of complementary products in a 'line'
    - The availability of accessories and suppliers for product use or maintenance

- **Intangible attributes**
  - Image
  - Perceived value

These features are interlinked. A product has a tangible **price**, but you obtain the **value** that you perceive the product to have. The suitability of the product for its purposes (ease of use, convenient storage, low maintenance) may be important to you. So may its aesthetic qualities (looks good, your favourite colour, says 'modern'). So may its 'esteem' value (rare, high quality, trendy, impressive to friends, sentimental value). Whether or not you perceive the product as offering 'value for money' depends not only on how much you pay for it – but what value you get from it.

EXAM TIP

Get used to thinking about the full range of product attributes. What, for example, really accounts for the phenomenal success of the i-Pod, and its resistance to competition from other MP3 player brands?

1.1.2 Product levels

It is useful for marketers to think of a product, and its attributes, at different levels.

Figure 5.1: Levels of product

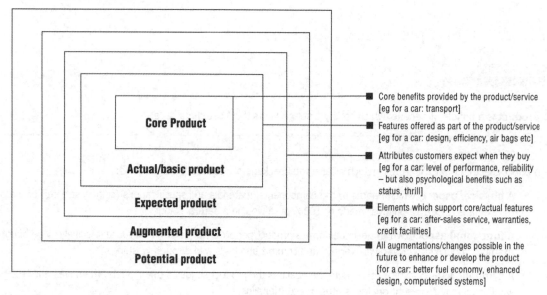

KEY CONCEPTS

Concept

The **core/generic product** is those benefits that all the products in the category would have – all cars, for example, provide transport

The **augmented product** is the core product plus extra benefits that differentiate it from other products in the category. These might include warranty, delivery, installation, after-sales support

Many products are marketed at the **augmented product** level – the total package of the customer's experience of purchasing and consuming the product/service is relevant.

The **expected product** level is also important, because of the potential for customers to be dissatisfied (by disappointed expectations) or delighted (by exceeding expectations).

The **potential product** is important in providing the marketing organisation with future avenues to develop the product (and marketing message) in order to stay competitive and 'fresh' in the market.

1.2 Product classification

KEY CONCEPTS

Concept

Products can be classified as **consumer goods** or **industrial goods**. Consumer goods are sold directly to the person who will ultimately use them. Industrial goods are used in the production of other products.

FMCG stands for Fast Moving Consumer Goods – items such as packaged food, beverages, toiletries, and tobacco.

Consumer goods can be classified as follows.

Convenience goods	The weekly groceries are a typical example. There is a further distinction between **staple goods** (eg bread and potatoes) and **impulse buys**, like the bar of chocolate that you find at the supermarket checkout. **Brand awareness** is extremely important in this sector.
Shopping goods	These are the more durable items that you buy, like furniture or washing machines. This sort of purchase is usually only made after a good deal of advance planning and shopping around.
Speciality goods	These are items like jewellery or the more expensive items of clothing.
Unsought goods	These are goods that you did not realise you needed! Typical examples are new and sometimes 'gimmicky' products, such as 'wardrobe organisers', or fire resistant car polish!

ACTIVITY 1

Application

Think of three products that you have bought recently, one low-priced, one medium-priced, and one expensive item. Identify the product attributes that made you buy each of these items and categorise them according to the classifications shown above.

Industrial goods can be classified as follows.

- **Installations**, eg major items of plant and machinery like a factory assembly line
- **Accessories**, such as PCs
- **Raw materials**, for example plastic, metal, wood, foodstuffs and chemicals
- **Components**, eg the Lucas headlights on Ford cars, the Intel microchip in most PCs
- **Supplies**, such as office stationery and cleaning materials

1.3 Branding

"Branding is the culmination of a range of activities across the whole marketing mix, leading to a brand image that conveys a whole set of messages to the consumer ... about quality, price, expected performance and status". Blythe, J. (2008)

A **brand** is a name, term, sign, symbol or design intended to identify the product of a seller and to differentiate it from those of competitors.

Branding is a very general term covering brand names, designs, trademarks, symbols, jingles and the like. A **brand name** refers strictly to letters, words or groups of words which can be spoken. A **brand image** distinguishes a company's product from competing products in the eyes of the user.

Branding might be discussed under any of the four Ps. For instance, part of the branding of a Rolls Royce is the unmistakeable design of the product; or you might buy a 'cheaper brand' of washing-up liquid if you are concerned about price. However, as the definition above suggests, most brands are created and maintained by **marketing communications** such as advertising and promotions.

Branding is now apparent in just about all markets. Not long ago – and this is still the case in many less developed countries – most products were sold unbranded. Today even salt, oranges, nuts and screws are often branded. There has been a limited return recently in some developed countries to 'generics': cheap products packaged plainly and not heavily advertised. This apparent lack of branding is in fact establishing a brand identity itself, as with 'no frills' brands.

MARKETING AT WORK

Application

Tesco has been named the most valuable brand on the high street, worth £8.6bn, almost £4bn more than rival Sainsbury's. A report has said that Tesco's top ranking was "almost inevitable" following sales of £32bn and its market leading share in the supermarket and convenience store markets. Brands in the study were valued after looking at public sales figures for the last five years and attributing a score to measures such as future growth, price positioning, customer service and brand heritage.

Tesco's strong brand is likely to give it a better chance to weather tougher times on the UK high street, because consumers need more reasons to buy.

www.brandrepublic.com – accessed 12 May 2008

A brand identity may begin with a name, such as 'Kleenex' or 'Ariel', but extends to a range of visual features which should assist in stimulating demand for the particular product. The additional features include typography, colour, package design and slogans.

In addition, of course, a brand shares the attributes of a product: it is a bundle of tangible and intangible benefits which deliver customer value.

ACTIVITY 2

Application

What characteristics do the following brand names suggest to you?

- Brillo (scouring pads)
- Pampers (baby nappies)
- Cussons Imperial Leather (soap)
- Kerrygold (butter)
- Hush Puppies (shoes)

1.3.1 Objectives of branding

The key benefit of branding is product differentiation and recognition. Products may be branded for a number of reasons.

- It aids **product differentiation**, conveying a lot of information very quickly and concisely. This helps customers readily to identify the goods or services and thereby helps to create a customer loyalty to the brand. It is therefore a means of increasing or maintaining sales.

- It maximises the impact of **advertising** for product identification and recognition. The more similar a product (whether an industrial good or consumer good) is to competing goods, the more branding is necessary to create a separate product identity.

- Branding leads to a **readier acceptance** of a manufacturer's goods by wholesalers and retailers.

- It reduces the importance of **price differentials** between goods.

- It supports **market segmentation**, since different brands of similar products may be developed to meet specific needs of categories of uses. (Think of all the cereal brands produced by Kellogg's, for example.)

- It supports **brand extension** or **stretching**. Other products can be introduced into the brand range to 'piggy back' on the articles already known to the customer (but ill-will as well as goodwill for one product in a branded range will be transferred to all other products in the range).

- It **eases the task of personal selling**, by enhancing product recognition.

The relevance of branding does not apply equally to all products. The cost of intensive brand advertising to project a brand image nationally may be prohibitively high. Goods which are sold in large numbers, on the other hand, promote a brand name by their existence and circulation.

The decision as to whether a brand name should be given to a **range of products** or whether products should be branded **individually** depends on quality factors.

- If the brand name is associated with quality, all goods in the range must be of that standard.

- If a company produces different quality (and price) goods for different market segments, it would be unwise to give the same brand name to the higher and the lower quality goods because this would deter buyers in the high quality/price market segment.

1.3.2 Branding strategies

Brand extension is the introduction of new flavours, sizes etc to a brand, to capitalise on existing brand loyalty. Examples include the introduction of Persil washing up liquid and Mars ice cream. New additions to the product range are beneficial for two main reasons.

- They require a lower level of marketing investment (part of the 'image' already being known).

- The extension of the brand presents less risk to consumers who might be worried about trying something new. (Particularly important in consumer durables with relatively large 'investment' in a car, stereo system or the like.)

Multi-branding is the introduction of a number of brands that all satisfy very similar product characteristics. This can be used where there is little or no brand loyalty, in order to pick up buyers who are constantly changing brands.

The best example is washing detergents. The two majors, Lever Brothers and Procter & Gamble, have created a barrier to fresh competition as a new company would have to launch several brands at once in order to compete.

Family branding uses the power of the brand name to assist all products in a range. This strategy is being used more and more by large companies, such as Heinz. In part it is a response to retailers' own-label (family branded) goods. It is also an attempt to consolidate expensive television advertising behind one message rather than fragmenting it across the promotion of individual items.

1.4 Product range planning

KEY CONCEPT   Concept

A company's **product range** (or product portfolio, assortment or mix) is all the product lines and items that the company offers for sale.

A company's product range can be described in the following terms.

Characteristic	Defined by:
Width/Breadth	Number of product lines: eg cosmetics, haircare, toiletries and health products
Depth	Average number of items per product line: eg cosmetics including moisturiser, cleanser, toner, lipstick, eyeshadow etc.
Consistency	Closeness of relationships in product range for the benefit of users and production/distribution processes

1.4.1 Managing the product range

There are benefits to be gained from using a systematic approach to the management of the product range. It can be **reduced** (eg by discontinuing a product) or **extended** by:

- Introducing variations in models or style (eg a paint manufacturer introducing different colours, types and pot sizes)

- Differentiating the quality of products offered at different price levels (eg 'premium' paints and 'value' paints)

- Developing associated items (eg a paint roller and brushes, paint trays, colour charts)

- Developing new products with little technical or marketing relationship to the existing range (eg wallpaper and DIY accessories – or something completely different)

Managing the product range also raises broad issues such as:

- What role a product should play in the range. ('Flagship' brand? Profit provider? Niche filler? New market tester/developer? Old faithful, retaining customer loyalty?) The roles of products in the mix should create a balanced range, with sufficient **cash-generating** products to support **cash-using** (declining or new/market-developing) products

- How resources should be allocated between products

- What should be expected from each product

- How far products should be integrated within the brand image and be recognisable as part of the brand family

Marketing is not an exact science and there is no definitive approach or technique which can determine how resources should be shared across the product range. There are, however, techniques which can aid decision making. Ultimately the burden of the decision is a management responsibility and requires judgement, but tools such as the **BCG matrix** (see below) and the **product life cycle** (see Section 4) can help the decision-making process.

1.4.2 The BCG matrix

The **BCG matrix** classifies products or brands on the basis of their market share and according to the rate of growth in the market as a whole, as a way of assessing their role in the product range.

Figure 5.2: The BCG matrix

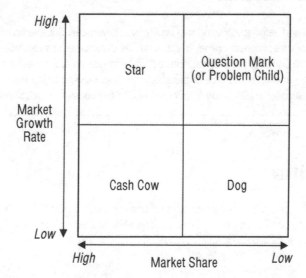

On the basis of this classification, each product may fall into one of four broad categories.

- **Question mark** (or problem child): A small market share in a high growth industry. The generic product is clearly popular, but customer support for the particular brand is limited. A small market share implies that competitors are in a strong position and that if the product is to be successful it will require substantial funds, and a new marketing mix. If the market looks good and the product is viable, then the company should consider a 'build' strategy to increase market share: increasing the resources available for that product to permit more active marketing. If the future looks less promising, then the company should consider withdrawing the product. What strategy is decided will depend on the strength of competitors, availability of funding and other relevant factors.

- **Star**: A high market share in a high growth industry. The star has potential for generating significant earnings, currently and in the future. At this stage it may still require substantial marketing expenditure as part of a 'maintain' strategy, but this is probably regarded as a good investment for the future.

- **Cash Cow**: A high market share in a mature slow-growth market. Typically, a well established product with a high degree of consumer loyalty. Product development costs are typically low and the marketing campaign is well established. The cash cow will normally make a substantial contribution to overall profitability. The appropriate strategy will vary according to the precise position of the cash cow. If market growth is reasonably strong then a 'holding' strategy will be appropriate, but if growth and/or share are weakening, then a 'harvesting' strategy may be more sensible: cut back on marketing expenditure and maximise short-term profit.

- **Dog**: A low market share in a low-growth market. Again, typically a well established product, but one which is apparently losing consumer support and may have cost disadvantages. The usual strategy would be to consider divestment, unless the cash flow position is strong, in which case the product would be harvested in the short term, prior to deletion from the product range.

1.5 The digital revolution

Information and communications technology (ICT) is itself a product. The so-called 'digital revolution' has radically changed the market and introduced a host of new products and services.

- Technology components, tools and services are sold in both consumer and B2B markets: think of PCs, mobile phones, digital cameras, i-Pods (and their accessories) Internet services, web page design services, database and other software packages and ICT consultancy.

- ICT enables information to be sold as a product/service: think of subscriptions to on-line databases, publications and news services; business consulting via the Internet.

- ICT enables service provision: think of online banking, telephone banking, online travel reservations, online education/learning provision, dating/friendship communities.

 MARKETING AT WORK

Application

ICT is now used to add value to conventional products and services. For example, if you send a parcel by international courier, you can track its progress online. If you study by distance education, you can use TV, video, CD-ROM and online (e-learning) methods to enhance the interest, interactivity and demonstration aspects of the curriculum. Even a tin of baked beans is enhanced – as a total package of benefits – by its packaging being electronically bar-coded: providing information to the retailer and supplier (sales value/frequency) and to the consumer (recording special offers and use-by-dates).

2 Packaging

 "Packaging of the product is equally part of the product, since the packaging can itself convey benefits".
Blythe, J. (2008). Look through the Brand Republic website at packaging related articles
(www.brandrepublic.com). ∎

2.1 Functions of packaging

Product **packaging** fulfils a number of functions.

- Protection of contents from damage or deterioration

- Distribution, helping to transfer products from the manufacturer to the customer (eg bulk storage packs)

- Selling, as the design and labelling provide information and convey an image

- User convenience, as an aid to storage and carrying (eg aerosol cans and handy packs)

- Compliance with government regulations eg providing a list of ingredients and contents by weight, as in food packaging

- Promotion, as packs can be used to print sales promotion information

- Management information, as bar codes can be used to track sales

2.2 The qualities required of a pack

A number of different criteria may be used to plan and evaluate packaging.

In industries where **distribution** is a large part of total costs, packaging should include the following.

- Protect, preserve and convey the product to its destination in the desired condition
- Use vehicle space cost effectively
- Fit into the practices of mechanised handling and storage systems
- Be space efficient, but also attractively display items
- Convey product information to shoppers effectively
- Preserve the product's condition

Packaging is an important **aid to selling** in the following ways.

- Help to promote the advertising/brand image
- Shape, colour and size relate to customer motivation (for 'value' or 'quantity')
- Appropriate size for the expected user of the product (eg family size packets)
- Promote impulse buying (eg new FMCG products, snack foods, etc)
- Convenience pack (tubes, aerosols) where this is important
- Maintain product quality standards
- Attract attention of potential customers in-store

Where a product cannot be differentiated by design techniques, the packaging therefore takes over the design selling function. This is particularly so for basic commodities such as flour.

Printable surfaces can be used for **product labelling and information** (some of which is required by law) and also promotional messages, sales promotions and coupons.

 MARKETING AT WORK Application

Weight Watchers is repackaging its low-calorie cakes and sponges to make them appear more indulgent. The range will also be expanded with the addition of Weight Watchers' Mini Victoria Sponges, Apple Crumble Slices and Belgian Chocolate Slices.

Finsbury Food Group, which produces the cakes for Weight Watchers wants to develop packaging that is more appealing. Weight Watchers also plans to update the branding of its savoury and hot meal products.

www.brandrepublic.com – accessed 12 May 2008

Values integral to the packaging itself (size, environment-friendliness, convenience, attractiveness, protection of product quality) are part of the overall benefit and image bundle of the product. The sustainability of resources, and therefore the importance of recycling, is having a major impact upon companies' packaging decisions.

 MARKETING AT WORK Application

The National Trust, which introduced a charge on 1 May 2008 in its shops and garden centres, has managed to slash plastic bag usage by 85%, or 1m bags a year. It said just 5% of its customers were now taking the disposable option.

"We are really pleased at how quickly customers have reacted and adapted their shopping habits by investing in durable alternatives in which to carry their purchases," said the National Trust's Stuart Richards, adding that in the trust's shops, sales of reusable jute bags have soared as plastic bag use has fallen away.

www.guardian.co.uk

Packaging must appeal not only to consumers, but also to distributors. A sales outlet wants a package design which helps to sell the product, but also minimises the likelihood of breakage, or extends the product's shelf life, or makes more economic use of shelf space.

The **packaging of industrial goods** is primarily a matter of maintaining good condition to the point of use. In itself this is a selling aid in future dealings with the customer. Large, expensive and/or fragile pieces of equipment must be well packaged.

3 Services

'Products' is a generic term and can, in many case, include 'services' for the practical purpose of marketing. There are very few pure products or services. Most products have some service attributes and many services are in some way attached to products.

"In effect, all products are on a continuum between the purely physical product (for example a bag of cement) to the purely service (life insurance). Even at these extremes there are no pure products: a bag of cement still has to be stocked by a builders' merchant, and an insurance policy still has a physical document to prove that it exists." Blythe, J. (2009) ▪

KEY CONCEPT

Concept

Services include:

'*those separately identifiable but intangible activities that provide want-satisfaction, and that are not, of necessity, tied to, or inextricable from, the sale of a product or another service. To produce a service may or may not require the use of tangible goods or assets. However, where such use is required, there is no transfer of title (permanent ownership) to these tangible goods.*' (Cowell, 1995)

'*goods that are largely or mainly non-physical in character, such as personal services, travel and tourism, medical care or management consultancy.*' (Brassington and Pettitt, 2006)

MARKETING AT WORK

Application

At McDonald's for example, customers receive their product (the Big Mac) but the experience of ordering and receiving the food is also a significant element in the transaction. The additional service elements of the marketing mix (covered in detail in Chapter 9) are **people** (the staff at McDonald's, using our example), **process** (the procedure for ordering and serving of the burger) and **physical evidence** (various elements of the McDonald's experience such as the appearance of the staff, the cleanliness of the restaurant, the presence of a playground for those with children).

The marketing of services presents a number of distinct problems. As a consequence, particular marketing practices must be developed. There are many service industries which are highly market-oriented (for instance, in retailing, transport hire, cleaning and hotel groups).

MARKETING AT WORK

Application

Enterprise Rent-A-Car is the number one car rental company in North America and the recipient of awards for achievement in many areas. Its customer service focus is described at **www.thetimes100.co.uk**:

"The management team at Enterprise Rent-A-Car developed a simple but highly effective way of finding out what keeps customers happy. They created a questionnaire for customers based on two questions:

1.   How would you rate your last Enterprise experience?

This is ranked on a scale from 'completely satisfied' to 'completely dissatisfied'.

2.   Would you rent from Enterprise again?

This is a novel type of customer survey. A major problem with customer surveys is that the response rate is very low because the surveys are long and complicated. The opposite is true in this case.

The results of the survey form part of the Enterprise Service Quality index (ESQi). This is the basis for measuring performance of the various rental branches of Enterprise."

www.thetimes100.co.uk – accessed 14 May 2008

There are, however, many service industries which remain relatively unaffected by marketing ideas and practices, or which have only just begun to adopt them (for example, public sector and legal services). Marketing ideas are likely to become much more important as competition within the service sector intensifies.

  ACTIVITY 3   Application

What evidence have you seen that legal services (for example) have begun to adopt marketing ideas and practices?

3.1 The rise of the service economy

In terms of employment, more people now work in the service sector than in all other sectors of the economy. In terms of output, the major contributors to national output are the public and private service sectors. The extension of the service sector and the application of 'market principles' across what were previously publicly-owned utilities has made a large number of service providers much more marketing conscious.

The service sector extends across the **public sector** in the legal, medical, educational, military, employment, credit, communications, transportation, leisure and information fields. Some are 'not-for-profit', but increasingly there are profits involved as services are run as businesses.

The **private sector** includes areas such as arts, leisure, charities, religious organisations and educational institutions, as well as business and professional services involved in travel, finance, insurance, management, the law, building, commerce, and entertainment.

3.2 Marketing characteristics of services

The following characteristics of services distinguish them from goods.

- **Intangibility**: services cannot be touched or tasted
- **Inseparability**: services cannot be separated from the provider
- **Heterogeneity** (variability, or lack of 'sameness'): the standard of service will vary with each delivery
- **Perishability**: services cannot be stored for provision 'later'
- **Ownership**: service purchase does not transfer ownership of property

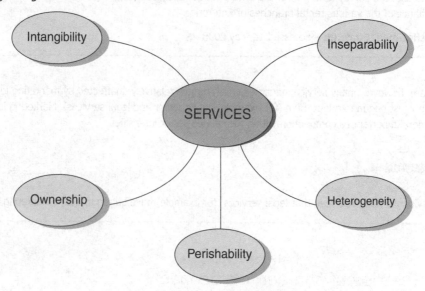

We will look at each characteristic in detail, along with its marketing implications, in Chapter 9 of this text.

 EXAM TIP

Application

You will need to be able to illustrate how the unique characteristics of services affect an organisation's extended marketing mix. Cite the characteristics of services, and note that the 'extended marketing mix' consists of the full 7Ps – product, price, place, promotion, people, processes and physical evidence. The new syllabus specimen examination paper for *Marketing Essentials* contains a 25-mark question on the importance of a co-ordinated services marketing mix. Services marketing is discussed in detail in Chapter 9.

4 The product life cycle

4.1 What is the product life cycle?

 KEY CONCEPT

Concept

The **product life cycle** uses a 'biological' analogy to suggest that products are born (or introduced), grow to reach maturity and then enter old age and decline.

The profitability and sales position of a product can be expected to change over time. The 'product life cycle' is an attempt to recognise distinct stages in a product's sales history. Here is the classic representation of the life cycle.

Figure 5.4: The product life cycle

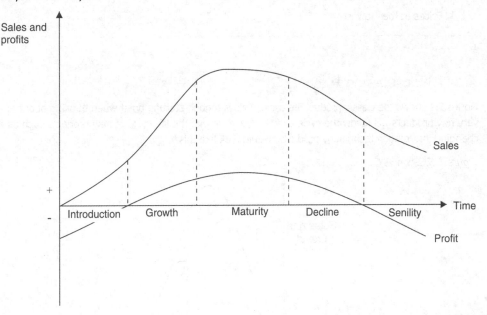

- **Introduction**. A new product, following development, takes time to find acceptance by consumers and there is slow growth in sales. Only a few firms sell the product, unit costs are high due to low output and there may be early teething troubles with production technology. **Prices may be high** to cover production costs and sales promotion expenditure. For example, pocket calculators, video cassette recorders and mobile telephones were all very expensive when launched. The product, initially, is a loss maker.

- **Growth**. If the new product gains market acceptance, sales will rise more sharply and the product will start to make profits. New customers buy the product and, as production rises, unit costs fall. Since demand is strong, **prices tend to remain fairly static for a time**. However, the prospect of cheap mass production and a strong market will attract competitors, so that the number of producers increases. With increased competition, manufacturers must spend a lot of money on product improvement, sales promotion and distribution to obtain a dominant or strong market position.

- **Maturity**. The rate of sales growth slows down and the product reaches a period of maturity, which is probably the longest period of a successful product's life. Most products on the market are at the mature stage of their life, and prices are stable. Eventually sales will begin to decline so that there is overcapacity of production. Severe competition occurs, profits fall and some producers leave the market. The remaining producers seek means of prolonging the product life by modifying it and searching for new market segments.

- **Decline**. Most products reach a stage of decline, which may be slow or fast. Many producers are reluctant to leave the market, although some inevitably do because of falling profits. If a product remains on the market too long, it will become unprofitable and the decline stage in its life cycle then gives way to a 'senility' or '**obsolescence**' stage.

 EXAM TIP Application

Different promotional and pricing strategies are appropriate at different stages of the life cycle. A question on the September 2009 paper asked about promotional strategies appropriate to the maturity phase, when competition is at its peak. There is no way of knowing how long such a phase might last, but examples might be:

- Intensive distribution

- Repositioning/new versions for various market segments

- Major promotional campaigns

- Maintaining loyalty and awareness
- Prices at their lowest

4.1.1 Non-classic PLC

Figure 5.4 shows the classic product life cycle. This is a good starting point when thinking about any product, even though very few products will follow the cycle exactly. For example, the life cycle of new products such as the 'cyber pet', or fast changing information technology products, would look like this.

Figure 5.5: Short PLC

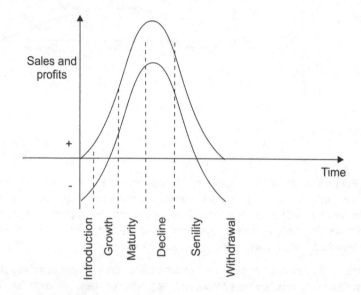

The product goes through all stages at a rapid rate. A short introduction phase leads to extreme sales growth, but maturity is short-lived, and decline is just as rapid as growth was. Often products are withdrawn completely as they have become unprofitable.

"Some products, for example computer games, may go through the entire life cycle in a matter of months. Others, like pitta bread, have a life cycle measured in thousands of years, and may never become obsolete". Blythe, J. (2008)

ACTIVITY 4

 Application

Where do you consider the following products or services to be in their product life cycle?

- Digital cameras
- Baked beans
- MP3 players
- Cigarettes
- Carbon paper
- Mortgages
- Writing implements
- Car alarms
- Organically grown fruit and vegetables

4.2 Criticisms of the product life cycle

Criticisms of the practical value of the PLC include the following.

- The stages cannot be easily defined.

- The traditional bell-shaped curve of a product life cycle does not always occur in practice. Some products have no maturity phase and go straight from growth to decline. Others have a second growth period after an initial decline. Some have virtually no introductory period and go straight into a rapid growth phase, while others (the vast majority of new products in fact) do not succeed at all.

- Strategic decisions can change a product's life cycle: for example, by repositioning a product in the market, its life can be extended. If strategic planners 'decide' what a product's life is going to be, opportunities to extend the life cycle might be ignored.

- Competition varies in different industries and the strategic implications of the product life cycle will vary according to the nature of the competition. The 'traditional' life cycle presupposes increasing competition and falling prices during the growth phase of the market and also the gradual elimination of competitors in the decline phase. This pattern of events is not always true.

  EXAM TIP • *Do not know which phase when* Application

Limitations of the product life cycle appear on the specimen paper.

4.3 BCG and PLC

You may have spotted a relationship between the BCG matrix, described earlier in the chapter, and the classic product life cycle. The typical new product is likely to appear in the 'question mark (or problem child)' category to begin with (introduction). If it looks promising, and with effective marketing, it might be expected to become a 'star' (growth). Then, as markets mature, a 'cash cow' (maturity) and finally a 'dog' (decline). The suggestion that most products will move through these stages does not weaken the role played by marketing. Poor marketing may mean that a product moves from being a question mark (problem child) to a dog without making any substantial contribution to profitability. Good marketing may enable the firm to prolong the 'star' and 'cash cow' phases, maximising cash flow from the product.

5 New product development

 "There is a strong positive relationship between a firm's innovative activities and its ability to survive and prosper, so many companies place a strong emphasis on developing new products to replace those which become obsolete, or which are superseded by competitors' offerings." Blythe, J. (2008)

 KEY CONCEPT Concept

New product development (NPD) is the process of developing new products from idea stage through to launch on the market. The NPD sequence typically includes: conception; screening of ideas; business analysis; product development and marketing mix planning; test marketing; and commercialisation and launch.

5.1 Why develop new products?

New product development is important for maintaining customer satisfaction through change; refreshing or extending the product range; and adapting to environmental opportunities and threats. These will all contribute towards the success of a company's long-term business strategy.

There are a number of reasons why a company may consider extending its product mix with the introduction of new products.

- To meet the **changing needs/wants of customers**: a new product may meet a new need (eg for environmentally friendly alternatives) or meet an existing need more effectively (eg digital cameras).
- To **match competitors**: responding to innovations and market trends before or shortly after competitors, so as not to miss marketing opportunities.
- To **respond to environmental threats and opportunities**: capitalising on opportunities presented by new technology, say (digital cameras), or other products (accessories and supplies for digital cameras); minimising the effects of threats such as environmental impacts (developing 'green' alternatives) or safety concerns (developing new safety features).
- To **extend the product/brand range** as part of a product development or diversification growth strategy as described in the previous chapter in the context of planning and the marketing audit. New products can bring new customers to the brand and enable cross-selling of products in the mix.
- To **extend the 'maturity' stage of the PLC** for a product, by modifying it to maintain interest, simulate re-purchase (because it is 'new and improved') and/or target as yet unreached market segments.
- To **refresh the product range**, as products go into the decline stage of their life cycle. Some products may become obsolete and need updating. Others will simply be deleted, and the company will need to replace them in the product mix in order to maintain brand presence and profitability.

5.2 New products

New products may be genuinely innovative, but 'newness' may also mean 'adapted', 'repackaged' or 'introduced' in a new market.

What is a new product?
- One that opens up an entirely new market
- One that replaces an existing product
- One that broadens significantly the market for an existing product

An old product can be new if:
- It is introduced to a new market
- It is packaged in a different way
- A different marketing approach is used
- A mix variable is changed – for example, a new price is set, or a new distribution channel is used

 ACTIVITY 5   Application

Can you think of examples of new products and 'new' old products to fit into each of the above categories?

 MARKETING AT WORK   Application

There are **degrees of 'newness'**!

- **The unquestionably new product**, such as new medicines for the treatment of AIDS and cancer. Marks of such a new product are technical innovation, high price, possible initial performance problems and limited availability.
- **The partially new product**, such as the DVD player. The main mark of such a product is that it performs better than the equivalent old product.
- **Major product change**, such as the digital camera. Marks of such a product are radical technological change altering the accepted concept of the order of things (eg no need to get your films developed: print them out at home or share them by e-mail).
- **Minor product change**, such as styling changes. The motor industry does this all the time.

5.2.1 Sources of new products

New products may arise from a number of sources.

- Licensing (eg Formica, Monopoly)
- Acquisition (buy the organisation making it)
- Internal product development (your own Research and Development team)
- Customers (listen to and observe them, analyse and research) and sales people that have contact with them
- External freelance inventors
- Competition (eg Dyson's bagless vacuum cleaners, or Apple's i-Pod MP3 player, now copied by other manufacturers)
- Patent agents
- Academic institutions (eg the pharmaceutical industry funds higher education research)
- PEST factor changes, presenting new opportunities and threats

5.3 New product development (NPD) process

New products should only be taken to advanced development if there is evidence of:

- **Adequate demand**
- Compatibility with existing **marketing ability**
- Compatibility with existing **production ability**

The stages of new product (or service) development are as follows.

Figure 5.6: NPD

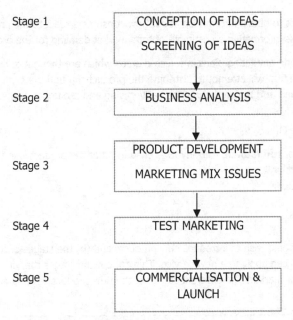

The mortality rate of new products is very high. To reduce the risk of failure new product ideas must be screened. Only the best will make it to the next development stage.

5.3.1 Conception and screening of ideas

The **concept** for the new product could be **tested on potential customers** to obtain their reactions. Some caution does however need to be exercised when interpreting the results.

- When innovative new designs are tested on potential customers it is often found that they are conditioned by traditional designs and are dismissive of new design ideas.

- However, testers may say they like the new concept at the testing stage, but when the new product is launched it is not successful because people continue to buy old favourites.

5.3.2 Business analysis

A thorough business analysis is required for each product idea, projecting future sales and revenues, giving a description of the product so as to provide costs of production, providing estimates of sales promotion and advertising costs, the resources required, profits and return on investment. Other factors such as the product life cycle, legal restrictions, competitors' reactions among others, must also be evaluated. Products which pass the business evaluation will be developed. A timetable and a budget of resources required and of cost must be prepared, so that management control can be applied to the development project.

5.3.3 Product development

Money is invested to produce a working **prototype** of the product, which can be tried by customers. This stage ensures that the product can be produced in sufficient quantities at the right price. The form which the product **test** takes will depend very much on the type of product concerned. The test should replicate reality as closely as possible.

- If the product is used in the home, a sample of respondents should be given the product to use at home.

- If the product is chosen from amongst competitors in a retail outlet (as with chocolate bars), then the product test needs to rate response against competitive products.

- If inherent product quality is an important attribute of the product, then a 'blind' test could be used.

- An industrial product could be used for a trial period by a customer in a realistic setting.

The marketing mix for the product will need to be planned at this stage.

5.3.4 Test marketing

The purpose of **test marketing** is to obtain information about how consumers react to the product. Will they buy it, and if so, will they buy it again? With this information an estimate of total market demand for the product can be made.

A market test involves implementing marketing plans in selected areas which are thought to be 'representative' of the total market. In the selected areas, the firm will attempt to distribute the product through the same types of sales outlets it plans to use in the full market launch, and also to use the intended advertising and promotion plans.

5.3.5 Commercialisation and launch

Finally the product is developed for **full launch**. This involves ensuring that the product is in the right place at the right time, and that customers know about it.

  EXAM TIP

Application

Think about (a) why a company would wish to introduce new products and (b) the stages of the product development sequence. Do not forget that NPD can apply to a new service. Think about the stages that are involved – and be able to apply them to a specific product or market. The different stages of the new product development process appear on the specimen paper.

6 Product and service adoption

"New products are not immediately adopted by all consumers. Some consumers are driven to buy new products almost as soon as they become available, whereas others prefer to wait until the product has been around for a while before risking their hard-earned money on it". Blythe, J. (2008)

Concept

The **diffusion** of a new product refers to the spread of information about the product in the market place. **Adoption** is the process by which consumers incorporate the product into their buying patterns.

The classification of adopters is shown below.

Figure 5.7: Adoption of new products

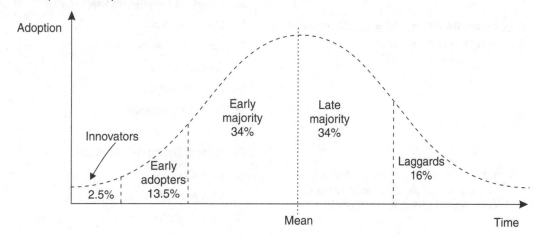

The types of adopters are described below.

Innovators – these are people who like to own the latest products, and value being the 'first' to have them amongst their group of friends and family members.

Early adopters – these people are open to new ideas, but they prefer to wait and see how the product goes after its initial launch, and to observe the experience of the innovators.

Early majority – these will buy the product when they are sure that there is no risk with the product.

Late majority – of similar numbers to early majority, the late majority will only buy the new product when most other people already have one.

Laggards – these people adopt products only when they have no choice but to do so.

Innovators and **early adopters** are thought to operate as 'opinion leaders' and are therefore targeted by companies in order to influence the adoption of a product by their friends.

The main problem with this model is that the categories appear to add up to 100% of the target market. This does not reflect marketers' experience. Some potential consumers do not adopt/purchase at all. It has consequently been suggested that an additional category is needed: **non-adopters,** or **non-consumers**.

Jobber (2006) has written a very clear chapter about managing products (chapter 9). See website www.thetimes100.co.uk *for useful case studies on marketing and business practice*

Learning objectives	Covered
1 Explain and illustrate the principles of product and planning	☑ Branding
	☑ Product lines/ranges (depth and breadth)
	☑ Packaging eg sustainability, design eg recycling
	☑ Service support
2 Explain the concept of the Product Life Cycle, (PLC) and its limitations as a tool for assessing the life of the product/service	☑ Stages of the product life cycle (development, introduction, growth, maturity, decline, obsolescence)
	☑ Limitations including failure of the product to succeed/no measurable outcome
3 Explain the importance of new products and services into the market	☑ Changing customer needs
	☑ Digital revolution
	☑ Long-term business strategies
4 Explain the different stages of the process of New Product Development	☑ Idea generation
	☑ Screening new ideas
	☑ Concept testing
	☑ Business analysis
	☑ Product development
	☑ Test marketing
	☑ Commercialisation and launch
5 Explain the process of product and service adoption explaining the characteristics of customers at each stage of adoption	☑ Innovators
	☑ Early adopters
	☑ Early majority
	☑ Late majority
	☑ Laggards

1   What is the 'symbolic' aspect of a product?

2   What is an 'augmented' product?

3   What is 'brand extension'?

4   Fill in the blanks:

     "In the context of the BCG matrix, a 'question mark' has _____ market share in a _____ industry. A 'cash cow' has _____ market share in a _____ industry".

5   Why does packaging need to appeal to distributors?

6   What are the three Ps of the services mix?

7   What are the distinguishing characteristics of services? Give a brief explanation of each.

8   What might happen if a declining product stays on the market for too long?

9   "The traditional bell-shaped curve of a product life cycle does not always occur in practice". What does this mean?

10   What is the sequence for new product development?

11   What is the difference between 'testing a concept' on consumers, and 'test marketing'?

12   What buying behaviour characterises the 'late majority'?

---

1   This depends upon the products you have chosen. The table in paragraph 1.2 should have helped if you were stuck for inspiration.

2   Here are some suggestions.

     •   Brillo (scouring pads) – 'brilliant', shining, clean
     •   Pampers (baby nappies) – comforting, caring, soft
     •   Cussons Imperial Leather (soap) – quality, tradition, masculinity
     •   Kerrygold (butter) – Ireland, farmland, high quality, sunshine, yellow
     •   Hush Puppies (shoes) – comfort, softness, friendliness

3   The most obvious example (in the UK, at least) is the proliferation of companies offering to help out if you have an accident at work. It is very difficult to avoid their TV ads. For instance Claims Direct was launched in 1996 by a former London cabbie called Tony Sullman, and has since grown to become the largest direct-response advertiser in the market. The "personal injury compensation specialist" has a panel of more than 300 solicitors and claims that over 75 per cent of cases are successful.

4   You could perhaps pin down some of these items, but most are open to discussion, especially if you take an international perspective. For many you may consider that the PLC is not valid, and you will not be alone, as the discussion within the chapter has shown.

5   You should try to think of your own examples, but these suggestions may help.

New product

Entirely new market	Web 'browsers', National Lottery
Replacing an existing product	Centrino replacing Celeron processors; digital cameras replacing film, MP3 replacing CD
Broadening the market	Cable for satellite, TV and telephones

'New' old product

In a new market	German confectionery (in the UK)
New packaging	Smarties in a hexagonal tube replacing the cylinder
New marketing	French wine competing

---

1   The symbolic aspect of a product represents the qualities that the product suggests to buyers – for example, a label stating 'low in fat' will suggest health benefits.

2   An augmented product is the core product plus those extra benefits that differentiate it from other products in the category, such as guarantees or after-sales support.

3   Brand extension is the introduction of new flavours, sizes etc to a brand, to build upon existing brand loyalty.

4   A 'question mark' has **small** market share in a **high growth** industry. A 'cash cow' has **high** market share in a **low growth** industry.

5   Packaging needs to appeal to distributors because, for example, sales outlets want package designs which will help to sell the product, reduce the risk of breakage, extend shelf life or make better use of available shelf space.

6   People, process and physical evidence.

7
- Intangibility: services cannot be touched or tasted
- Inseparability: services cannot be separated from the provider
- Heterogeneity (or lack of 'sameness'): the standard of service will vary with each delivery
- Perishability: services cannot be stored for provision 'later'
- Ownership: service purchase does not transfer ownership of property

8   It may decline to such an extent that it becomes obsolete, taken over by innovative new products. This is possibly what is happening to older style 'cathode ray tube' (CRT) televisions, with the market being taken over by LCD and plasma models.

9   The classic pattern is not always followed. Some products have no maturity phase and go straight from growth to decline. Others have a second growth period after an initial decline. Some have virtually no introductory period and go straight into a rapid growth phase, while others do not succeed at all.

10   The NPD sequence typically includes: conception; screening of ideas; business analysis; product development and marketing mix planning; test marketing; and commercialisation and launch.

11   'Testing a concept' involves gauging initial reactions to the product before committing resources to further development. 'Test marketing' follows that development, and involves implementing marketing plans in selected areas which are thought to be representative of the total market.

12   The late majority will only buy a new product when most other people already have one.

References

Anon (2008) "*Weight Watchers overhauls cake packaging*" Marketing, 7 May 2008 **www.brandrepublic.com** accessed 12 May 2008.

Blythe, J (2009) <u>Principles and Practice of Marketing</u>, 2nd edition, South-Western/Cengage Learning

Blythe, J (2008) <u>Essentials of Marketing</u>,4th edition, FT Prentice Hall.

Brassington, F and Pettitt, S (2006) <u>Principles of Marketing</u>, 4th edition, FT Prentice Hall.

Cowell, D (1995) <u>The Marketing of Services</u>, CIM, Cookham

Dibb S, Simkin L, Pride W.M., Ferrell O.C. (2005) <u>Marketing: Concepts and Strategies</u>, 5th edition, Houghton Mifflin.

Jobber, D (2009) <u>Principles and Practice of marketing</u> 6th edition, McGraw Hill Higher Education

Osborne, H "*Plastic bag charge hailed as a huge success*", Guardian.co.uk, 1 May 2009 – accessed 3 June 2010

Chapter 6

Pricing

Topic list

1   The role of price in the mix
2   Influences on pricing decisions
3   Price setting strategies

Introduction

In this chapter, we develop our coverage of the marketing mix by introducing basic concepts behind pricing strategy and decisions.

In section 1, we look at the role of price in the marketing mix, and then in section 2 we explore a range of internal and external factors which influence pricing decisions. This focuses on the key factors of objectives, costs, competition and demand.

In section 3 we suggest a range of pricing policies and tasks that an organisation might adopt to achieve its marketing objectives.

Syllabus linked learning objectives

By the end of the chapter you will be able to:

Learning objectives	Syllabus link
1 Explain the importance of price as an element of the marketing mix	3.5
2 Identify and illustrate a range of different pricing approaches that are adopted by organisations as effective means of competition	3.6

1 The role of price in the mix

Concept

Price can be defined as a measure of the value exchanged by the buyer for the value offered by the seller.

Pricing decisions are important to the firm. This may be stating the obvious, but it is worth making it clear that pricing is very important as it is the only element of the marketing mix which generates income, revenue and profits, rather than creating costs.

All profit organisations, and many non-profit ones, face the task of pricing their products or services. Price can go by many names: fares, fees, rent, assessments among others.

Price was once the single most important decision made by the sales department. In those production-oriented times, price was viewed as the major factor in satisfying customer needs, and a price change was the usual reaction to competitor activity.

Today, though, marketing managers view price as just one of the factors involved in customer satisfaction. In fact it is sometimes suggested that marketing aims to make price relatively unimportant to the consumers' decision making process. There is certainly some truth in this view. The other elements of the marketing mix are concerned with adding value to the product and tailoring it to the consumers' needs, to ensure that the choice between two products is not simply based on their different prices.

However, the role of price in the marketing mix is still significant, and should not be underestimated. It contributes towards the organisation's business and financial objectives in the following ways.

- As noted above, pricing is the only element of the mix which generates revenue rather than creating costs.

- It also has an important role as a competitive tool to differentiate a product and organisation, and thereby exploit market opportunities.

- Pricing must be consistent with other elements of the marketing mix, since it contributes to the overall image created for the product.

Application

Morgan, a fashion retailer which targets women aged 18 to 35, has struggled to compete in the UK with rival high-street brands such as Topshop and H&M. It has also faced competition from discount chains such as Primark and New Look.

Morgan has stuck to its traditional fashion model, stocking just two collections a year, and while the price of fashion in the UK has steadily been getting lower, it has struggled to keep pace due to its inflexible pricing model. One commentator said:

"The key problem for Morgan is a lack of clear brand positioning. The high-street fashion market in the UK is brutally competitive; consumer expectations are high and retailers require a tightly run operation to meet those expectations and still turn a profit.

Shoppers want to see the very latest fashions in-store and online, at extremely keen prices. Premium pricing can be an option, but consumers want value for money, and product quality and brand values must support this.

As women happily mix Primark shoes with a Prada top, there must be clarity in consumer minds about what the brand is offering. Morgan's pricing is mid-point and its image is indistinct."

On 31 December 2008, Morgan announced that it had gone into administration.

ACTIVITY 1

In what circumstances would you expect price to be the main factor influencing a consumer's choice?

EXAM TIP

Remember that at its most basic level a price aims to produce the desired level of sales in order to meet the objectives of the business. Pricing must take into account the internal needs of, and the external constraints on, the organisation.

2 Influences on pricing decisions

Pricing decisions are affected by a range of factors, both internal (to the organisation) and external (in the competitive environment).

Internal factors	External factors
• **Marketing objectives**: profit maximisation; market share leadership; brand targeting and positioning	• **Competition:** the extent of competition in the market; whether there is non-price competition; competitor pricing and promotions.
• **Marketing mix strategy**: factoring in the cost/ price implications of quality, distribution, brand differentiation	• **Demand**: the sensitivity of customer demand for the product to change in price (elasticity of demand) in the given market.
• **Costs**: at least setting the lowest viable price at which the company can afford to sell the product.	• **Customer perceptions** of price and what it means for quality and value
• **Price-setting methodologies**: negotiated by sales force; set by management	• **Suppliers and intermediaries**: impacting on costs; reacting to price decisions to protect their own margins.
• **Product portfolio strategies**: launch/new-product incentive pricing; 'loss leaders' to support the product range	• **PEST factors**: economic factors determining affordability; government price watchdogs; social responsibility dictating affordability; changing perceptions of 'value'; technology lowering production costs.

2.1 Business objectives

Pricing decisions are guided by one or other of two business objectives.

Maximise profits	Maintain or increase market share
Charge as **high** a price as possible. This depends on how good your product is and how much demand is affected by higher prices.	Charge a **lower** price than competitors, or the **same** price. You would do this if you want to hold on to existing customers and/or attract new ones.

Either approach may be used in specifying pricing objectives, and they may appear in combination. It is important that pricing objectives are consistent with overall **corporate objectives**: you might not want to raise prices, for example, if the corporate objective is to be an accessible, ethical low-cost provider of essential services.

2.2 Costs

In practice, cost is the most important influence on price. In cost-based pricing, costs are estimated and then a profit margin is added to set the price. There are a number of reasons for the predominance of **cost-based pricing**.

- Easier assessment of performance
- Emulation of successful large companies
- Belief by management in a 'fair return' policy
- Fear of government action against 'excessive' profits
- Tradition of production orientation rather than marketing orientation
- Tacit collusion in industry to avoid competition
- Easier planning and administration of cost-based pricing strategies based on internal data

There are two types of cost-based pricing: **full cost pricing** and **cost-plus pricing**. These are examined in section 3 on price setting strategies.

  ACTIVITY 2 Application

Look at the following advertisement for SWATCH.

FROM PLASTIC TO PLATINUM

WORLDWIDE

INDIVIDUALLY NUMBERED LIMITED EDITION OF 12,999

£1,000 INC VAT

- *Most exclusive Swatch ever produced.*
- *950 Platinum case and crown.*
- *Stainless steel presentation case with acrylic glass inlay.*
- *Interchangeable royal blue leather and padded plastic straps.*
- *Limited availability in the UK.*

Suggest how Swatch might have chosen the price of £1,000.

2.3 Competition

Prices may be set on the basis of what competitors are charging, rather than on the basis of cost or demand. This sometimes results in '**going rate**' pricing. Some form of average level of price becomes the norm, including standard price differentials between brands.

2.3.1 Price as a competitive tool

In established industries dominated by a few major firms, it is generally accepted that a price initiative by one firm will be countered by a price reaction by competitors. Consequently, in industries such as breakfast cereals (dominated in Britain by Kellogg's, Nabisco and Quaker) or canned soups (Heinz, Crosse & Blackwell and Campbell's) a certain **price stability** might be expected without too many competitive price initiatives.

A firm may respond to **competitor price cuts** in a number of ways.

- **Maintain existing prices**, if the expectation is that only a small market share would be lost, so that it is more profitable to keep prices at their existing level. Eventually, the rival firm may drop out of the market or be forced to raise its prices.

- **Maintain prices but respond with a non-price counter-attack**. This is a more positive response, because the firm will be securing or justifying its price differential with enhanced product quality, improved back-up services or other augmented features.

- **Reduce prices**, to protect the firm's market share. The main beneficiary from the price reduction will be the consumer.

- **Raise prices and respond with a non-price counter-attack**. The extra revenue from the higher prices might be used to finance the promotion of product improvements, which in turn would justify the price rise to customers.

2.3.2 Price leadership

 KEY CONCEPT Concept

Price leaders are firms whose market share and share of the capacity in the industry are great enough for them to be able to set the prices in the market.

A **price leader** will dominate price levels for a class of products: increases or decreases by the price leader provide a direction to market price patterns. The price-dominant firm may lead without moving at all. (This would be the case if other firms sought to raise prices and the leader did not follow: then the upward move in prices would be halted.)

The role of price leader is based on a track record of having initiated price moves that have been accepted by both competitors and customers. Often, this is associated with a mature, well established management group, efficient production and a reputation for technical competence. A price leader generally has a large, if not necessarily the largest, market share.

2.3.3 Non-price competition

In some market structures, price competition may be avoided by tacit agreement, leading to concentration on **non-price competition**: the markets for cigarettes and petrol are examples of this. Price-setting here is influenced by the need to avoid retaliatory responses by competitors, which could result in a breakdown of the tacit agreement and profit-reducing price competition. Price changes based on real cost changes are led in many instances by a 'representative' firm in the industry, followed by other firms.

Whether agreements exist at all is hard to prove: competitors are exposed to the same market forces and so might be expected to set similar prices. This is a problem for government agencies, such as the Office of Fair Trading, when attempting to establish if unethical pricing agreements exist.

2.3.4 Competitive bidding

Competitive bidding is a special case of competition-based pricing. Many supply contracts, especially concerning local and national government purchases (where it is compulsory) involve would-be suppliers submitting a sealed bid or **tender**.

The firm's submitted price needs to take account of expected competitor bid prices. Often the firms involved will not even know the identity of their rivals but successful past bids are often published by purchasers and it is possible to use this data to calculate a realistic bid.

2.4 Demand

KEY CONCEPT

Concept

Demand is defined as a want which can be paid for.

Prices may be based on the intensity of demand: strong demand may lead to a high price, and weak demand to a low price. The concept of **price elasticity** illustrates how demand can be affected by price changes.

2.4.1 Price elasticity of demand

In classical economic theory, price is the major determinant of demand. More recently, emphasis has been placed on other factors. The significance of other elements of the marketing mix: product quality, promotion, personal selling, distribution and brands has grown.

KEY CONCEPT

Concept

Price elasticity is measured as:

$$\frac{\% \text{ change in sales demand}}{\% \text{ chage in sales price}}$$

As you might expect, 'elasticity' indicates how much demand will 'stretch' or how far a change in price will affect demand. The more elastic demand is, the more demand will *increase* if you *lower* the price slightly – and the more demand will *decrease* if you *raise* the price slightly. In other words, if demand is elastic, buyers are very sensitive to price and price changes: if it is inelastic, price is not a key factor in demand.

2.4.2 Price discrimination

A firm might successfully charge higher prices for the same product to people who are willing to pay more. This is called price discrimination, or differential pricing.

By market segment	By product version	By time
A cross-channel ferry company would market its services at different prices in England, Belgium and France.	Software is written top-down and the full version is sold at a premium price.	Travel companies are successful price discriminators, charging more to rush hour commuters whose demand is inelastic at certain times of the day.
Services such as cinemas and hairdressers are often available at lower prices to old age pensioners and/or students.	For less advanced users all the software company has to do is take features out: there is little extra cost.	Other examples are off-peak travel bargains or telephone charges.

Price discrimination will only be effective under certain conditions.

- The market must be **segmentable** in price terms, and different sectors must show **different intensities of demand**. Each of the sectors must be identifiable, distinct and separate from the others, and be accessible to the firm's marketing communications.

- There must be little or no chance of a **black market** developing, so that those in the lower priced segment can resell to those in the higher priced segment.

- There must be little chance that competitors can/will **undercut** the firm's prices in the higher priced (and/or most profitable) market segments.

- The **cost** of segmenting and administering the arrangements should not exceed the extra revenue derived from the price discrimination strategy.

2.5 Price sensitivity

Subjective perception is important in the way customers react to price and price changes.

 KEY CONCEPT

Concept

Price sensitivity refers to the effect a change in price will have on customers.

Price sensitivity will vary amongst purchasers. Those who can pass on the cost of purchases will be least sensitive, and will respond more to other elements of the marketing mix.

- Provided that the price fits the corporate budget, the business traveller will be more concerned about an hotel's level of service and quality of food. In contrast, a family on holiday are likely to be very price sensitive when choosing an overnight stay.

- In industrial marketing, the purchasing manager is likely to be more price sensitive than the engineer who might be the actual user of new equipment. The engineer places product characteristics as first priority, the purchasing manager is more price oriented.

Research on price sensitivity of customers has shown that in general the following apply.

- Customers have a good concept of a **'just price'** – a feel for what is fair for the benefits offered.

- For **special purchases**, customers search for price information before buying, become price aware when wanting to buy, but forget soon afterwards

- Customers will buy at what they consider to be a **bargain price**, without full regard for their present needs and the level of the price itself

- **Down payment and instalment price** are more important than total price

- In times of rising prices, the **price image** tends to lag behind the current price

- If there are **substitute goods**, especially close substitutes, customers will be more sensitive to price. For example, in a greengrocer's shop, a rise in the price of one fruit such as apples or pears is likely to result in a switch of customer demand to other fruits, many fruits being fairly close substitutes for each other.

- Over **time**, consumers' demand patterns are likely to change. If the price of something is increased, the initial response might be a small change in demand. But as consumers adjust their buying habits in response to the price increase, demand might fall substantially.

2.6 Other factors influencing pricing decisions

Several factors influence the pricing decisions of an organisation.

- **Intermediaries' objectives**

  If an organisation distributes products or services to the market through independent intermediaries, the objectives of these intermediaries have an effect on the pricing decision. Intermediaries aim to maximise their own profits rather than those of suppliers. Conflict over price can arise between suppliers and intermediaries which may be difficult to resolve.

Many industries have traditional margins for intermediaries. To deviate from these might well cause problems for suppliers. In some industries, notably grocery retailing, the power of intermediaries allows them to dictate terms to suppliers.

- **Competitors' actions and reactions**

An organisation, in setting prices, sends out signals to competitors and they are likely to react in some way. In some industries (such as petrol retailing) pricing moves in unison. In others, price changes by one provider may initiate a **price war**, with each provider attempting to undercut the others.

- **Suppliers**

An organisation's suppliers may attempt to increase prices on the basis that the buying organisation is able to pay a higher price. (This argument is sometimes used by trade unions negotiating the price for the supply of labour.)

- **Quality connotations**

In the absence of other information, customers tend to judge quality by price. A price change may send signals to customers concerning the quality of the product. A rise may be taken to indicate improvements, a reduction may signal reduced quality. Any change in price needs to take such factors into account.

- **New product pricing**

Most pricing decisions for existing products concern price changes, which have a **reference point** from which to move (the existing price). A new product has no reference points. It may be possible to seek alternative reference points, such as the price in another market where the new product has already been launched, or the price set by a competitor.

- **The economy**

In times of **rising incomes**, price may become a less important marketing variable. When income levels are falling and/or unemployment levels rising, price will become more important. In periods of **inflation** the organisation's prices may need to change in order to pass on increases in the prices of supplies, labour, rent and other overheads.

- **Product range**

Most organisations market not just one product but a range of products. The management of the pricing function is likely to focus on the profit from the whole range, using low-cost products to attract customers, who can then be encouraged to buy related products with higher profit margins.

- **Social responsibility**

Ethical considerations are involved, such as whether to exploit short-term shortages (or life-and-death products such as some pharmaceuticals) through higher prices.

- **Government**

Some organisations are compelled by government to charge certain prices. For instance, in the UK Oftel have a say in how much British Telecom is allowed to charge.

 MARKETING AT WORK   Application

Customers and competitors now have greater **access to price information**. You could view the many online price comparison sites as a threat, especially if your product or your retail outlet comes out as the most expensive!

One of many examples of a **price comparison site** is **DealTime** (www.dealtime.co.uk) where you can check the prices of dozens of products. Categories include Appliances (Fridges, Vacuum Cleaners, Washing Machines, etc), Books, Cars (Motor Insurance, Car Loans), Used Cars, Computers, Electronics (Digital Cameras, DVD Players, Televisions, etc), Finance (Loans, Life Insurance, Insurance, etc), Flowers & Wine, Health & Beauty (Women's Fragrance, Face Makeup, Skin Care, etc), Home & Garden, Jewellery, Lingerie , Mobile Phones, Software, Toys & Games, Travel Insurance, Hotels, Car Hire, Video Games.

Several **online catalogues** use price in a way that has not been so easily available before. For instance, if you need to buy a gift for someone and have no bright ideas you can visit the website of, say, Argos, click on Gifts, and specify the price you want to pay and the sort of person you're buying for (toddler, teenager, 'for him', for her', etc) and be presented with lots of ideas.

Also relevant here is the growth of **online auctions**. Effectively this means that the customer decides the price (s)he is willing to go pay.

The use of ICT may also enable suppliers to **reduce prices** (especially for products/services sold online), because of the reduction in sales and administration costs enabled by 'self-service' marketing by e-commerce, m-commerce (using mobile phones) and telephone ordering. There are often special discounts available if customers order online, for example.

3 Price setting strategies

Companies may undertake any of a variety of pricing strategies, depending on their objectives and the industry they operate in. Pricing strategies can be used to pursue a number of marketing objectives.

3.1 Cost-based pricing

In practice, cost is the most important influence on price.

3.1.1 Techniques of cost analysis

While you will not need an in-depth knowledge of cost analysis for this exam, it is worth being aware of the key techniques and concepts.

- **Fixed costs** are costs which do not vary according to how many units are being produced or sold (eg salaries, advertising costs)

- **Variable costs** are costs which vary directly according to how many units are being produced or sold (eg materials costs, sales force commissions). Marginal cost pricing may be used – this involves the calculation of only those costs that rise as output increases. This will not cover all costs - for example, costs such as factory rent which stay the same no matter how many units are produced.

- **Contribution** is the amount that a product or project contributes to covering fixed costs.

It is calculated as:

- Selling price/revenue *minus* variable cost

- If a product or marketing plan generates sufficient contribution to cover fixed costs, it may be worth pursuing in the short term.

- Breakeven analysis is used to calculate how much of a product/service must be output at a given price, in order for sales revenue to equal the total costs of producing/marketing it. The breakeven quantity (BEQ) equals:

$$\frac{\text{Fixed costs}}{\text{Contribution}}$$

This calculation enables marketers to calculate the effect of different prices on the breakeven point/quantity.

3.1.2 Full cost pricing

Full cost pricing is a form of cost-based pricing which takes account of the full average cost of production of a product, including an allocation for overheads, under what is called absorption costing. A profit margin is then added to determine the selling price. This method is often used for non-routine jobs which are difficult to cost in advance, such as the work of solicitors and accountants where the price is often determined after the work has been performed.

3.1.3 Cost-plus pricing

KEY CONCEPT

Concept

Cost-plus pricing means basing the price calculation on the firm's production costs, plus a predetermined allowance for profit.

Under cost-plus pricing, only the more easily measurable direct cost components such as labour and raw material inputs are calculated in the unit cost, whilst an additional margin incorporates an overhead charge and a residual profit element. This method is used where overhead allocation to unit costs is too complex or too time consuming to be worthwhile.

A common example occurs with the use of **mark-up pricing**.

KEY CONCEPT

Concept

Mark-up is the amount of profit calculated as a proportion of the bought-in price.

This is used by retailers and involves a fixed margin being added to the buying-in price. In the UK, for example, fast moving items such as cigarettes carry a low 5-8% margin (also because of tax factors); fast moving but perishable items such as newspapers carry a 25% margin; while slow moving items which involve retailers in high stockholding costs, such as furniture or books, carry 33%, 50% or even higher mark up margins.

Since the cost-plus approach leads to **price stability**, with price changing only to reflect cost changes, it can lead to a marketing strategy which is reactive rather then proactive.

3.1.4 Limitations of cost-based pricing

There is very limited consideration of **demand** in cost-based pricing strategies.

- From a marketing perspective, cost-based pricing may reflect **missed opportunities**, as no account is taken of the price consumers are *willing* to pay for the brand, which may be higher than the cost-based price.

- Particular problems may be caused for a **new brand**, as initial low production levels in the introduction stage may lead to a very high average unit cost and consequently a high price. A longer term perspective may be necessary, accepting short-term losses until full production levels are attained.

3.2 Price skimming

KEY CONCEPT

Concept

Price skimming involves setting a high initial price for a new product (in order to take advantage of those buyers prepared to pay a high price for innovation) and then gradually reducing the price (to attract more price sensitive segments of the market).

This strategy is an example of price discrimination over time and is favoured in the following situations.

- Insufficient market capacity, and competitors cannot increase capacity
- Buyers are relatively insensitive to price increases
- High price perceived as high quality

This is the opposite of penetration pricing.

3.3 Penetration pricing

 KEY CONCEPT

Penetration pricing is pricing a new product low in order to maximise market penetration before competitors can enter the market.

The organisation sets a relatively low price for the product or service, to maximise sales by stimulating growth of the market and/or obtaining a larger share of it. This strategy was used by Japanese motor cycle manufacturers, for example, to enter the UK market. It worked! UK productive capacity was virtually eliminated and the imported Japanese machines could later be sold at a much higher price and still dominate the market.

Sales maximising objectives are favoured when the following apply.

- Unit costs will fall with increased output (in other words, there are economies of scale)
- The market is price sensitive and relatively low prices will attract more sales
- Low prices will discourage any new competitors

 EXAM TIP

The techniques of 'price skimming' and 'penetration pricing' are examined on the specimen paper. Loss leaders (see below) are specifically mentioned in the syllabus.

3.4 Product line pricing

 KEY CONCEPT

Product line pricing is the application of differential pricing policies to products that are co-dependent in terms of demand.

When a firm sells a **range of related products**, or a product line, its pricing policy should aim to maximise the profitability of the line as a whole. The pricing must be consistent with its brand image.

- There may be a **brand name** which the manufacturer wishes to associate with high quality and high price, or reasonable quality and low price. All items in the line will be priced accordingly. For example, all major supermarket chains have an 'own brand' label which is used to sell goods at a slightly lower price than the major named brands.

- If two or more products in the line are complementary, one may be priced as a **loss leader** (a low profit-margin item) in order to attract customers and demand for the related products.

- If two or more products in the line share **joint production costs** (joint products), prices of the products will be considered as a single decision. For example, if a common production process makes one unit of joint product A for each unit of joint product B, a price for A which achieves a demand of, say, 17,000 units, will be inappropriate if associated with a price for product B which would only sell, say, 10,000 units. 7,000 units of B would be unsold and wasted.

 KEY CONCEPT

A **loss leader** is an item which is charged at a deliberately low price in order to make money elsewhere – retailers often use them to attract people into their stores, where the intention is that they will also spend money on items with high margins.

ACTIVITY 3

An organisation has declared that its primary pricing objective for its new product is 'early cash recovery'. It wants to recover its investment in the product as quickly as possible. What are some possible reasons for having such an objective?

3.5 Promotional pricing

KEY CONCEPT

Concept

Promotional pricing is pricing that is related to the promotion of a product, generally over the short term only.

Pricing and promotion are often co-ordinated. According to Dibb, Simkin, Pride and Ferrell (2001) there are four main types of promotional pricing.

- **Price leaders** – products that are sold at or below cost to attract customers in the hope that they will buy other, full priced items. This tactic is often used in department stores and supermarkets.

- **Special event pricing** – pricing that is linked to an event or a holiday to increase sales volume. An example is the 'Buy 2, get the 3rd free' often seen at Christmas.

- **Everyday low pricing** – this involves the reduction of prices for a prolonged period, supported by cutting costs elsewhere in the operation (such as distribution costs, or cutting down on other promotions).

- **Experience curve pricing** – the fixing of a low price that competitors cannot hope to match, in order to increase market share. A company can do this when it has been able to reduce manufacturing costs through improvements in processes that have been accumulated through experience.

EXAM TIP

To find an appropriate pricing strategy, you have to consider the nature of the product: is it exposed to competition or could a premium price strategy be justified by the niche nature of the product or the prospect of enthusiastic early adopters?

You may like to remember the key factors in pricing strategy as the four Cs = Costs, Customer (demands), Competition and Company (objectives).

" Jobber's (2009) on pricing looks at the alternative approaches to pricing and includes some useful diverse case studies in airline and bathroom pricing strategies. He also considers the ethical issues associated with pricing." ■

Learning objectives	Covered
1 Explain the importance of price as an element of the marketing mix	☑ Brings together the marketing mix elements to fulfil customer needs
	☑ Income, revenue and profit generation
	☑ Contributing to the organisation's business and financial objectives
	☑ Limitations of price as a competitive tool
2 Identify and illustrate a range of different pricing approaches that are adopted by organisations as effective means of competition	☑ Absorption costing
	☑ Cost base and marginal costing
	☑ Cost plus
	☑ Price skimming
	☑ Penetration pricing
	☑ Loss-leader
	☑ Promotional pricing

1 Pricing decisions are guided by one or other of two business objectives. What are they?

1 ....

2 ....

2 Why might a cost-based approach to price setting be problematic from a marketing point of view?

3 List three factors that might influence a farmer's pricing policy.

4 List four ways of responding to a price cut by a competitor

5 What is price elasticity?

6 In practice, what is the biggest influence on setting prices?

7 Give an example of product line pricing.

8 What is the opposite of penetration pricing?

1   You might have identified a number of different factors here. Perhaps the most important general point to make is that price is particularly important if the other elements in the marketing mix are relatively similar across a range of competing products. For example, there is a very wide variety of toothpastes on the market, most of them not much differentiated from the others. The price of a particular toothpaste may be a crucial factor in its sales success.

2   One possibility is that the cost of the product was established (to make sure of breaking even), VAT added since it makes a significant difference for the customer, and comparisons were made with items of similar quality and rarity on the market. A range of possible prices, based on this data, might then have been presented to potential customers to see how they reacted to them. Data may also have been collected about the results of similar exercises by other watchmakers (or the like) in the past.

3   The objective of 'early cash recovery' would tend to be used in the following conditions:

    •   The business is high risk
    •   Rapid changes are expected (maybe in fashion or technology)
    •   The innovator is short of cash!

1   Maximise profits; Maintain or increase market share.

2   Because it does not take proper account of the price consumers may be willing to pay and because in the case of a new product it does not take account of the typical pattern of the product life cycle or the diffusion of innovation.

3   The main one will be intermediaries' objectives. Many farmers have gone out of business in recent years because, they claim, supermarkets drive down the prices they can obtain for their goods. Other factors may play a part: for instance competition from cheap imported goods, the quality of their goods (eg organic vegetables), government subsidies or quotas.

4   Maintain existing prices; maintain prices but respond with extra advertising; reduce prices; raise prices and respond with extra features or higher quality.

5   A measure of how much demand will 'stretch', or how far a change in price will affect demand

6   Cost

7   If two or more products in the line are complementary, one may be priced as a loss leader (a low profit-margin item) in order to attract customers and demand for the related products.

8   Price skimming. Instead of setting a price low to get into the market, a company deliberately sets prices high in order to take advantage of those buyers prepared to pay a high price for innovation, and then gradually reduces the price to attract more price sensitive segments.

BPP
LEARNING MEDIA

Blythe, J (2009) <u>Principles and Practice of Marketing</u>, 2nd edition, South-Western/Cengage Learning

Blythe, J (2008) <u>Essentials of Marketing</u>, 4th edition, FT Prentice Hall.

Jobber D (2009) <u>Principles and Practice of marketing</u>, 6th edition, McGraw Hill Higher Education

Brassington, F and Pettitt, S (2006) <u>Principles of Marketing</u>, 4th edition, FT Prentice Hall.

Dibb S, Simkin L, Pride WM, Ferrell OC (2005) <u>Marketing: Concepts and Strategies</u>, 5th edition, Houghton Mifflin.

Chapter 7
Channel decisions

Topic list

1   The role of place in the mix
2   Channels of distribution
3   Channel decisions
4   Internet distribution

Introduction

Availability is a critical factor in managing the marketing mix. In this chapter, we examine the various decisions regarding channels of distribution that an organisation might need to make to satisfy customer requirements most effectively – and profitably.

When selecting a distribution channel many factors come into play. How much support should be given to dealers? How far should marketing efforts be integrated up to the point of sale? What are the characteristics of the product or service? What do competitors do?

Distribution involves certain basic processes.

- Bringing buyers and sellers into contact
- Offering a sufficient choice of goods to meet the needs of buyers
- Persuading customers to develop a favourable opinion of a particular product
- Distributing goods from the manufacturing point to retail outlets
- Maintaining an adequate level of sales
- Providing appropriate services (eg credit, after-sales service)
- Maintaining an acceptable price

The choice of channels of distribution will depend on how far a manufacturing company wishes to carry out these processes itself, and how far it decides to delegate them to other organisations.

In this chapter we explore key issues in channel decisions and supply chain management including the role of distribution in the marketing mix (section 1), the various channels of distribution that are available to modern marketers (section 2) and the factors involved in making channel decisions (section 3). Finally, the impact of the Internet and new digital technologies upon distribution channels is described in section 4.

Syllabus linked learning objectives

By the end of the chapter you will be able to:

Learning objectives	Syllabus link
1 Define the different channels of distribution, and the role they play in a coordinated marketing mix	3.7
2 Explain the factors that influence channel decisions and the selection of alternative distribution channels	3.8

1 The role of place in the mix

 "... people can only buy products that are available and easily obtained". Blythe, J. (2008) ■

 KEY CONCEPT

Concept

Place is concerned with the selection of distribution channels used to deliver goods to the consumer. The 'place' element of the marketing mix is really concerned with the processes by which the product reaches the consumer in a convenient way. Other terms for 'place' include distribution, delivery systems or channels.

The importance of place within the marketing mix should not be underestimated. If you get it right for your market it can be a crucial source of competitive advantage. Marketing effort will be futile if the product is not actually in the right place at the right time so that the customer has the choice of buying your product, not your competitors'.

The choice of a particular distribution policy, such as whether or not to use wholesalers or retailers, may result in the company delegating at least part of its marketing function to others. We look at factors governing such a decision in section 3.

 EXAM TIP

Application

While there is no specific question on distribution on the specimen paper for *Marketing Essentials*, it is important to realise that distribution plays a major role, and will form part of any answer to a question (particularly in Section B) about the characteristics of an overall marketing mix for a given company. The structure of distribution channels can vary widely depending upon the market, customer needs and the type of product. It is easy to see how a Section B question could be structured to test your ability to apply your knowledge to a scenario.

1.1 Benefits of effective distribution management

The benefits of effective distribution management include the following.

- **Customer value** through more choice and customisation; better quality control; faster delivery; less likelihood of stockouts; service-driven supply planning; convenient, safe and undamaged handling, storage, transport and display of goods.

- **Cost savings** that can be made when a properly planned approach is undertaken, allowing long, steady production runs and minimising inefficient stock holding.

- **Closer links between suppliers and manufacturers**, for example, using EDI (Electronic Data Interchange), e-commerce and relationship marketing (particularly in B2B markets, where direct supply from manufacturer to buyer is far more likely than the use of intermediaries).

 MARKETING AT WORK

Application

Blythe (2008) gives a good illustration of the importance of distribution in the marketing mix.

'In some ways the physical distribution of a product is part of the bundle of benefits that make up that product. For example, a jacket bought through mail order offers convenience benefits which a chain store jacket does not. Conversely, the chain-store purchase may include hedonistic benefits (the fun of shopping around, the excitement of finding a real bargain) which the mail-order company does not supply. Even when the actual jacket is identical, the benefits derived from the distribution method are different".

2 Channels of distribution

KEY CONCEPTS

Concept

The term **channels of distribution** refers to the methods by which goods or services are transferred from producers to consumers.

Physical distribution is another commonly used term and is concerned again with the handling and movement of outbound goods from an organisation to its customers. Distribution might be direct or indirect.

Another common term in this area is **logistics**, which is concerned with inbound raw materials and other supplies, as well as with outbound goods. It also covers strategic issues such as warehouse location, materials management, stock levels and information systems.

2.1 Distribution functions

A variety of functions are involved in distribution.

- **Transport**

  This function may be provided by the supplier, the distributor or may be sub-contracted to a specialist. For some products, such as perishable goods, transport planning is vital.

- **Stock holding and storage**

  For production planning purposes, an uninterrupted flow of production is often essential. A good stock or inventory control system is designed to avoid stockouts whilst keeping stockholding costs low.

- **Local knowledge**

  As production has tended to become centralised in pursuit of economies of scale, the need to understand and be 'close to' local markets has grown.

- **Promotion**

  While major promotional campaigns for national products are likely to be carried out by the supplier, the translation of the campaign to local level is usually the responsibility of a distributor or retail outlet.

- **Sales displays**

  Presentation of the product at the local level is often the responsibility of the distributor. Specialist help from merchandisers can be bought in if required.

ACTIVITY 1

Application

For many types of goods, producers invariably use retailers as middlemen in getting the product to the customer. Try to think of some of the disadvantages of doing this, from the producer's point of view.

- added final cost
- not in control of display
- lots of competition
- reliability for business.

2.2 Intermediaries

"Intermediaries provide important services in smoothing the path between producers and consumers, almost invariably reducing costs by increasing efficiency". Blythe, J. (2009) ▮

Companies may distribute direct to customers, or choose from a wide range of intermediaries: retailers, wholesalers, dealers, agents, franchisees and multiple stores.

KEY CONCEPT

Concept

An **intermediary** is someone who 'mediates' or brings about a settlement between two persons: in this case between the original supplier and the ultimate buyer.

There are a variety of types of intermediary and several may intervene before a product gets from the original provider and the final buyer.

Figure 7.1: Intermediaries

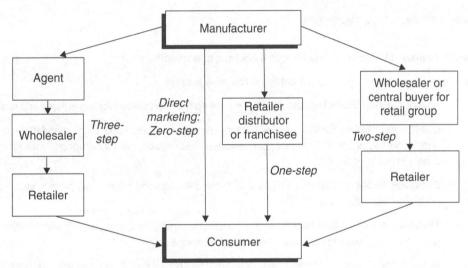

- Retailers are traders operating outlets which sell directly to households. They may be classified by:
    - Type of goods sold (eg hardware, furniture, food, clothes)
    - Type of service (self-service, counter service)
    - Size and/or ownership
    - Location (rural, city-centre, suburban or out of town shopping mall)

- Wholesalers stock a range of products from potentially competing manufacturers, to sell on to other organisations such as retailers. Many wholesalers specialise in particular products.

- Distributors and dealers contract to buy a manufacturer's goods and sell them to customers. Their function is similar to that of wholesalers, but they usually offer a narrower product range, sometimes (as in the case of most car dealers) the products of a single manufacturer. In addition to selling on the manufacturer's product, distributors often promote the products and provide after-sales service.

- Agents differ from distributors, in that they do not purchase and resell the goods, but sell goods on behalf of the supplier and earn a **commission** on their sales.

- Multiple stores (eg supermarkets, department stores) buy goods for retailing direct from the producer, sometimes under their 'own label' brand name.

- Direct marketing methods include:

    - Mail order
    - Telephone selling
    - Door-to-door selling
    - Personal selling in the sale of industrial goods
    - Sales through retail outlets owned by the supplier
    - TV shopping channels
    - E-commerce (Internet selling via online marketing – see section 4)

 KEY CONCEPTS

 Concept

Direct marketing is marketing without intermediaries.

Direct marketing methods are covered in more detail in the next chapter on marketing communications.

Franchises are independent organisations which in exchange for an initial fee and (usually) a share of sales revenue are allowed to trade under the name of a parent organisation. For example, few of the Kall Kwik chain of High Street print shops are actually owned by Kall Kwik – most are run by franchisees. Other examples are McDonalds, KFC and Benetton.

 MARKETING AT WORK

 Application

Kodak Express Malaysia: Promotion of franchise opportunities

As a Kodak Express member, you will enjoy the following benefits.

- **Kodak Express Branding**: the right to use the Kodak Express logo for advertising and promotions in the store.

- **Quality Monitoring Service:** Kodak's engineers will advise and make recommendations on how to maintain our print quality according to international Kodak quality standards. With this support, your store will be able to provide quality prints to consumers.

- **Exclusive Rebates**: Exclusive only to you, these discounts and rebates will provide your business with a leading edge over the rest.

- **Training**: one of the best benefits in the franchise program. Each year, Kodak will organise at least four training sessions to help you improve your business performance.

- **Retail Shop Concept**: A new store concept for the Kodak Express shops is specially designed to project Kodak Express as a young, vibrant and professional retail store to consumers.

- **360-degree Checklist Program**: your Business Support Executive will conduct checks and monitoring exercises in your store regularly. The quality of the photos processed, the visual displays and the quality of staff service will be measured to ensure that your store meets the quality requirements to stay competitive in the market.

- **Best Kodak Express Award**: designed to reward members who provide consistently good service and quality prints to consumers. Every year, the top ten Kodak Express Award winners will receive cash prizes and public recognition in local papers.

- **Newsletter**: one of the ways which you will be kept updated on the latest products, services and trends in the photo-retailing industry.

- **Advertisements**: you will benefit from the advertising plans and strategies initiated by Kodak.

- **Annual Conference**: an annual event where members will not only interact and discuss ways to improve the Kodak Express program, but also gain knowledge.

A franchise agreement is, in effect, a contractual virtual marketing system which co-ordinates and integrates marketing and distribution activities. A package of services (product advice, marketing approaches, operating procedures and quality control for example) is offered by the franchisor to the franchisee in return for a payment. Franchises are generally exempt from EU competition law, as the theory is that they increase competition and encourage better distribution.

Advantages of franchising

For the franchisor:

- Control over some aspects of operations

- Quality control

- Shelter from poor performance

- Access to local knowledge (particularly in new or international markets) without capital outlay

- Secured distribution

For the franchisee:

- Direct benefits from sales and profits

- Access to franchisor resources / buying power / expertise

- Financial incentive to manage the business well

- Local ownership and motivation

Disadvantages of franchising

For the franchisor:

- Lack of total control over entire operation

- Potential for conflict over levels of support

- Possibility of inconsistent service delivery

- Expensive initial outlays (such as training)

For the franchisee:

- Can be left 'out in the cold'

- Some control may be retained centrally (eg marketing, pricing, product features)

Risk of conflict

 MARKETING AT WORK   Application

The vending machine is a familiar feature of the landscape – on railway platforms (for tickets or chocolate bars), in waiting rooms and anywhere that people may be passing by or simply passing the time. Vending machines can distribute anything from travel tickets, cash from your bank account and dry cleaning orders to food and drink, and offer the latest DVDs for hire, all for 24 hours a day with no requirement for sales staff – although there are costs associated with restocking and servicing They can now even deliver clothing.

"Japanese trainer and sports fashion brand Onitsuka Tiger has launched what it claims to be the UK's first trainer vending machine. The machine, which can vend 24 pairs of trainers in 6 sizes, was launched today in Carnaby Street, London. The brand intends to roll out the concept across the UK. As part of the launch, Onitsuka Tiger is giving shoppers in the Carnaby Street area the chance to win a free pair of trainers until Wednesday."

---

3   Channel decisions

Choosing distribution channels is important for any organisation, because once a set of channels has been established, subsequent changes are likely to be costly and slow to implement. Distribution channels fall into one of two categories: **direct** and **indirect** channels.

As hinted at in the previous section, direct distribution means the product going directly from producer to consumer without the use of a specific intermediary. These methods are often described as **active**, since they typically involve the supplier making the first approach to a potential customer.

Indirect distribution means systems of distribution, common among manufactured goods, which use an intermediary; a wholesaler or retailer for example (as described in the previous section). In contrast to direct distribution, these methods are **passive**, in the sense that they rely on consumers to make the first approach by entering the relevant retail outlet.

ACTIVITY 2

Application

One factor influencing the choice between direct and indirect methods is the average order size for a product. What do you think the relationship might be between average order size and the occurrence (or non-occurrence) of direct distribution?

Independently owned and operated distributors may well have their own objectives and these are likely to take precedence over those of the manufacturer or supplier with whom they are dealing. Suppliers may solve the problem by buying their own distribution route or by distributing direct to their customers. Direct distribution is common for many industrial and/or customised product suppliers. In some consumer markets direct distribution is also common, particularly with the advent of e-commerce via the Internet (as we will see in section 4).

3.1 General principles

A number of considerations will determine the choice of distribution strategy:

*   The number of **intermediate stages to be used**. There could be zero, one, two or three intermediate stages of selling (as shown in Figure 7.1 above). In addition, it will be necessary to decide how many dealers at each stage should be used – ie how many agents should be used, how many wholesalers should be asked to sell the manufacturer's products, and what the size of the direct sales force should be.

*   **The support that the manufacturer should give to the dealers**. It may be necessary to provide an efficient after-sales and repair service, or to agree to an immediate exchange of faulty products returned by a retailer's customers, or to make weekly, bi-weekly or monthly stock-checking visits to retailers' stores. To help selling, the manufacturer might need to consider advertising or sales promotion support, including merchandising.

*   **The extent to which the manufacturer wishes to dominate a channel of distribution**. A market leader, for example, might wish to ensure that its market share of sales is maintained, so that it might, for example, wish to offer exclusive distribution contracts to major retailers.

*   **The extent to which the manufacturer wishes to integrate its marketing effort up to the point of sale with the consumer**. Combined promotions with retailers, for example, would only be possible if the manufacturer dealt directly with the retailer (and did not sell to the retailer through a wholesaler).

3.2 Factors in channel decisions

In setting up a channel of distribution, the supplier has to take several factors into account.

*   Customers

- Nature of the goods or services
- Distributor characteristics
- Competitors' channel choice
- The costs associated with available channels
- The supplier's own characteristics

3.2.1 Customers

The **number** of potential customers, their **buying habits** and their **geographical proximity** are key influences. The use of mail order and Internet purchases for those with limited time or mobility (remote rural location, illness) is an example of the influence of customers on channel design.

Different distribution strategies may be adopted for **consumer** and **industrial** markets. Industrial channels tend to be more direct and shorter.

Industrial markets are generally characterised as having fewer, higher-value customers purchasing a complex total offering of products/services which fulfil detailed specifications. Industrial distribution channels therefore tend to be more direct and shorter, allowing partnership level relationships. There are specialist distributors in the industrial sector, which may be used as well as, or instead of, selling directly to industrial customers.

There have traditionally been fewer direct distribution channels from the manufacturer to the consumer in the consumer market. Even with the advent of e-commerce in some sectors, it is still more usual for companies in consumer markets to use wholesalers and retailers to move their product to the final consumer.

3.2.2 Nature of the goods or service

Some product characteristics have an important effect on design of the channel of distribution.

Characteristic	Comment
Perishability	Fresh fruit and newspapers must be distributed very quickly or they become worthless. Speed of delivery is therefore a key factor in the design of the distribution system for such products. Fragile items need extra care and minimal handling.
Customisation	Customised products tend to be distributed direct. When a wide range of options is available, sales may be made using demonstration units, with customised delivery to follow.
After-sales service/technical advice	Extent and cost must be carefully considered, staff training given and quality control systems set up. Suppliers often provide training programmes for distributors. Exclusive area franchises giving guaranteed custom can be allocated, to ensure distributor co-operation; the disadvantage of this is that a poor distributor may cost a supplier dearly in a particular area.
Franchising	Franchising has become an increasingly popular means of getting products to the customer. The supplier gains more outlets more quickly, and exerts more control than is usual in distribution.
Value	Highly valuable items might be better suited to direct delivery.

 ACTIVITY 3

Application

How might a service organisation choose channels of distribution?

3.2.3 Distributor characteristics

The location, customer base, performance and reliability, promotion and pricing policies of different types of distributor, and specific distribution outlets, will have to be evaluated. Selling to supermarket chains in the UK, for example, is now very difficult as the concentration of grocery retailing into a few large chains has increased the power of the buyers. Some products (such as emergency medical supplies) will be dependent upon faultlessly reliable delivery systems.

3.2.4 Competitors' channel choice

For many consumer goods, a supplier's brand will sit alongside its competitors' products. For other products, distributors may stock one name brand only (for example, in car distribution) and in return be given an exclusive area. In this case new suppliers may face difficulties in breaking into a market because the distribution channel is in effect controlled by the competition.

3.2.5 Costs

There are considerable costs associated with distribution. In addition to the costs of importing goods from overseas suppliers, or exporting to overseas customers, products will often need to be stored (in warehouses for example) or held somewhere (such as on the shop floor, for the use of which rent will usually be payable) awaiting sale or collection. The cheapest method of transport (by road, as opposed to by air) will not always be the most effective.

3.2.6 Supplier characteristics

A strong financial base gives the supplier the option of buying and operating their own distribution channel: Boots the Chemist is a good example in the UK. The market position of the supplier is also important: distributors are keen to be associated with the market leader, but other brands may experience distribution problems.

3.3 Making the channel decision

Producers have to decide the following.

- **What types of distributor** are to be used (wholesalers, retailers, agents)?

- **How many of each type will be used?** This depends on what degree of market exposure is required.

    - Intensive, blanket coverage
    - Exclusive, appointed agents for exclusive areas
    - Selective, some but not all in each area

- **Who will carry out specific marketing tasks?**

    - Credit provision
    - Delivery
    - After-sales service
    - Training
    - Display

- How will the **effectiveness** of distributors be evaluated?

    - In terms of cost?
    - In terms of sales levels?
    - According to the degree of control achieved?
    - By the amount of conflict that arises?

To develop an integrated system of distribution, the supplier must consider all the factors influencing distribution, combined with a knowledge of the merits of the different types of channel.

3.4 Direct distribution versus indirect distribution

Factors favouring the use of direct distribution	Factors favouring the use of intermediaries
(a) The need for an expert sales force to demonstrate products, explain product characteristics and provide after-sales service. Publishers, for example, use sales reps to keep booksellers up-to-date with new titles or to arrange for the return of unsold books.	(a) Insufficient resources to finance a large sales force.
	(b) A policy decision to invest in increased productive capacity, rather than extra marketing effort.
	(c) The supplier may have insufficient in-house marketing 'know-how' in selling to retail stores.

Factors favouring the use of direct distribution	Factors favouring the use of intermediaries
(b) Intermediaries may be unwilling or unable to sell the product.	(d) The product line may be insufficiently wide or deep for a sales force to carry. A wholesaler can complement a limited range and make more efficient use of his sales force.
(c) Existing channels may be linked to other producers.	
(d) The intermediaries willing to sell the product may be too costly, or they may not be maximising potential sales.	(e) Intermediaries can market small lots as part of a range of goods. The supplier would incur a heavy sales overhead if its own sales force took 'small' individual orders.
(e) Where potential buyers are geographically concentrated, the supplier's own sales force can easily reach them (typically an industrial market).	(f) Large numbers of potential buyers spread over a wide geographical area (typically consumer markets).
(f) Where e-commerce is well established, potential buyers can be reached online.	

3.4.1 Multiple channels

A producer serving both industrial and consumer markets may decide to use:

- **Intermediaries** for the **consumer** division
- **Direct selling** for the **industrial** division.

For example, a detergent manufacturer might employ a small sales team to sell to wholesalers and large retail groups in their consumer division. It would not be efficient for the sales force to approach small retailers directly.

3.5 Distribution strategy

There are three main strategies.

- Intensive distribution involves blanket coverage of distributors in one segment of the total market, such as a local area.

- Using selective distribution, the producer selects a group of retail outlets from amongst all retail outlets. The choice of selected outlets may be based on reflecting brand image (eg 'quality' outlets), or the retailers' capacity to provide after-sales service ('specialist' outlets).

- Exclusive distribution is where selected outlets are granted exclusive rights to stock and sell the product within a prescribed market segment or geographical area. Sometimes exclusive distribution or franchise rights are coupled with making special financial arrangements for land, buildings or equipment, such as petrol station agreements.

  ACTIVITY 4   Application

Discount factory shops, often situated on factory premises from where manufacturers sell seconds or retailers' returns, are well-established in the UK but developers have begun to group such outlets together in purpose-built malls.

What would you suggest are the advantages of this method of distribution for customers and manufacturers?

4 Internet distribution

4.1 ICT and distribution channels

Information and communication technology (ICT) has enabled direct marketing of products and services to consumers/business users, cutting short distribution channels, by:

- **Facilitating conventional direct sales**: offering sales force information linked to central databases, allowing personalised direct mail and online mail order catalogues.

- Empowering customers to **purchase direct from virtual stores and auctions**. e-commerce and its B2B equivalent (e-purchasing) via the Internet has exploded in many sectors over recent years, especially in markets such as music and books, apparel, travel products, banking services, groceries and specialist goods.

- **Facilitating home delivery** of goods, eg by allowing remote ordering, payment and tracking – and 'virtual' supply (eg by downloading information, software, books or music direct from the Internet).

- The **computerisation of purchase systems and record keeping**, covering stock control, purchase requisitions, purchase orders, expediting/tracking of deliveries, goods receipts and the generation of reports.

- Electronic Data Interchange (EDI) allows direct transfer of queries, information, orders, invoices and payments via cable or telecommunication link between supplier and purchaser.

- **Point-of-sale data capture systems**, such as bar-coding and electronic point of sale (EPOS) systems, which allow stock and sale information to be recorded in a database and processed as management information for retailers and suppliers.

- Warehousing data capture systems, using barcodes and scanners to carry out inventory checks and re-ordering.

Increasingly, the online shopping experience is simulating 'place', with familiar processes (eg 'shopping carts' and 'checkouts'), access to people (eg e-mail contact or voice/phone options) and physical evidence (eg downloadable/printable order confirmations, vouchers and brochures).

 MARKETING AT WORK _____ Application

'TriSenx is planning to take [virtual shopping] one step further, by allowing users to not only download scents, but to print out flavours that can be tasted. The Savannah, Ga., based company has developed a patented technology that allows users to print smells onto thick fibre paper sheets and taste specific flavours by licking the paper coated with the smell.

'Just as advertisers used scratch and sniff technology a couple of decades ago, they will likely use the novelty of digital scents to peddle their products now. Coca-Cola could embed their cola smell into banner ads, which could be triggered by a user scrolling over the ad. Suddenly, you're thirsty for a Coke. Sounds like pretty effective advertising.

'Consumers may also benefit from this aromatic technology. With online spending on the rise, shoppers will now be able to sample some of the goods that they buy, including flowers, candy, coffee and other food products. Soon, you'll be able to stop and smell the roses without leaving your workstation.'

www.trisenx.com

 EXAM TIP _____ Application

The application of the Internet to the work of the marketer is very likely to be examined under this new syllabus – developments in the communications field are highly relevant for the marketing profession. Look out for examples from your own experience or your own organisation that you can use in your answers, particularly to Section B questions.

4.2 Information and delivery

Information gathering is still the most common Internet activity, whether it be information about a historical fact, a medical problem or, hopefully, about your product. At present the five most common online purchase categories are books, CDs, clothing, toys and games, and computer software, but many buyers for other types of product do their initial 'window shopping' online and then go to a more conventional distribution outlet to actually make their purchase.

The Internet is perfect for the display of many types of product – anything, in fact, that customers do not need to be able handle physically, but which can be adequately shown off in words, still and moving pictures and sound.

For businesses, the advantage is that it is much cheaper to provide the information in electronic form than it would be to employ staff to man the phones on an enquiry desk or walk the shop floor, and much more effective than sending out mailshots that people would either throw away or forget about.

The Internet can be used to get certain products directly into people's homes. Anything that can be converted into digital form can simply be uploaded onto the seller's site and then downloaded onto the customer's PC (even some mobile phones). The Internet offers huge opportunities to producers of text, graphics/video, and sound-based products. Much computer software is now distributed in this way.

 MARKETING AT WORK   Application

For most companies, the Internet presents a golden opportunity to be part of a global distribution network with unparalleled means of enhancing brand awareness and improving market share. Luxury brands are different, with many of them yet to join the worldwide web. How can they harness the web's incredible reach, while maintaining a brand's uniqueness and exclusivity?

The answer, for many luxury brands, has been to avoid online marketing altogether. But the web is evolving – customers can say what they think, whenever they wish, to however many people, plus they can shop around for the best service and price. This unregulated exchange of opinions, reviews, and information between consumers means luxury brands have to relinquish some of the control they have traditionally exerted.

'Online' needs to be viewed as an extension of the brand-building process, offering more opportunities to reinforce key values. For instance, Louis Vuitton's website offers consumers a glimpse of what lies beneath the brand – product quality. The website also lets users taste the brand's exclusive identity by inviting them to personalise a Louis Vuitton product online.

Then there is the question of service. Many digital marketers are bewildered when it comes to replicating the high standards of in-store service in an online setting. It can be argued however that the potential interactivity of a website is eminently better suited to reinforcing a brand than a flat, broadcast TV ad.

Luxury brands could do well to learn from certain high fashion brands. Diesel has created a community of online consumers around the so-called 'Diesel Cult'. Members can go online to listen to music, watch videos, post new pieces of art and talk about exotic places they have visited. They can interact with one another and, crucially, do the sort research that affects their purchasing decisions. This online community reinforces Diesel's brand values and brand experience in a way that no other medium can compete with.

www.brandrepublic.com

4.3 Knowing the customer

Web servers (the computers that host websites) automatically log certain information about visitors, such as the time of their visit, their name and location of the service they are using to connect to the Internet, what pages they visited and what features they used.

If a visitor chooses to register with a website and provide a little further information such as their post code, sex and age, offerings can be closely tailored to the needs of the visitor. This is as good, or possibly much better than, any local knowledge a conventional distributor can offer.

The customisation is done by means of dynamically-generated pages: the page you see is only created when you request it and it is built up from elements that are of direct relevance to you: clothes in your favourite colour (if they are available in your size), your local weather forecast or even your favourite background music. The information is a combination of your customer profile and information on products and services that are a direct part of the organisation's information system.

How have ICT developments impacted on the functions of distribution listed in paragraph 2.1?

- Transport
- Stock holding and storage
- Local knowledge
- Promotion
- Sales displays

(McDonald (2007) raises some useful questions and answers in respect to distribution in chapter 10 of his book). ∎

Learning objectives	Covered
1 Define the different channels of distribution, and the role they play in a co-ordinated marketing mix	☑ Wholesaling
	☑ Retailing
	☑ Direct marketing
	☑ Internet marketing
	☑ Vending
	☑ Telephone selling
	☑ Franchising
	☑ Digital/e-channels
2 Explain the factors that influence channel decisions and the selection of alternative distribution channels	☑ Multiple channels
	☑ Location of customers
	☑ Compatibility
	☑ Nature of the goods/services
	☑ Geographic/environmental/terrain
	☑ Storage and distribution costs
	☑ Import/export costs

1 Draw a diagram illustrating possible intermediaries between a manufacturer and a consumer.

2 The ideas in the table below are jumbled. Rearrange them into the proper order.

Product characteristic	Issue
Perishability	Training required
After-sales service	More sales outlets
Franchising	Demonstration units are used
Customisation	Speedy delivery

3 Why is it important for companies to have what is termed 'local knowledge' and how does this impact upon distribution choices?

4 An organisation has limited financial resources and a small assortment of products, but potentially a global market. Which type of distribution should it use?

5 Fill in the blank: " _____ distribution is common for many industrial and/or customised product suppliers."

6 When would using 'surface' transport be preferable to using air freight over a long distance?

7 What is 'intensive distribution'?

8 For what is the Internet still most commonly used for?

1   Your answers might include some of the following points.

   (a)   The intermediary of course has to take his 'cut', reducing the revenue available to the producer.

   (b)   The producer needs an infrastructure for looking after the retailers – keeping them informed, keeping them well stocked – which might not be necessary in, say, a mail order business.

   (c)   The producer loses some part of his control over the marketing of his product. The power of some retailers (for example W H Smith in the world of UK book publishing) is so great that they are able to dictate marketing policy to their suppliers.

2   Other things being equal, if the order pattern is a small number of high-value orders, then direct distribution is more likely to occur. If there are numerous low-value orders, then the cost of fulfilling them promptly will be high and the use of intermediaries is likely.

3   It depends very much on the type of service.

   •   Hairdressers cannot deliver their own haircutting skills through an intermediary: the customer would get a different haircut and a different experience. (On the other hand, a self-employed hairdresser may rent a 'seat' in a number of different salons. This is not dissimilar to distributing via a retailer.)

   •   A train company has little option but to deliver transport services using the existing railway infrastructure. There are all manner of possible outlets for ticket sales.

   •   Insurance companies often deliver though agents who get paid commission, but they also use direct selling, for instance distributing via a mixture of the Internet, telesales or DRTV and conventional post.

4   Prices can be as much as 50% below conventional retail outlets, and shoppers can choose from a wide range of branded goods that they otherwise might not be able to afford. They can also turn a shopping trip into a day out, as factory outlet centres are designed as 'destination' shopping venues, offering facilities such as playgrounds and restaurants.

     Manufacturers enjoy the ability to sell surplus stock at a profit in a controlled way that does not damage the brand image. They have also turned the shops into a powerful marketing tool for test-marketing products before their high street launch, and selling avant-garde designs that have not caught on in the main retail market.

5   Impact of ICT developments on the functions of distribution:

   •   Managing income materials/components

   •   Inventory/stock management

   •   Managing flow of outbound goods

   •   Packaging/transport management

   •   Quality assurance and control

   •   Information management

   •   Banner advertising on websites

   •   Long, steady production runs: cost savings

   •   Minimising inefficient stock holding

   •   Timely supply of channel/customer demand

   •   Goods undamaged, preserved, safe, convenient for handling, storage, transport, display

   •   Customer value through reduced incidence of defective products

   •   Partnership throughout value chain, feedback for planning and control

1

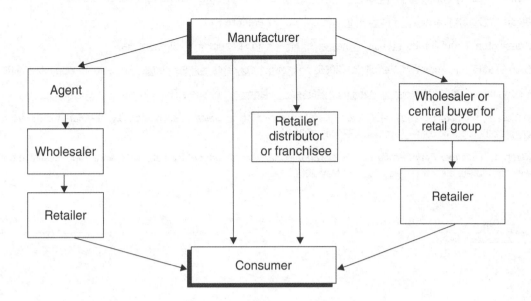

2

Product characteristic	Issue
Perishability	Speedy delivery
After-sales service	Training required
Franchising	More sales outlets
Customisation	Demonstration units are used

3   As production has tended to become centralised in pursuit of economies of scale, the need to understand and be 'close to' local markets has grown. This can mean that distributors who have knowledge of customers in a particular geographical area need to be chosen – very important when considering international distribution.

4   In theory the organisation should use an intermediary. However, effective internet distribution may make direct selling possible, especially if the product can be distributed over the internet (such as some software packages).

5   Direct

6   When, for example, speed is not vital in delivering the product, or its weight makes air freight prohibitively expensive.

7   Intensive distribution involves blanket coverage of distributors in one segment of the total market, such as a local area.

8   Information gathering prior to purchase

Blythe, J (2009) Principles and Practice of Marketing, 2nd edition, South-Western/Cengage Learning

Blythe, J (2008) Essentials of Marketing, 4th edition, FT Prentice Hall

Brassington, F and Pettitt, S (2006) Principles of Marketing, 4th edition, FT Prentice Hall

Dibb S, Simkin L, Pride WM, Ferrell OC (2005) Marketing: Concepts and Strategies, 5th edition, Houghton Mifflin

McDonald, M (2007) Malcolm McDonald on Marketing Planning, Reissue edition, Kogan Page, London.

McCusker, G *"Luxury brands: Viewpoint – Can luxury ever shine online?"* Revolution UK, 14 March 2008, from www.brandrepublic.com – [accessed 22 May 2008].

Kemp, E "*Onitsuka Tiger introduces trainer vending machine to London*" Marketing, 14 April 2008, available online from: www.brandrepublic.com – [accessed 22 May 2008].

Chapter 8
Marketing communications

Topic list

1 Overview of marketing communications
2 Marketing communications tools
3 Marketing communications media

Introduction

This chapter examines the last of the four Ps – promotion. The word 'promotion' implies that the seller is doing all the talking, yet in a market-orientated business (following relationship marketing principles) there is a two-way dialogue, where the buyer's response is as important as the seller's message. Hence the growth of the term 'marketing communications' – which is the term used by the syllabus and the one that you are most likely to see in the exam.

It could be argued that all the other Ps are merely elements of the marketing communications mix: product and packaging have a quality and design that 'communicates' a great deal to the customer; price speaks volumes; and the choice of distribution outlet says something else again.

Following an introductory overview, this chapter outlines some of the tools used in marketing communications (section 2) and the media that can be employed (section 3). There have been major changes in the way organisations communicate with their audiences. New technology, new media and changes in the way that people spend their time (working from home, shopping habits and leisure patterns etc) have meant that companies have to find new ways to reach people. Direct marketing (see section 2) is now a more significant part of the marketing plan for many products, along with interactive forms such as the Internet (see section 3).

Syllabus linked learning objectives

By the end of the chapter you will be able to:

Learning objectives	Syllabus link
1 Evaluate a range of marketing communications tools that comprise the marketing communications mix and consider their impact in different contexts	3.9
2 Evaluate the range of marketing communications media and consider their impact in different contexts	3.10

1 Overview of marketing communications

1.1 An integrated approach

The basic **promotional mix** consists of advertising, sales promotion, personal selling and PR, but more promotional methods are appearing all the time, particularly with the development of information and communication technologies. Figure 8.1 indicates the extensive range of tools that can be used to communicate with a customer or potential customer.

Figure 8.1: The marketing communications mix

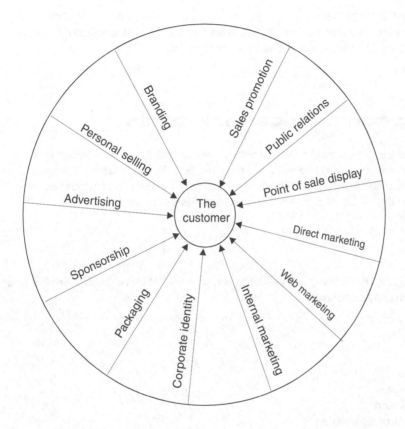

  EXAM TIP

Application

Note that in addition to some of those listed on the 'wheel' above, the syllabus also mentions direct response advertising and digital technologies (such as SMS marketing messages sent to your mobile phone). Pay careful attention to the uses and advantages/disadvantages of each tool or approach, then look at the broader criteria covered in this chapter. Don't forget to read exam questions very carefully for context (consumer/B2B, industry and so on).

1.2 Above or below 'the line'?

Promotional activities are often classified as **above-the-line** and **below-the-line**.

KEY CONCEPTS

Concept

Above-the-line promotion is advertising placed in paid-for media, such as the press, radio, TV, cinema and outdoor/transport poster sites. The 'line' is one in an advertising agency's accounts, above which are shown its earnings on a commission basis, from the buying of media space for clients.

Below-the-line promotion is a blanket term for a range of non-commissionable marketing communication activities. (Agency earnings on a fee basis are shown below the 'line' in their accounts.) More specifically, it refers to activities such as direct mail, sales promotions, sponsorship and exhibitions or trade shows.

2 Marketing communications tools

The range of promotional tools continues to grow. The variety of media that can be used for 'above the line' campaigns has expanded, both in the printed advertising field and in the broadcast field. There are literally thousands of publications aimed at different target groups. In the broadcast field the number of television stations steadily increases through satellite, cable and digital television, and the number of commercial radio stations has also grown considerably.

KEY CONCEPT

Concept

Advertising is 'any paid form of non-personal presentation and promotion of ideas, goods or services by an identifiable sponsor'. (American Marketing Association)

Why advertise?

- To promote **sales**
- To create an **image**
- To support **sales staff**
- To offset **competitor advertising**
- To **remind and reassure**

This section examines the marketing communications tools that are specifically listed in the syllabus.

2.1 Direct response advertising

KEY CONCEPT

Concept

Direct response advertising seeks *'an immediate response from the consumer in terms of purchase, or request for a brochure, or a visit to the shop'.* Blythe, J. (2008). It does not involve the use of intermediaries.

Direct response advertising may involve traditional advertising in a newspaper or magazine with a cut out (or stuck on) response coupon; loose inserts with response coupons or reply cards; direct-response TV or radio advertisements, giving a call centre number or website address to contact.

Advertising on interactive TV includes a 'pop up' button which gives you the option to interact by transferring to a website. DRTV (home shopping) is presently conducted mainly through the use of television commercials or infomercials (which combine information with a commercial), which direct customers to a website or telephone order lines. In the UK, cable and satellite also provide a number of channels exclusively devoted to shopping.

Direct response advertising enables detailed measurement of the effectiveness of ads on different stations, at different times, in different formats.

Direct mail tends to be the main medium of direct response advertising. The main reason for this is that other major media such as newspapers and magazines are familiar to people for advertising in other contexts. Direct mail has a number of strengths as a direct response medium.

- The advertiser can target down to **individual level**.

- The communication can be **personalised**. Known data about the individual can be used, while modern printing techniques mean that parts of a letter can be altered to accommodate this.

- The medium is good for **reinforcing interest** stimulated by other media such as TV. It can supply the response mechanism (a coupon) which is not yet available in that medium.

- The opportunity to use **different creative formats** is almost unlimited.

- **Testing potential is sophisticated**: a limited number of items can be sent out to a 'test' cell and the results can be evaluated. As success is achieved, so the mailing campaign can be rolled out.

2.2 Personal selling

Personal selling encompasses a wide variety of tasks including prospecting, information gathering and communicating as well as actually selling.

  KEY CONCEPT Concept

Personal selling is the presentation of products and persuasive communication to potential clients by sales staff employed by the supplying organisation. It is the most direct and longest established means of promotion within the promotional mix.

Personal selling, or sales force activity, must be undertaken within the context of the organisation's overall marketing strategy. For example, if the organisation pursues a **'pull'** strategy, relying on massive consumer advertising to draw customers to ask for the brands, then the role of the sales force may primarily be servicing, ensuring that retailers carry sufficient stock, allocate adequate shelf space for display and co-operate in sales promotion programmes.

Conversely, with a **'push'** strategy, the organisation will rely primarily on the sales force to persuade marketing intermediaries to buy the product.

2.2.1 Sales roles

A salesperson might perform any of six different activities.

Activity	Salesperson's role
Prospecting	Gathering additional potential customers
Communicating	Communicating information to existing and potential customers about the company's products and services can take up a major proportion of the salesperson's time
Selling	Approaching the customer, presenting benefits, answering objections and closing the sale
Servicing	Providing services to the customer, such as technical assistance, arranging finance and speeding delivery
Information gathering	Feedback and marketing intelligence gathering
Allocating	Allocating products to priority customers, in times of product shortages

2.2.2 The selling process

Personal selling is part of an integrated promotional strategy. It will be supported by a range of other activities such as advertising and PR, lead generation and sales support information.

Elements of the selling process can be depicted as follows.

Figure 8.2: Elements of personal selling

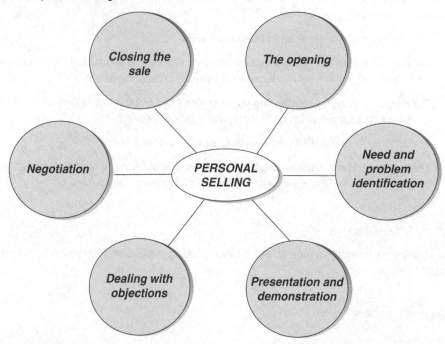

The stages need not occur in any particular order. Objections may occur during the presentation; negotiation may begin during problem identification; and if the process of selling is going well, the salesperson may try to close the sale.

The salesperson's job begins before meeting the buyer. **Preparation** could include finding out about the buyer's personal characteristics, the history of the trading relationship, and the specific requirements of the buyer and how the product being sold meets those requirements. In this way, the salesperson can frame sales presentations and answers to objections.

At the other end, the selling process does not finish when the sale is made. Indeed, the sale itself may only be the start of a long-term **relationship** between buyer and seller.

Personal selling will be **supported** by a range of other marketing communication activities.

- **Product advertising, public relations and sales promotion**, drawing consumer attention and interest to the product and its sources *and* motivating distributors/retailers to stock and sell the product.

- **'Leads'** (interested prospective customers) generated by contacts and enquiries made through exhibitions, promotional competitions, enquiry coupons in advertising and other methods.

- **Informational tools** such as brochures and presentation kits. These can add interest and variety to sales presentations, and leave customers with helpful reminders and information.

- **Sales support information**: customer/segment profiling; competitor intelligence; access to customer contact/transaction histories and product availability. (This is an important aspect of customer relationship management, enabling field sales teams to facilitate immediate response and transactions without time-lags to obtain information.)

2.2.3 The advantages and disadvantages of personal selling

Personal selling is often appropriate in **B2B markets**, where there are fewer, higher-value customers who are looking for a more complex total offering tailored to a more specific set of requirements.

A number of advantages are associated with using personal selling when compared to other promotional tools.

- Personal selling contributes to a relatively **high level of customer attention** since, in face-to-face situations, it is difficult for a potential buyer to avoid a salesperson's message.

- Personal selling enables the salesperson to **customise the message** to the customer's specific interests and needs.

- The two-way communication nature of personal selling allows **immediate feedback** from the customer so that the effectiveness of the message can be ascertained.

- Personal selling communicates a larger amount of **technical and complex information** than would be possible using other promotional methods.

- In personal selling there is a greater ability to **demonstrate** a product's functioning and performance characteristics.

- Frequent interaction with the customer gives great scope for the **development of long-term relations** between buyer and seller.

The main disadvantage of personal selling is the **cost** inherent in maintaining a salesforce. In addition, a salesperson can only interact with one buyer at a time. However, the message is generally communicated more effectively in the one-to-one sales interview, so the organisation must make a value judgement between the effectiveness of getting the message across against the relative expense.

2.3 Sponsorship

 KEY CONCEPT   Concept

Sponsorship involves supporting an event or activity by providing money (or something else of value, such as prizes for a competition), usually in return for naming rights, advertising or acknowledgement at the event and in any publicity connected with the event. Sponsorship is often sought for sporting events, artistic events, educational initiatives and charity/community events and initiatives.

Sponsorship is often seen as part of a company's socially responsible and community-friendly public relations profile: it has the benefit of positive associations with the sponsored cause or event. The profile gained (for example, in the case of television coverage of a sporting event) can be cost-effective compared to TV advertising). However, it relies heavily on awareness and association: unless additional advertising space or 'air time' is part of the deal, not much information may be conveyed.

Marketers may sponsor local area or school groups and events – all the way up to national and international sporting and cultural events and organisations. Sponsorship has offered marketing avenues for organisations which are restricted in their advertising (such as alcohol and tobacco companies) or which wish to widen their awareness base among various target audiences.

- There is wide corporate involvement in mass-support sports such as football and cricket.

- Cultural sponsorship (of galleries, orchestras or theatrical productions) tends be taken up by financial institutions and prestige marketing organisations.

- Community event sponsorship (supporting local environment 'clean-up' days, tree planting days, charity fun-runs, books for schools programmes) is often used to associate companies with particular values (for example, environmental concern, education) or with socially responsible community involvement.

2.3.1 The purpose of sponsorship

The objective of the organisation soliciting sponsorship is most often financial support – or some other form of contribution, such as prizes for a competition, or a prestige name to be associated with the event. In return, it will need to offer potential sponsors satisfaction of *their* objectives.

The objectives of the **sponsor** may be:

- **Awareness creation** in the target audience of the sponsored event (where it coincides with the target audience of the sponsor)

- **Media coverage** generated by the sponsored event (especially if direct advertising is regulated, as for tobacco companies)

- Opportunities for **corporate hospitality** at sponsored events

- **Association** with prestigious or popular events or particular values

- Creation of a **positive image** among employees or the wider community by association with worthy causes or community events

- Securing **potential employees** (for example, by sponsoring vocational/tertiary education)

- **Cost-effective** achievement of the above (compared to, say, TV advertising)

Sponsorship as a promotional technique also has limitations.

- Sponsorship by itself can only communicate a restricted amount of information (unless integrated with advertising and other initiatives).

- Association with a group or event may also attach negative values (such as sports-related violence and alcohol abuse).

 ACTIVITY 1

 Application

List some examples of sporting, artistic, educational and community sponsorships that you are aware of in your country (or internationally).

- What image of the sponsoring company or brand does association with that particular event/group/cause create?

- How much promotional coverage (advertising, publicity) does the sponsor get as a result of sponsorship: how much information about the organisation or brand is conveyed?

2.4 Public relations

Public relations aims to enhance goodwill towards an organisation from its publics.

 KEY CONCEPT

 Concept

The Institute of Public Relations has defined **public relations** as 'the planned and sustained effort to establish and maintain goodwill and mutual understanding between an organisation and its publics'.

This is an important discipline, because although it may not directly stimulate sales, the organisation's image is an important factor in whether it attracts and retains employees, whether consumers buy its products/services, whether the community supports or resists its presence and activities and whether the media reports positively on its operations.

An organisation can be either reactive or proactive in its management of relationships with the public.

- **Reactive public relations** is primarily concerned with the communication of what has happened and responding to factors affecting the organisation. It is primarily defensive.

- In contrast, **proactive public relations** practitioners have a much wider rôle and thus have a far greater influence on overall organisational strategy. The scope of the PR function is much wider, encompassing communications activities in their entirety.

2.4.1 Scope of public relations

Organisations will have to deal with more than one public, including consumers, business customers, employees, the media, financial markets and wider society.

The scope of PR is very broad. Some frequently used techniques are as follows.

- **Consumer marketing support**

    - Consumer and trade press releases (to secure media coverage)
    - Product/service literature (including video and CD-ROM)
    - Special events (celebrity store openings, product launch events etc)
    - Publicity 'stunts' (attention-grabbing events)

- **Business-to-business communication**

    - Corporate identity design (logos, liveries, house style of communications)
    - Corporate and product videos
    - Direct mailings of product/service literature and corporate brochures
    - Trade exhibitions and conferences

- **Internal/employee communications**

    - In-house magazines and employee newsletters (or intranet pages)
    - Recruitment exhibitions/conferences
    - Employee communications: briefings, consultation, works councils

- **Corporate, external and public affairs**

    - Corporate literature

    - Corporate social responsibility and community involvement programmes: liaison with pressure and interest groups

    - Media relations: networking and image management through trade, local, national (and possibly international) press

    - Lobbying of local/central government and influential bodies

    - Crisis and issues management: minimising the negative impacts of problems and bad publicity by managing press/public relations

- **Financial public relations**

    - Financial media relations
    - Design of annual and interim financial reports
    - Facility visits for analysts, brokers, fund managers
    - Organising shareholder meetings and communications

2.5 Direct marketing

 KEY CONCEPT

Concept

Direct marketing creates and develops a direct relationship between the consumer and the company on an individual basis.

(a)   The Institute of Direct Marketing in the UK defines direct marketing as 'The planned recording, analysis and tracking of customer behaviour to develop relational marketing strategies'.

(b)   The Direct Marketing Association in the US defines direct marketing as 'An interactive system of marketing which uses one or more advertising media to effect a measurable response and/or transaction at any location'.

Direct marketing involves use of a wide variety of media to communicate directly with the target market and to elicit a measurable response.

2.5.1 Features of direct marketing

It is worth studying these definitions and noting some key words and phrases.

- **Response**. Direct marketing is about getting people to respond by post, telephone, e-mail or web form to invitations and offers.

- **Interactive**. The process is two-way, involving the supplier and the customer.

- **Relationship**. Direct marketing is in many instances part of an on-going process of communicating with and selling to the same customer.

- **Recording and analysis**. Response data are collected and analysed so that the most cost-effective procedures may be arrived at.

Direct marketing helps create and develop **direct one-to-one relationships** between the company and each of its prospects and customers. This is a form of **direct supply**, because it removes all channel intermediaries apart from the advertising medium and the delivery medium: there are no resellers. This allows the company to retain control over where and how its products are promoted, and to reach and develop business contacts efficiently.

2.5.2 Tools of direct marketing

Direct marketing tools include direct mail, e-mail, text message, DRTV advertising (section 2.1) and telemarketing.

Direct marketing is the fastest growing sector of promotional activity. It now embraces a range of techniques, some traditional – and some based upon new technologies.

- **Direct mail** (DM): a personally addressed 'written offering' (letter and/or sales literature) with some form of response mechanism, sent to existing customers from an in-house database or mailing list.

 MARKETING AT WORK   Application

Computers now have the capacity to operate in three new ways which will enable businesses to operate in a totally different dimension.

Customers can be tracked individually. Thousands of pieces of information about each of millions of customers can be stored and accessed economically.

Companies and customers can interact through, for example, phones, mail, E-mail and interactive kiosks. ... for the first time since the invention of mass marketing, companies will be hearing from individual customers in a cost-efficient manner.

Computers allow companies to match their production processes to what they learn from their individual customers - a process known as 'mass customisation' which can be seen as 'the cost-efficient mass production of products and services in lot sizes of one'.

There are many examples of companies which are already employing or experimenting with these ideas. In the US Levi Strauss, the jeans company, takes measurements and preferences from female customers to produce exact-fitting garments. The approach offers the company tremendous opportunities for building learning relationships.

The Ritz-Carlton hotel chain has trained staff throughout the organisation to jot down customer details at every opportunity on a guest preference pad. The result could be the following: You stay at the Ritz-Carlton in Cancun, Mexico, call room service for dinner, and request an ice cube in your glass of white wine. Months later, when you stay at the Ritz-Carlton in Naples, Florida, and order a glass of white wine from room service, you will almost certainly be asked if you would like an ice cube in it.

- **E-mail**: messages sent via the Internet from an e-mail database of customers. E-mails can offer routine information, updates and information about new products: e-mail addresses can be gathered together via enquiries and contact permissions at the company's website.

- **Mobile phone text messaging (SMS)**. Messages can be sent via mobile phone to a captive audience, catching them wherever they are. This form of marketing is still in its infancy, but with the proliferation of mobile phone usage it is likely to be very significant, at least in terms of numbers reached. It is also becoming increasingly sophisticated, with '3G' (third-generation) mobile phone technology. SMS marketing is governed by the Mobile Marketing Association in the UK.

- **Direct response advertising** as described at paragraph 2.1 above.

- **Mail order**. Mail order brochures typically contain a selection of items also available in a shop or trade outlet, which can be ordered via an order form included with the brochure and delivered to the customer. Mail order extends the reach of a retail business to more (and more geographically dispersed) customers.

- **Catalogue marketing** is similar to mail order, but involves a complete catalogue of the products of the firm, which typically would not have retail outlets at all. Electronic catalogues can also be downloaded on the internet, with the option of transferring to the website for transaction processing, and on CD-ROM.

- **Call centres** and **telemarketing**. A call centre is a telephone service (in-house or outsourced by the marketing organisation) responding to or making telephone calls. This is a cost-effective way of providing a professionally trained response to customer callers and enquirers, for the purposes of sales, customer service, customer care or a contact point for direct response advertising.

 KEY CONCEPT

Concept

Telemarketing is the planned and controlled use of the telephone for sales and marketing opportunities. Unlike all other forms of direct marketing it allows for immediate two-way communication.

 MARKETING AT WORK

Application

A survey of recent direct mail campaigns includes the following creative ideas to overcome 'junk mail' resistance and marketing fatigue.

- **Great Ormond St Hospital, (UK)**

  How do you make it clear that a new ultrasound scanner would mean that surgeons could avoid unnecessary surgery when diagnosing children? Send a donation request in a clear package, that asks "If you could see inside every envelope, would you open every one?"

- **Oroverde, Tropical Rainforest Founding (Germany)**

  How do you remind potential donors of the precarious state of the world's rainforests? Send them a paint-by-numbers kit with only one colour included: black.

- **Genesis Energy (New Zealand)**

  How do you let customers know you're there to help them save on their energy bills? Print your energy-saving tips in fluorescent ink, so they can read them with the lights off.

- **First Direct bank (UK)**

  How do you show customers that you're still the most thoughtful bank? Send them a single sock that they can marry to the odd one we all have in our sock drawer.

2.6 Sales promotion

Sales promotion techniques add value to a product in order to achieve a specific marketing objective.

 KEY CONCEPT   Concept

The Institute of Sales Promotion (ISP) defines **sales promotion** as 'a range of tactical marketing techniques, designed within a strategic marketing framework, to add value to a product or service, in order to achieve a specific sales and marketing objective'.

Sales promotion activity is typically aimed at increasing short-term sales volume, by encouraging first time, repeat or multiple purchase within a stated time frame ('offer closes on such-and-such a date'). It seeks to do this by adding value to the product or service: consumers are offered something extra – or the chance to obtain something extra – if they purchase, purchase more or purchase again.

 EXAM TIP   Application

It is worth being aware of the potential for confusion between the terms 'promotion' (used as another way of saying 'marketing communications' in general) and 'sales promotion' (which is a specialist term reserved for the techniques involved). In an exam, especially if you are reading through questions fairly quickly, it is all too easy to answer the 'wrong' question.

2.6.1 Objectives of sales promotion

The following are examples of consumer sales promotion objectives, stated in broad terms.

- Increase **awareness and interest** amongst target audiences
- Achieve a **switch in buying behaviour** from competitor brands
- **Incentivise consumers** to make a forward purchase of your brand
- **Increase display space** allocated to your brand
- **Smooth seasonal dips** in demand for your product
- Generate a **customer database** from mail-in applications

Sales promotion objectives will link into overarching marketing and marketing communications objectives. For example:	
Marketing objective	Increase 'Brand X' market share by 2 percentage points between January and December 20XX
Marketing communications objective	To contribute to brand share gain of 2% in 20XX by increasing awareness of 'Brand X' from 50% to 70% among target consumers
Sales promotion objective	To encourage trial of 'Brand X' among target consumers by offering a guaranteed incentive to purchase

2.6.2 Consumer sales promotion techniques

Consumer promotion techniques include reduced price, coupons, gift with purchase and competitions and prizes.

The range of consumer **sales promotion techniques** can be depicted as follows.

Figure 8.3: Consumer sales promotion techniques

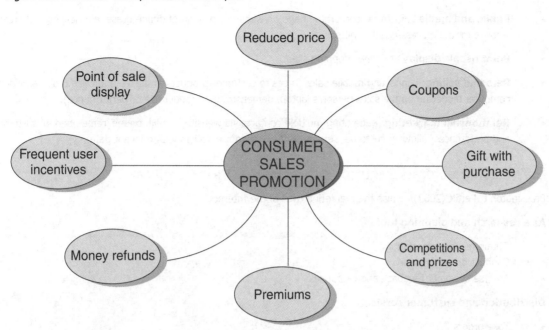

- **Price promotions**: for example discounted selling price or additional product on current purchase, or coupons (on packs or advertisements) offering discounts on next purchase

- **'Gift with purchase'** or **'premium'** promotions: the consumer receives a bonus, gift or refund on purchase or repeat purchase, or on sending in tokens or proofs of multiple purchases

- **Competitions and prizes** for example, entry in prize draws or 'lucky purchase' prizes, often used both to stimulate purchase (more chances to win) and to capture customer data.

- **Frequent user (loyalty) incentives** for example, Air Miles programmes, points-for-prizes cards.

 MARKETING AT WORK   Application
_____   - - - - - - - - - - - - - - - - - -

It is reckoned that two-thirds of purchases result from in-store decisions. Attractive and informative point-of-sale displays are therefore of great importance in sales promotion.

Point of sale materials include product housing or display casing (such as racks and carousels), posters and leaflet dispensers. Their purpose is to:

- Attract the attention of buyers
- Stimulate purchase in preference to rival brands
- Increase available display and promotion space for the product
- Motivate retailers to stock the product (because they add to store appeal)

2.7 Technological developments

Information and communication technology (ICT) is adding impact, speed, interactivity and fun to the full range of promotional methods and tools. **Digital technologies** and the imaginative use of **websites** are creating endless possibilities.

- **Advertising**: using direct response advertising, web-advertising, CD-ROM and video packages, and mobile phone advertisements.

- **Direct marketing**: using e-mail or mobile text messages instead of conventional mail shots.

- **Sales promotion**: online vouchers, discounts, loyalty schemes, 'SMS to win', competitions.

- **Public and media relations**: corporate image on websites, posting of online press releases, special areas of the website for trade/press/client publics.

- **Point of sale display** at online shopping sites.

- **Personal selling**: connecting mobile sales forces to customer/product databases and sales tools (eg video or computer modelling on the sales person's laptop, demonstrating product use or performance).

- **Relationship marketing**: generating multiple contacts via website, e-mail, phone 'remembering' customer details and preferences; allowing customer service staff to 'recognise' callers with relevant data.

2.7.1 Internet marketing

Brassington & Pettitt (2003) itemise the marketing uses of the Internet.

As a research and planning tool

- Obtain market information
- Conduct primary research
- Analyse customer feedback and responses

Distribution and customer service

- Take orders
- Update product offerings
- Help the customer to buy
- Process payments
- Raise customer service levels
- Reduce marketing and distribution costs
- Distribute digital products (music, software etc)

Communication and promotion

- Generate enquiries
- Enable low-cost direct communication
- Reinforce corporate identity and present company in a good light
- Produce and display product catalogues and product information
- Entertain, amuse and build goodwill
- Inform investors, suppliers and employees of developments

  EXAM TIP

Application

You should of course be aware of these technological developments, but also realistic about their current application. It is important for marketers to be aware of what ICT – especially the Internet – can't do. It may be able to deliver some products/services in 'real time', or very fast: information, music and images, educational material and banking transactions. However, many products will still have to be physically delivered. The Internet is global in its reach, and so products will have to be delivered internationally. This takes resources, logistics, infrastructure and time.

Because of the promotional strengths of the Internet, there is great potential for customer disappointment if the product does not live up to the sophistication of the promises – or if it cannot be delivered in a reasonable condition or within a reasonable period of time.

3 Marketing communications media

'Promotion is all about getting the message across to the customer (and the consumer) in the most effective way, and the choice of method will depend on the message, the receiver and the desired effect.' Blythe, J. (2008)

The general criteria for selecting a medium to convey the promotional message to the appropriate audience are as follows.

- The advertiser's specific **objectives** and plans
- The **size of the audience** which regularly uses the medium
- The **type of people** who form the audience of the medium
- The **suitability** of the medium for the message
- The **cost** of the medium in relation to its ability to fulfil the advertiser's objectives
- The susceptibility of the medium to **testing and measurement**

  ACTIVITY 2   Application

Brainstorm a list of media which might be suitably targeted (by factors in the media themselves, or in the media habits of the target audiences) for advertising the following products/services.

- A local garage offering car service, maintenance and parts

- An up-market restaurant

- A software package for use by accountants (based on UK law and regulation)

- A new brand of washing powder

- A microchip for use in engineering applications

3.1 Television

Because of the high exposure, glamour and audio-visual impact of television, it has become the favoured medium for launching new products, raising brand awareness and building brand loyalty, re-positioning brands and also motivating the employees and supply chain partners of the advertising organisation. This perception is encouraged by advertising agencies, whose commission on TV airtime is many times higher than on print space and other media.

3.1.1 Viewership

It is a complex matter to access not just how many sets are owned and switched on at particular times, but how many people are actually watching – let alone consciously taking in what is being transmitted.

The size of the television audience for a given programme (and advertising) is measured in **ratings**: rating points, or TVRs. One TVR point represents 1% of all homes which have a TV set in the region to which the programme is broadcast. Ratings are used by TV stations to monitor the popularity of their programmes, and to set advertising rates. The advertiser pays for the number of TVRs allocated to given advertising spots.

- A programme with 20 TVRs is seen by 20% of homes with a TV. This is the number of people who will (in theory) see an ad once.

- If you placed an ad in four programmes, each with a rating of 20 TVRs, you would achieve 80 TVRs. However, some homes might have seen the ad all four times, while others may have missed it altogether.

- Gross Rating Points (GRPs) are a measure of probable reach multiplied by probable frequency. If you buy 280 GRPs, about 70% of households should have four opportunities to see your ad.

- Target Audience Rating Points (TARPs) measure reach and frequency against specific demographic audiences, across a wide range of criteria (geographic, gender, age, socio-economic bracket). These are the most effective guide for advertisers, since they allow the media planner to devise a schedule which will deliver the largest relevant audience for the available budget.

Reach refers to the size of the audience which is exposed to an ad, both net (number of people reached) and gross (including cumulative multiple exposures).

Frequency refers to the number of times an ad is run, opportunities to see (OTS) the ad; or 'impacts'.

Ratings are measurements of television audiences, which multiply reach by frequency (or OTS) to give the probable coverage and repetition of an ad, with (TARPS) or without (GRPs) breakdown by demographic criteria.

3.1.2 Scheduling TV ads

In addition to TARPs, which suggest where and when to schedule ads in order to reach an optimum number of target viewers an optimum number of times, the advertiser should consider the following.

- Daytime audiences are more responsive. Direct responses to TV ads are greatest between 12 noon – 2pm and 2pm – 4pm on weekdays.

- Audiences show greater recall of ads at the beginning of a long commercial break. The more ads they see, the lower the recall of each.

- Audiences tend to watch through commercial breaks in the middle of TV programmes, because they do not want to miss any of the programme. However, viewers are reluctant to take action in response to ads during the programme, so direct-response ads are more successful during end breaks. (Most people respond within 15 minutes of the ad spot.)

- Advertising guru David Ogilvy suggests that while most advertisers use 30-second ads, 90-second or even two minute ads can be more effective (as with long-copy press ads) especially for complex or expensive products.

- Very short (10-second) ads can also be effective, and offer much higher TARPs for the available budget, since you can get more exposures. However, the greater impact of longer commercials usually offsets the reduced TARPs which longer ads deliver.

- Repetition of ads increases TARPs, but is subject to the law of diminishing returns. It is essential for the message to sink in, but people easily become habitual and cease to notice or be motivated by the ad. One strategy is to have a set of related ads which can be rotated, reinforcing but varying the message.

 ACTIVITY 3

Application

All other things being equal, and subject to detailed research, at what time of day, or in what kind of programme, might you advertise the following products on TV?

- Shoe polish
- Home disinfectant
- Car repairs
- Chat/introduction lines

3.2 Cinema

Cinema advertising takes advantage of high audio-visual impact and a captive audience but still requires a high quality and entertainment value.

Cinema advertising best suits 'lifestyle' products.

- Branded consumer goods with high style and profile, aimed mainly at young adults (such as jeans and alcohol)
- Local services in the area of the cinema (particularly restaurants)

3.3 Billboards

Poster advertising is one of the oldest media for consumer goods advertising. Sites on walls, hoardings and bus shelters can be leased for a fee per calendar month. In addition, many vehicles (buses, trucks and taxis) now carry external advertising, and some are tailor-made to do so (advertising 'floats'). Trains and buses also offer internal advertising positions. Size and visibility of the sites are the main consideration.

3.4 Press and magazines

 KEY CONCEPT   Concept

Press or print media includes newspapers: (daily and weekly, morning and evening, national and regional) and **magazines**, periodicals and journals (general appeal, special interest and trade)

3.4.1 Advertising in the press

Print media offer different types of advertising.

- **Classified advertising**. The classified sections of publications offer small spaces for text-only ads. The advantage is that classified space is very cheap, and the publication usually typesets the ad for you. The disadvantage is the difficulty of attracting attention with so much competition and so little space: icons, headline, styles and impactful/incentive copy are required to make an ad stand out.

- **Semi-display advertising** allows you to use borders, typographic features and illustrations to attract attention (although on a crowded page, white space and simplicity may be more effective). Small ads in the Yellow Pages are a good example.

- **Display advertising** offers further opportunity for creativity: the advertisers design and provide their own artwork or film, constrained only by the technical specifications (size, colour) of the publication. Full-colour magazine ads are a good example. 'Long copy' advertisements break the usual simple visual style of display advertising by including lots of detailed information.

- **Advertorials** are advertisements presented as edited copy, in order to take advantage of the perceivably objective authority of editorial matter. Features on health and beauty, advice, house and garden are often advertisements for the products and services 'reviewed' or 'recommended'.

- **Loose inserts** or 'drop outs' are printed leaflets (produced by the advertiser) inserted into magazines and newspapers. They usually work out 4 or 5 times more expensive than advertising space – but draw up to 5 or 6 times as many responses as a full-page advertisement.

Print media is bought in column inches (or centimetres) or standard page divisions (quarter, half or full page, or 'junior' page). The cost/rate differs according to several criteria.

- The size of the ad
- The number of colours in the ad and the production quality of the publication
- Position of the ad for which a premium may be charged
- The readership number of the publication
- The potential for readership targeting or niche marketing
- The prestige of the publication and the spending power of its readership.

3.4.2 Positioning press ads

Media research into **'traffic per page'** (the reading and noting of different pages in a print publication) suggests the following.

- Early pages are read more than late pages
- Right-hand pages have higher noting scores than left-hand pages
- Pages opposite relevant or popular editorial content do better than pages opposite other advertising

Cover space is particularly sought after because of its high visibility, and usually also because the covers are printed on better quality paper for colour production. The outside front cover is likely to be most expensive, followed by outside back, inside front (especially if opposite the contents page) and inside back.

MARKETING AT WORK

Business-to-business magazines are used regularly for work purposes by more decision-makers than any other medium. 87% of decision-makers are regular users. B2B magazines dominate all other media in terms of usefulness to business decision-makers.

When asked for eleven types of information, which medium was most useful, B2B magazines not only achieved the highest score in every case but also did so by wide margins.

The typical pattern was that, for a given type of information, the proportion of decision-makers who declared that B2B magazines were the most useful medium was usually around four to six times larger than for the medium in second place. The remaining eight media then tailed away with few people thinking them the most useful source.

The eleven types of information for which B2B publications were so pre-eminent were:

- Providing thorough coverage of your sector
- Helping you to stay in touch with what's going on in your sector
- Helping you to understand how your sector is changing
- Helping you to learn from the successes and mistakes of others
- Keeping you up-to-date with news of product launches
- Providing you with information about new products and services
- Helping you select new suppliers
- Looking for jobs, or helping you to keep up-to-date with the job market
- Helping you to spot new business opportunities
- Containing advertising which is useful to you
- Helping you to do your job better

Source: Periodical Publishers' Association survey

3.5 Web advertising

3.5.1 Websites

"Websites fall into two main categories: presence websites, which merely give information about the company and usually include contact telephone and email addresses, and interactive websites, where customers can navigate around the site, obtain more information about the company and its products, and even place orders". Blythe, J. (2009)

Advertising using a website on the internet offers two main marketing opportunities, namely **distribution** and **communication**.

KEY CONCEPTS

E-commerce is about transactions involving the exchange of goods and services, for payment, using the internet and related digital facilities. In business-to-consumer marketing, some industries have been revolutionised: low cost airlines conduct virtually all their bookings online.

Internet marketing is about the application of the internet and related digital facilities to help determine and satisfy marketing objectives.

Web advertising is generally acknowledged to be when an advertiser pays to place advertising content on another website.

A **banner advertisement** is "a typically rectangular graphic displayed on a web page for purposes of brand-building or driving traffic to a site. It is normally possible to perform a click through to access further information from another website. Banners may be static or animated". Banner adverts can be targeted at a particular audience.

The ability to reach customers directly and so avoid many channel intermediaries reduces transaction costs and is a prime goal for most organisations. The use of the Internet as a communications medium is equally attractive, facilitating interactivity and a two-way dialogue that no other method of communication can support.

Smith and Chaffey (2001) (referred to by Brassington & Pettitt (2006)) describe the benefits of e-marketing as the '5Ss':

* **Sell** goods and services online, to a global market
* **Serve** customers in new and better ways
* **Save** money, with fewer of the overheads that are associated with traditional ways of doing business
* **Speak** to customers directly
* **Sizzle** with a well designed website that can engage and entertain the visitor

"Whatever its purpose, and however much is spent on it, a website should provide a powerful supplementary marketing tool. It should have all the creative flair of an advertisement, the style and information of a company brochure, the personal touch and tailored presentation of face-to-face interaction and, not least, always leave the visitor clear as to what action should be taken next". Brassington, F. & Pettitt, S. (2006)

A good website should be:

* Continually updated
* Easy to navigate
* Informative
* Quick to load and respond

The most common form of web advertising occurs when the advertiser uses a range of sites (often via a search engine such as Yahoo!) to drive visitors to its corporate site. Companies are still learning what works with web advertising, and what does not. There are two basic types of promotion associated with the Internet, online and offline.

KEY CONCEPTS

Concept

Online promotion uses communication via the Internet itself to raise awareness. This may take the form of links from other sites, targeted email messages or banner advertisements.

Offline promotion uses traditional media such as TV or newspaper advertising to promote a website address (URL). Offline marketing communications are usually required to support the online communications and facilities.

MARKETING AT WORK

Application

There are some tricks to offline promotion that can be used to help the customer in finding the information they need on a website. When advertising in traditional media such as a newspaper or magazine, it is beneficial to highlight a specific page that is related to the offline promotion and the interests of the audience. For example:

* In an American magazine: www.jaguar.com/us
* In a phone advert from a company that sells other products: www.ericcsson.com/us/phones

By doing this, the user will be sent directly to the relevant information without having to navigate through the corporate site.

A similar technique is to use a different sub-domain to the main domain, or register a completely different domain name which is in keeping with the campaign, such as

www.fireandwater.com rather than Harper and Collins Publishers.

Increasingly, promotion of the website in the offline media is not simply flagging the existence of the web site as an afterthought via including the URL at the bottom of the advert, but highlighting the offers or services available at the web-site, such as special sales promotions or online customer service. Amazon commonly advertises in newspapers to achieve this.

3.5.2 Measuring the effectiveness of Internet advertising

This is based upon the behaviour of web users. When using the Internet, users will go through several stages.

- Be exposed to a **message** (for example through a banner advertisement)
- Look for more **information** by clicking on the banner
- Go to the **web page** of the advertiser

Based on this sequence, different types of ad effectiveness have been identified. These can be measured for different online advertisements of the same advertiser, on a daily basis if required, to monitor web ad effectiveness.

- Total **ad impressions** (number of contacts made by the ad)
- **'Click throughs'** (contact by a user with advertisement)
- **Ad transfer** (successful arrival of a user at the advertiser's website)

3.5.3 Other online advertising methods

These include:

- **Promotion in search engines and directories** (such as Google). A company may want to have its company web-site listed when a user types in a specific keyword, such as 'office equipment'. To achieve this, the website should be registered with each of the main search engines.

- **Links from other sites**. This involves making sure that the site is linked to as many related sites as possible.

- **Using email** for advertising new products directly to customers.

  EXAM TIP

Application

You should be aware of how the Internet can impact upon marketing activities, and the strategic significance of Internet technologies. Remember however, that traditional marketing communications are still important in the strategic promotional activities of organisations.

 MARKETING AT WORK

Application

Online advertisements are becoming ever more attention seeking. Animation, video and audio are moving the field beyond the normal banner advert. New formats are giving scope for greater creativity.

Newspapers, which invested heavily in putting their content online, are at the forefront of experimenting with the new formats to attract advertising revenue to their sites.

The use of interactive banner adverts is also increasing, adding value to the advertisement by providing services such as:

- Entering a destination to show the cheapest fare
- Filling in an e-mail address to receive further information

3.6 Comparing different media

3.6.1 Influential factors

The effective audience of a medium, and therefore the competitiveness of different media, is influenced by the following factors.

- **Opportunity to use the medium**. The potential audience will not be able to use TV during working hours, or magazines while driving, or cinema over breakfast. Radio in the morning and TV in the evening have bigger effective audiences.

- **Effort required to use the medium**. People usually use the medium that will cost them least effort. Print media require the ability to read and concentrate: television is comparatively effortless.

- **Familiarity with the medium**. People consume media with which they are familiar: hence the survival of print media, since the education system is still predominantly print-orientated. Electronic media are however gaining ground.

- **Segmentation by the medium**. The print media currently has the greatest capacity for segmentation into special-interest audiences. Commercial television segments to a limited extent through programming, and cable/satellite television to a greater extent, through the proliferation of channels. Some media only charge in proportion to the segment you are targeting, which is more cost effective than paying for the full circulation.

  ACTIVITY 4 Application

What opportunity, effort and familiarity issues might you consider when appraising the following media?

- A newly launched radio station
- Daytime television
- Posters on buses
- Web pages

3.6.2 Evaluating different advertising media

Advantages	Disadvantages
NEWSPAPERS – daily, metropolitan, national	• Circulation does not mean readership: wasted circulation paid for
• 'Mass' medium: large audience in single exposure	• Print/image reproduction of variable quality
• Targeted sections (auto, home, computers etc)	• No exclusivity: ad may be next to competitor's
• Reader navigation: seeking news, information	• Costs loaded for preferred positions
• Short lead time for production: accept ads 24-48 hours before publication	• Short life-span of news
• Flexibility of ad size	
• Tangibility of ad (can be torn out and kept)	
• Multiple readers/users	
• Allows detailed information (prices, phone numbers etc)	
• Allows still images	
• Allows response mechanisms (eg captions)	

Advantages	Disadvantages

NEWSPAPERS– local, free

- Low cost
- Geographical targeting
- High local readership
- Special sections (especially local real estate, entertainment etc)

- Circulation of free papers/weeklies not always monitored/audited
- Variable editorial content
- Subject to weather and junk mail rejection if letterbox dropped

MAGAZINES

- High circulation (major titles)
- Targeted audiences (special)
- High quality reproduction (colour photography etc)
- Potential high prestige
- Reader motivation (selection, subscription)
- Long shelf life and multiple use/readership
- Tangibility, detail, images, response mechanisms (see newspapers)

- High costs of production
- Hyper-segmentation (by interest and geography, may be insufficient circulation to support local outlets)
- Long lead times: copy/artwork required 1 – 3 months before publication, can be inflexible

TELEVISION

- 'Mass' medium: large audience at single exposure, almost universal ownership/access
- Detailed monitoring of exposure, reach, viewer habits
- Allows for high degree of creativity
- Realism: impact of sound + sight + movement
- High-impact visual images reinforce retention
- Allows demonstration
- Flexibility as to scheduling
- Allows association with desirable products

- Most expensive of all media costs
- High production costs
- Lack of selectivity (except via programming) of audience
- Lack of opportunity: does not reach commuters/workers
- Long lead times for booking and production: penalties for withdrawal: inflexibility
- Passive, unmotivated audience: 'zapping' by fast-forward and remote controls erodes reach

OUTDOOR MEDIA – poster sites, bus stops, buildings

- Flexible: sites, duration of lease
- Comparatively low cost
- Opportunity: exposure to commuters, shoppers

- Difficulty of verification of exposure/response
- Subject to weather
- Opportunity: site specific
- No audience selectivity (except by site)

CINEMA

- Glamorous
- High impact (large size, highly visual, loud sound, high quality)
- Captive audience (no TV 'zap' factor)
- Can segment by local area

- High cost
- Opportunity: site/time specific
- Poor verification of response
- Limited number of people reached per exposure

Advantages	Disadvantages
INTERNET	• Generally poor viewership
• Principally sight, but with sound and colour further possibilities are developing	• Consumer confidence in security low (but improving)
• Interactive, permitting direct response	• Possible to direct audience to information, but can be difficult to gain large audience without support from other media
• Able to track audience movements	• Not yet a mainstream media with broad customer appeal
• Message permanent, and can be down-loaded	• Speed of access depends on sophistication of technological link
	• No universal computing language yet agreed

Chris Fill's (2006) text titled 'Simply Marketing Communications' gives a thorough overview of the subject. It is an extensive text and highly worth trying to spend time reading. If you are unable to manage the entire text in the time you have available, at the very least you should attempt chapter 1. Chapter 1 of Smith & Taylor's (2004) text will also help you see how marketing communications require careful integration with the entire marketing mix. ■

Learning objectives	Covered
1 Evaluate a range of marketing communications tools that comprise the marketing communications mix and consider their impact in different contexts	☑ Direct response advertising
	☑ Personal selling
	☑ Sponsorship
	☑ Public relations
	☑ Direct marketing
	☑ Sales promotions
	☑ Digital technologies
	☑ Website
2 Evaluate the range of marketing communications media and consider their impact in different contexts	☑ Television
	☑ Cinema
	☑ Billboards
	☑ Press
	☑ Magazine
	☑ Web advertising
	☑ Sales promotions

1   What is 'below-the-line' promotion?

2   There are six tasks that a sales person may undertake. What are they?

     P.....................

     C.....................

     S.....................

     S.....................

     I.....................

     A.....................

3   List five reasons why a company may use advertising.

4   Draw a diagram showing the various types of consumer sales promotions.

5   Put the term from the list below into the first column in the appropriate space.

PR technique	Example
	Shareholder meeting
	In-house magazine
	Celebrity store opening
	Trade exhibition
	Government lobbying

Consumer marketing support	Business-to-business	Internal communications	Public affairs	Financial relations

6   Name some tools of direct marketing.

7   How can new digital technologies assist with relationship marketing?

8   Why is television the favoured medium for launching new products and building brands?

9   What are 'advertorials'?

10   Why is cover space particularly sought after when advertising in the press?

11   What are the characteristics of a good website?

12   What are the disadvantages of Internet advertising, when evaluating it against other media?

1   This will depend on your own research. You might have considered sports sponsorship, especially of large international events that are guaranteed to have huge audiences. The public has a high level of acceptance of sponsorship, with many recognising that if there is no sponsorship, there will be no sports event at all. Spiralling costs have meant that sponsors are increasingly prepared to consider involvement at the grass roots level rather than the higher cost, 'glamour' events. This in turn encourages the development of sport over the long term, and appeals to today's socially responsible consumer who is looking for genuine involvement to overcome his cynicism about corporate motives. The Football Association in the UK, for instance, now has a limited number of sponsorship partners, who are expected to get involved at all levels of the game.

2   Here are some suggestions.

- Local radio (in car), bus stop, poster sites (driver visibility), local paper 'Auto' section

- Local cinema (evening session, adult-appeal film), local paper 'Food' section, Good Food Guide (regional listing), local radio (classical music/news programmes?)

- UK accountancy journals (various), Underground Station posters in financial districts, direct mail.

- Commercial TV (especially daytime for housewives, poster sites (shopper visibility), women's and household magazines. (Assuming mainly female buyer decision.)

- Trade engineering journals, website of inventor

3   Suggested timing of advertisements:

- Assuming mainly professional male buyers, next to business news, news or evening/weekend sports.

- Assuming mainly female buyers/decision makers, daytime (cost effective), home/lifestyle programmes, prime time soaps (eg for launch).

- Assuming car-owner buyers, not during commuting hours: driving/car programmes, motor sports, home/lifestyle (women buyers).

- Assuming single buyers, late-night television.

4   Opportunity, effort and familiarity issues:

- Opportunity and effort are good with radio: effortless background, portable etc. Familiarity may be a constraint where station newly launched: listeners may not want to switch from old favourites, may not be able to recall frequency.

- Daytime TV minimal effort and good familiarity with regular users, but limited opportunity if target audience includes workers/school-age commuters.

- Bus posters: minimal effort (depending on size, length of copy, sight lines: can be a strain to read bus posters), good familiarity, good opportunity because moving around (outside posters) but limited by bus users only (inside).

- Web pages: high effort (to search, wait, use queries etc, requires technological know-how) improving familiarity (biased towards computer-literate), limited opportunity by virtue of technology, access and expertise required.

1   The term refers to activities such as direct mail, sales promotions, sponsorship and exhibitions or trade shows – the non-commissionable marketing communication activities.

2   Prospecting, communicating, selling, servicing, information gathering, allocating

3   To promote sales
    To create an image
    To support sales staff
    To offset competitor advertising
    To remind and reassure

4

5

PR technique	Example
Financial relations	Shareholder meeting
Internal communications	In-house magazine
Consumer marketing support	Celebrity store opening
Business-to-business	Trade exhibition
Public affairs	Government lobbying

6   Direct mail, email, text messaging (SMS), direct response advertising, telemarketing

7   Generating contacts via website; use of targeted e-mail; 'remembering' customer details using a database

8   Television has very high exposure and strong audio-visual impact

9   Advertorials are advertisements presented as edited copy, in order to lend them perceived objective authority

10 It has high visibility, and the covers are generally printed on better quality paper for colour production.

11 Continually updated; easy to navigate; informative; quick to load and respond

12 •   Generally poor viewership

    •   Consumer confidence in its is security low (but improving)

    •   Possible to direct audience to information, but can be difficult to gain large audience without support from other media

    •   Not yet a mainstream media with broad customer appeal – user expertise may be limited

    •   Speed of access depends on sophistication of technological link

    •   No universal computing language yet agreed

Blythe, J (2009) <u>Principles and Practice of Marketing</u>, 2nd edition, South-Western/Cengage Learning

Blythe, J (2008) <u>Essentials of Marketing</u>, 4th edition, FT Prentice Hall

Brassington, F and Pettitt, S (2006) <u>Principles of Marketing</u>, 4th edition, FT Prentice Hall

Dibb S, Simkin L, Pride WM, Ferrell OC (2005) <u>Marketing: Concepts and Strategies</u>, 5th edition, Houghton Mifflin

Fill, C (2006) <u>Simply Marketing Communications</u>, Prentice Hall, Harlow

Smith, P and Taylor, T (2004) <u>Marketing Communications: an integrated approach</u>, 4th edition, Kogan Page, London

References

BPP
LEARNING MEDIA

Chapter 9
Services marketing

Topic list

1   The services marketing mix
2   Characteristics and implications

Introduction

We have looked at the four Ps of the traditional marketing mix (product, price, place and promotion) in Chapters 5 to 8 of this Text.

In this chapter we consider services, briefly introduced in Chapter 5 – things you pay for but can't touch, like banking or education or cleaning. How do you market something when you can't show it to customers or give them something for their money that they can feel good about or show off to their friends?

Syllabus linked learning objective

By the end of the chapter you will be able to:

Learning objectives	Syllabus link
1 Explain the importance of a coordinated services marketing mix, its characteristics and implications for the marketing of service products	3.11

1 The services marketing mix

"Consumer orientation means that we should be looking at what the consumer thinks, needs and wants, not at defining our product in terms of its characteristics". Blythe, J. (2008) ▇

It is often argued when discussing the marketing of services (such as transport, insurance or hospitality), that four 'ingredients' are not enough to describe the marketing mix. This is because a service does not primarily involve a physical product. If you go on a train journey the ticket itself does not transport you to your destination and you don't get to keep the train.

Most products have some element of service in them, too. If you buy a product over the telephone your purchase may be enhanced by friendly and helpful service from the telesales assistant. The telesales assistant may be able to offer that help because the ordering process is managed by a sophisticated customer and product database, and a customer relationship management system.

It has therefore been suggested that another three Ps should be added to the usual four to make an **extended marketing mix**.

- Product
- Price
- Place
- Promotion

- **People**
- **Process**
- **Physical evidence**

 EXAM TIP   Application

The importance of the extended marketing mix in the marketing of space travel forms a question in Section B of the specimen paper for 25 marks. Although space travel might be very expensive, and a long way off for many, the principles of services marketing can still be applied to the few who can afford it! Be ready to apply your knowledge to a wide range of service industry scenarios – travel and tourism, hospitality, personal services such as hairdressing and financial services to name a few.

1.1 People

The higher the level of customer contact involved in the delivery of a product or service, the more crucial is the role of people. In many cases the delivery and the physical presence of the staff involved are completely inseparable.

In some cases, the physical presence of people actually performing the job is a vital aspect of customer satisfaction. Think of counter staff in a bank, or waiting staff in a restaurant, or builders who leave your house tidier than they found it. The people involved are performing or 'producing' the service, selling the service and also liaising with the customer to promote the service, gather information and respond to customer needs.

Organisations need to take measures to institute a customer orientation in all sectors of activity. People issues will include the following.

- Appearance
- Attitude
- Commitment (including quality/customer)
- Behaviour

- Professionalism
- Skills/competence
- Discretion/confidentiality
- Integrity/ethics

Managers must promote values of customer service in order to create a culture of customer service. This may entail any or all of the following.

- **Job design** to give people the authority they need to meet customer needs

- Careful policies of **recruitment and selection**

- Programmes of **training and development** to ensure that staff have both technical competence and 'people skills'

- Standardised **rules and practices**, to ensure consistent basic levels of service

- Effective programmes of **staff motivation and reward**, creating commitment to the organisation, quality and customers

- Effective **communication** of quality, service and customer care values

1.1.1 Why care about service quality?

Quality of service is an important issue for marketers because it is one of the most significant ways in which customers differentiate between competing products and services.

An organisation can give better service through any of the seven Ps – make a better product, do a special deal on price, open for longer hours, give more information in the brochure, refurbish its store and process orders more quickly. But the main way is through the P of people.

 KEY CONCEPT  Concept

Service quality is the totality of features and characteristics of that service which bears on its ability to meet stated or implied needs.

There are two ways that organisations can gain from improving their quality of service to customers.

- **Higher sales revenues** and **improved marketing effectiveness** may come through improved customer retention, positive word-of-mouth recommendations and the ability to increase prices.

- Better quality **improves productivity** and **reduces costs** because there is less rework, higher employee morale and lower employee turnover.

1.1.2 What is 'service quality'?

Quality can only be defined by customers, and occurs where a firm supplies products to a specification that satisfies their needs. Customer expectations serve as standards, so when the service they receive falls short of expectations, dissatisfaction occurs.

Service quality has a number of dimensions.

- **Technical quality** of the service encounter (ie what is received by the customer). Was the meal edible? Was the train on time? Were the shelves fully stocked? Problems of this sort must be addressed by improving the processes of production and delivery.

- **Functional quality** of the service encounter (ie how the service is provided). This relates to the psychological interaction between the buyer and seller and is typically perceived in a very subjective way.

  - **Relationships between employees**. For instance, do these relationships appear to be professional? Do they chat to each other whilst serving the customer? Does each appear to know their role in the team and the function of their colleagues? Do they know who to refer the customer to if there is a need for more specialist advice? Are they positive about their colleagues or unduly critical?

  - **Appearance and personality of service personnel**. For instance, do they seem interested in the customer and the customer's needs? Are they smartly presented? Do they convey an attractive and positive image? Do they reflect the organisation or brand (eg through uniform/livery)?

  - **Service-mindedness of the personnel**. For instance, do they appear to understand and identify with the needs of the customer? Do they convey competence? Do they show willingness to help?

- **Accessibility of the service to the customer**. For instance, do the service personnel explain the service in language which the customer can understand?

- **Approachability of service personnel**. For instance, do the service personnel appear alert, interested or welcoming? Or are they day-dreaming, yawning or looking at their watches?

Key elements in customer service are set out in the table below.

Tangibles	The quality of the service area, products and information must be consistent with the desired image.
Reliability	Getting it right first time is very important, not only to ensure repeat business, but as a matter of ethics, if the customer is buying a future benefit (as in financial services).
Responsiveness	Staff must be willing to deal with customer queries and problems, responding flexibly to needs.
Communication	Staff should provide appropriate information to customers in language they can understand.
Credibility	The organisation should be perceived as honest, expert and trustworthy, acting in the best interests of customers.
Security	The customer needs to feel that transactions are safe, and where necessary, private and confidential.
Competence	Service staff need to develop competence in meeting the needs of the customers and using systems efficiently.
Courtesy	Customers should experience service staff as polite, respectful and friendly.
Understanding customers' needs	Service staff need to listen to and meet customer needs rather than try to sell products. This is a subtle but important difference.
Access	Minimising queues, having a fair queuing system and speedy service are all factors in customer satisfaction.

1.1.3 Improving service quality and customer care

An organisation can use a number of methods to try to improve its quality of service and customer care.

- Development of a customer-orientated **mission statement** and **customer care policy**, with clear **senior management support** for quality improvement initiatives.

- **Customer satisfaction research**, both formal (eg customer surveys, customer panels, analysis of complaints data) and informal (eg tuning in to customer feedback at the point of sale/service).

- **Monitoring and control**: feedback should be communicated, and standards constantly reviewed.

- Customer **complaints and feedback** systems, with incentives to encourage customers to complain!

- **Employee involvement**: eg through the use of quality circles, project teams and other forms of internal communication on quality/service issues.

- Customer care **training and development**

- **Rewarding** excellent service

  EXAM TIP

Application

This topic came up in December 2009 in the context of staff morale, productivity and, therefore, good customer service.

1.2 Process

Concept

Process involves the ways in which marketing tasks are achieved. They include all administrative, ordering and customer service features.

- Procedures
- Policies
- Automation of processes
  (eg online or by automated telephony)

- Information flow to service units/customers
- Capacity levels, for continuous performance
- Speed/timing of service
- Queuing/accessibility arrangements

MARKETING AT WORK

Application

Efficient processes can become a marketing advantage in their own right. For example, computer company Dell's success is due as much to the remarkable efficiency of its ordering and customer information system as it is to the quality and manufacturing efficiency of its production system. The company's marketing line is 'Easy as Dell', which refers to the process and sums up Dell's competitive advantage in a nutshell. Take a look, even if you don't want to buy a computer: **www.dell.com**.

The level and quality of service which is available to the customer is especially sensitive. Process issues include the following.

- **Capacity utilisation**: matching resource/staff utilisation to anticipated demand, to avoid delays, bottlenecks and waste.

- **Managing customer contacts and expectations**: keeping people realistically informed and empowering staff to respond to changing needs.

1.2.1 Automated processes

Customer handling is increasingly automated in order to increase process efficiency. Examples include web-based transactions and information provision; voice mail systems (for recording customer telephone queries); and automated call handling (ACH) and interactive voice response (IVR) systems, which allow customers to select menu options (eg for call routing, product ordering or information requests) using telephone keypad or verbal responses. You may have used such a system for telephone bill payments or taxi bookings.

The automation of customer-handling operations can have a positive impact for the customer and supplier alike.

- The organisation is available for contact 24 hours, 7 days, a week

- Ordering can be conducted 'instantly' and at any time to suit the customer.

- Frequently asked questions (FAQs) and e-mail contacts can reduce waiting time for answers to customer queries.

- Customer information is made available to personalise the transaction and build customer relationships. This includes recognition of customer telephone numbers, for example, so that call centre staff can address customers by name and do not have to ask repeatedly for address and other details. On a fully automated level, it includes the personalisation of the customer's interface with a web page.

- Automation creates significant cost savings for the company: reducing the number of customer-service staff required, and enabling other to work from home or in (in-house or outsourced) call centres.

- Fewer 'missed' calls and better customer service supports customer attraction, retention and loyalty.

Customer Relationship Management (CRM) systems can be used to empower customers to control the purchase and service process. A well-constructed website can often provide better services than are usually received through a human-based call centre. Such a website lets customers easily information on products and services that helps them to investigate product features and even make purchases, without help from costly sales and support staff.

Negative impacts of automation, however, include the following.

- Customers (particularly in certain age or cultural groups) may simply want to talk to a human being
- Automation leads to the loss of customer service jobs
- Automated call management systems can frustrate the customer by creating a lengthy 'loop' of menus

1.3 Physical evidence

"Physical evidence gives the consumer something to refer to and to show other people if necessary. Since service products are usually intangible, the consumer of (say) an insurance policy will need some written evidence of its existence in order to feel confident in the product". Blythe, J. (2008) ▮

You receive monthly bank statements – but all they are, really, is reassurance in tangible form that the bank still has your money. The following are other examples of items of physical evidence that the marketer can use in the marketing mix.

Environment of service delivery	**Facilities**	**Tangible evidence of purchase**
• Colours	• Vehicles/aeroplanes	• Labels and other printed information
• Layout	• Equipment/tools	• Tickets, vouchers and purchase confirmations
• Staff uniforms		• Logos and other visible evidence of brand identity
• Noise levels		• Packaging
• Smells		
• Ambience		
• Website design		

The layout, décor and 'branding' of a bank or travel agency, for example, are likely to be an important part of the customer's experience of receiving services which are otherwise intangible. Likewise, the appearance, user-friendliness and branding of a company's website can give a visible and 'interactive' aspect to the encounter.

A service can be presented in tangible (and promotional) physical form: consider how travel tickets are presented in branded envelopes (or more sophisticated document wallets), with vouchers for added services, information leaflets and other added value elements – despite the fact that all the customer has purchased is the promise of a future benefit.

Note that physical evidences can be used as a **marketing communications** tool: staff livery uniforms, logos and corporate identity features, and promotional messages printed on vouchers/ envelopes/receipts are all promotional opportunities.

 ACTIVITY 1

Application

See if you can think of three customer-focused 'C' equivalents to People, Processes and Physical evidence. What might these three Ps look like from the customer's point of view? Look back to paragraph 1.3 of Chapter 2 if you are stuck.

2 Characteristics and implications

Services are increasingly important in developed economies. A service has five distinguishing characteristics: intangibility, inseparability, heterogeneity, perishability, and ownership. Each of these has marketing implications, as we shall see in this section.

The main differences between selling goods and services are shown below.

Issue	Comment
Customer's purchase perception of services	• Customers view service as having less consistent quality
	• Service purchasers have higher risks
	• Service purchasing is less pleasant
	• When services are bought greater consideration is given to the particular salesperson
	• Perception of the service company is an important factor when deciding to buy a service
Customer's purchase behaviour with services	• Customers may do fewer price comparisons with services
	• Customers give greater consideration to the particular seller of services
	• Customers are less likely to be influenced by advertising and more by personal recommendations
Personal selling of services	• Customer involvement is greater
	• Customer satisfaction is influenced by the salesperson's personality and attitude
	• Salespeople may have to spend more time reducing customer uncertainty

  ACTIVITY 2

Application

All levels of staff must be involved in customer service. To achieve this end, it is vital for senior management to promote the importance of customer service. How do you think that this might be achieved?

2.1 Services characteristics

As was introduced in Chapter 5, the following characteristics of services distinguish them from goods.

- **Intangibility**: services cannot be touched or tasted
- **Inseparability**: services cannot be separated from the provider
- **Heterogeneity** (variability, or lack of 'sameness'): the standard of service will vary with each delivery
- **Perishability**: services cannot be stored for provision 'later'
- **Ownership**: service purchase does not transfer ownership of property

'The result of this is that consumers are likely to spend more time on information-gathering, and will rely more heavily on word-of-mouth recommendations than they would when buying a physical product … a consumer looking for a doctor may want to know what experience and qualifications the doctor has to treat a particular complaint; few car buyers would be interested in the qualifications and experience of Ford's chief design engineer.' Blythe, J. (2008)

We will now look at each characteristic in detail, along with its marketing implications.

2.1.1 Intangibility

'Intangibility' refers to the lack of substance which is involved with service delivery. Unlike goods, there are no substantial material or physical aspects to a service: no taste, feel or visible presence. Clearly this creates difficulties and can inhibit the desire to consume a service, since customers are not sure what they will receive.

We can view insubstantiality as a continuum, as shown in Figure 9.1 below.

Figure 9.1: The Goods – Services Continuum

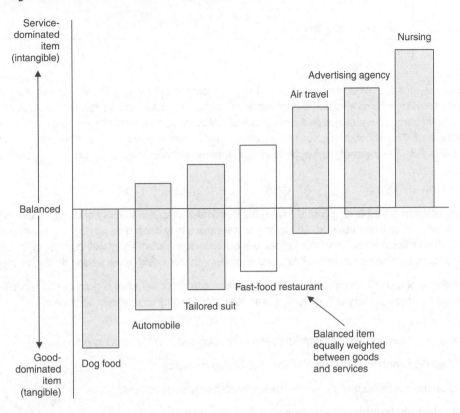

Marketers and consumers need to try to overcome this problem. The consumer needs information to avoid making a mistake, to obtain some grounds for forming a judgement and to cut down risk. The marketer wishes to make the choice of the product 'safer' and make the consumer feel more comfortable about paying for something they do not then own and which has no physical form.

Dealing with intangibility may involve the following.

*   **Increasing the level of tangibility**. Use physical or conceptual representations/illustrations to make the customer feel more confident as to what it is that the service is delivering: the 'physical evidences' component of the extended marketing mix.

*   **Focusing the attention of the customer on the principal benefits of consumption**. Communicating the benefits of purchasing the service so that the customer visualises its use. Promotion and sales material could provide images or records of previous customers' experience.

*   **Differentiating the service and reputation-building**. Enhancing perceptions of customer service and customer value by offering excellence in the delivery of the service. This reputation can be attached to brands, which must then be managed to secure and enhance their market position, (For example, the Virgin brand).

2.1.2 Inseparability

Services often cannot be separated from the provider. Think of having dental treatment or taking a journey. Neither exists until they are actually being experienced/consumed by the person who has bought them.

The 'creation' of many services is simultaneous with consumption, where the service is

- Made available
- Produced
- Sold
- Consumed

} all at the same time

Provision of the service may not be separable from the person or personality of the seller, to the extent that many consumers will develop a loyalty towards a trusted service provider (such as a hairdresser or a favourite restaurant). Consequently, increasing importance is attached to the need to instil values of quality, reliability and to generate a service ethic in customer-facing staff. This points up the need for excellence and customer orientation, and the need to invest in high quality people and high quality training: the 'people' component of the extended marketing mix.

2.1.3 Heterogeneity (variability, or lack of 'sameness' or consistency)

Many services face the problem of maintaining consistency in the standard of output. Variability of quality in delivery occurs because of the large number of variables involved. The quality of the service may depend heavily on who it is that delivers the service, or exactly when it takes place. Booking a holiday using standard procedures may well be quite different on a quiet winter's afternoon then on a hectic spring weekend, and may well vary according to the person dealing with your case.

It may also be impossible to obtain influence or control over customers' perceptions of what is good or bad service. From the customer's perspective it is, of course, very difficult to obtain an idea of the quality of service in advance of purchase/consumption.

In terms of marketing policy, heterogeneity highlights the need to develop and maintain processes for:

- Consistency of **quality control**, with clear and objective quality measures

- Consistency of **customer service** and customer care, standardising as far as possible

- Effective staff **selection, training** and **motivation** in customer care

- Adopting the **Pareto principle** and so identifying and responding most closely to potential 'troublespots'. (The Pareto principle states that 80% of the difficulties arise from 20% of events surrounding the service provision)

- **Monitoring** service levels and customer perceptions of service delivery

2.1.4 Perishability

Services cannot be stored: they are innately perishable. Seats on a bus or the services of a doctor exist only for periods of time. If they are not consumed, they 'perish'. They cannot be used later. They cannot be 'produced' in advance, to allow for peaks in demand.

This presents specific marketing problems. Meeting customer needs depends on staff being available as and when they are needed. This must be balanced against the need for a firm to minimise unnecessary expenditure on staff wages. Anticipating and **responding to levels of demand** is, therefore, a key planning priority, in order to avoid:

- Inadequate level of demand accompanied by substantial variable and fixed costs
- Excess demand resulting in lost custom through inadequate service provision

Policies must seek to **smooth out fluctuations** in the supply/demand relationship, or allow for contingencies. Examples include:

- Using price variations to encourage off-peak demand (eg on travel services)

- Using promotions to stimulate off-peak demand (eg free mobile calls between certain hours)

- Using flexible staffing methods to cover fluctuations in demand (eg part-time and temporary working, outsourcing to call centres)

2.1.5 Ownership

Services do not result in the transfer of property. The purchase of a service only gives the customer access to or the right to use a facility, not ownership. This may lessen the perceived customer value of a service – particularly if the benefit does not accrue until some time in the future (like a pension, or a voucher for future use).

There are two basic approaches to addressing this problem.

- **Promote the advantages of non-ownership**. This can be done by emphasising the benefits of paid-for maintenance, or a periodic upgrading of the product. Radio Rentals have used this as a major selling point with great success.

- **Make available a tangible symbol or representation of ownership** such as a certificate, voucher, merchandise item or simple receipt. This can come to embody the benefits enjoyed.

  ACTIVITY 3 Application

What are the marketing implications of the lack of ownership of a service received?

2.2 Service promotion

Promotional objectives for services are not much different to those for products.

- Build awareness and interest in the service and the service organisation
- Communicate and portray the benefits of the services available
- Build and maintain the overall image and reputation of the service organisation
- Advise customers of new channels
- Advise customers of special offers or modifications to the service
- Persuade customers to use or buy the service

However, in a service context there are four particular elements of the service that need to be taken into account.

- The **core service concept** and any auxiliary service
- The **accessibility** of the service
- The **interactive communications** that take place in delivering the service
- The **influence of the consumer** and other consumers receiving the service

Four **promotional methods** are generally used to influence the customer.

- Traditional selling
- Advertising and direct marketing
- Public relations and sales promotions
- The communication aspects of pricing policy

2.2.1 Guidelines for service promotion

A number of guidelines must be considered when designing promotional campaigns for service markets.

- Use **clear, unambiguous messages** to communicate the range, depth, quality and level of services

- **Emphasise the benefits of the services** rather than their technical details

- **Only promise what can be delivered**, to avoid disappointment

- **Advertise to employees**, as they are particularly important in many people-intensive services

- Obtain **maximum customer co-operation** in the service production process as the service is often an interactive system

- Build on **word-of-mouth communication** from one satisfied customer to another

- Provide **tangible evidence** to strengthen promotional messages. Use well known personalities to support the messages

- Develop **continuity in promotion** by the use of consistent and continuous symbols, themes, formats or images

- **Remove post purchase anxiety** by reassuring the buyer of the soundness of choice, especially where there is no tangible product

- **Personal selling** becomes more important in the promotion of services

ACTIVITY 4

Application

Do a little of revision:

(a)   What are the three service Ps?

(b)   What are the five characteristics of services that distinguish them from goods?

(c)   How could you charge different groups of people a different price for the same service?

EXAM TIP

Application

Services are an important area of the international economy and account for more employment than the manufacturing sector. They are likely to feature regularly on exam papers. You may be asked to illustrate how the unique characteristics of services affect a particular organisation's extended marketing mix – be able to cite the characteristics of services, and remember that the extended marketing mix is not just the extra three Ps, but the full seven!

2.3 Service marketing online

Many services can be distributed online as effectively, or almost as effectively, as if they were digital products like videos or software. That is because, at heart, many services consist of processing information.

The most obvious example of this is **online banking**, now offered by all major high street banks. Online banking allows you to look at your balance ('physical evidence' that they still have your money, or at least, visible evidence), transfer money between accounts, make payments and set up direct debits and standing orders. There is nothing that you can do online that you can't do by posting a letter, picking up the telephone and speaking, or visiting a branch, but it is less effort.

It is also less effort for the bank, of course, and less costly, because they are 'empowering' you to do things that a member of their staff would have done previously.

Much the same applies to any service where the outputs are **information**. Examples are accountancy, legal work, architectural plans, graphic design, education, entertainment/travel bookings – and many others.

ACTIVITY 5

Application

Online distribution of services, where possible, is massively convenient. Can you see any drawbacks?

Adrian Palmer's (2007) text titled 'Principles of Services Marketing' is another useful but extensive text. We would recommend that you read chapters 1 and 3.

Learning objective	Covered
1 Explain the importance of a coordinated services marketing mix, its characteristics and implications for the marketing of service products	☑ Co-ordinated approach to people, physical evidence and process
	☑ Characteristics/implications: inseparability, intangibility, variability, perishability and non-ownership

1 What are the marketing implications of the 'inseparability' of some services?

2 What does heterogeneity mean? Give an example.

3 Is self-service in petrol stations and restaurants merely a way of counteracting service marketing problems such as inseparability and perishability?

4 What are the marketing implications of the intangibility of services?

5 In what two ways can firms gain by improving their quality of service to customers?

6 Distinguish between technical and functional quality

7 Give some examples of "tangible evidence of purchase'

8 Give examples of two items at opposite ends of the product-services continuum.

9 Why can many services be distributed online?

10 What are the promotional objectives of services?

1

People	Care
Select, train and manage staff in service delivery	Communicate and implement customer care values
Processes	**Corporate Competence**
Organise, plan and control systems and operations	Understand customer expectations and convey commitment to deliver: customers don't need to know how things are done (much less how difficult they are to do...)
Physical evidence	**Consistency**
Manage all physical factors (premises, logos etc)	Ensure that customer contacts and experiences are alike, to establish recognition and positive associations

2   There must be continuous development of service-enhancing practice.

- Policies on selection
- Programmes of training
- Standard, consistent operational practices ('McDonaldisation')
- Standardised operational rules
- Effective motivational programmes
- Managerial appointments
- The attractiveness and appropriateness of the service offer
- Effective policies of staff reward and remuneration

3   Possible marketing implications

(a)   Promote the advantages of non-ownership. This can be done by emphasising, in promotion, the benefits of paid-for maintenance, and periodic upgrading of the product. Radio Rentals have used this as a major selling proposition with great success.

(b)   Make available a tangible symbol or representation of ownership (certificate, membership of professional association). This can come to embody the benefits enjoyed.

(c)   Increasing the chances or opportunity of ownership (eg time-shares, shares in the organisation for regular customers).

4   (a)   These were mentioned earlier in this chapter: people, process and physical evidence.

(b)   Look back at Chapter 5 if you had trouble remembering, and skim read it to check that you could explain the marketing implications if asked.

- **Intangibility**: services cannot be touched or tasted
- **Inseparability**: services cannot be separated from the provider
- **Heterogeneity** (or 'sameness'): the standard of service will vary with each delivery
- **Perishability**: services cannot be stored
- **Ownership**: service purchase does not transfer ownership of property

(c)   Differential pricing or price discrimination is possible in some markets, for example in transport customers are charged more if they travel during the rush hour, and hotels and holiday companies charge more at peak times of year.

5   Security is the major risk. Sensitive accounting or legal data could be intercepted or go to the wrong person in the organisation if sent by e-mail. Some legal documents still need to be original paper documents, physically signed and witnessed by the relevant parties. Some customers simply don't like doing business this way: they value the personal contact and find it reassuring. All customers will get highly frustrated if your website is down when they want to use your service. You, in turn, are at the mercy of your customers' telephone connection.

1   Services often cannot be separated from the provider, so it is important to generate a customer service ethic in the staff who deliver the service.

2   It means lack of sameness or consistency (lack of 'homogeneity'). A good example is a train journey. You may catch the same train to work every day, but it will not always arrive at the same time. A telephone sales person may be pleasant and polite one day and grumpy the next. There are countless other examples.

3   No. It is usually a way of employing fewer people!

4   Strategies are required to do three things.

    •   Increase the degree of tangibility
    •   Focus attention on benefits
    •   Differentiate the service

5   Higher revenue and improved productivity

6   Technical quality of the service encounter refers to what is received by the customer.

    Functional quality of the service encounter refers to how the service is provided, typically perceived in a very subjective way.

7   Labels and other printed information

    Tickets, vouchers and purchase confirmations

    Logos and other visible evidence of brand identity

    Packaging

8   Dog food – nursing; carton of milk – hairdressing; tin of paint – train journey. All completely unrelated but illustrating the point that some items are purely 'product', while others are almost totally made up of 'service'.

9   A lot of the time, these services consist of processing information, which can be completed online very easily. Examples are online banking or booking flights using an airline's website.

10 They follow the same principles as with products:

    •   Build awareness and interest in the service and the service organisation
    •   Communicate and portray the benefits of the services available
    •   Build and maintain the overall image and reputation of the service organisation
    •   Advise customers of new channels
    •   Advise customers of special offers or modifications to the service
    •   Persuade customers to use or buy the service

References

Blythe, J (2009) <u>Principles and Practice of Marketing</u>, 2nd edition, South-Western/Cengage Learning

Blythe, J (2008) <u>Essentials of Marketing</u>, 4th edition, FT Prentice Hall

Brassington, F and Pettitt, S (2006) <u>Principles of Marketing</u>, 4th edition, FT Prentice Hall

Dibb S, Simkin L, Pride WM, Ferrell OC (2005) <u>Marketing: Concepts and Strategies</u>, 5th edition, Houghton Mifflin

Cowell, D (1995) <u>The Marketing of Services</u>, CIM, Cookham

Palmer, A (2007) <u>Principles of Services Marketing</u>, 5th edition, McGraw-Hill Higher Education

Chapter 10
Measuring marketing effectiveness

Topic list

1   Designing a co-ordinated mix
2   Segmentation and targeting
3   Positioning against the competition
4   Measuring marketing success

Introduction

This chapter is mainly concerned with the measurement of the success (or otherwise) of marketing activities. There may be annual targets (sales, budgets, expenditure budgets etc) against which performance can be measured on an ongoing basis. Alternatively, it may be decided to monitor how the market is responding to the marketing activity (such as via electronic point of sale information) in order to give continuous performance feedback.

Other measurement methods might include the following:

- Monitoring output against the marketing plan
- Measuring volume and/or growth of sales
- Comparing marketing activities this year against last year
- Monitoring market share
- Monitoring customer complaints and returns or (more happily) repeat sales and recommendations
- Gathering research on customer satisfaction, awareness and response to marketing
- Measuring the accuracy of budgets
- Comparing sales figures
- Measuring direct responses such as coupon redemption

This chapter begins with a consideration of the need for a co-ordinated approach to the marketing mix in section 1, and then goes on to describe the importance of segmentation, targeting and positioning in this context in sections 2 and 3.

As stated in the syllabus, it is important to be 'mindful of the target market, their needs and expectations' (in order to satisfy customers), and to be 'mindful of tactical competitive activities' (in order to compete effectively). This all leads in to section 4 which describes various means by which the success of marketing activities can be measured.

Syllabus linked learning objectives

By the end of the chapter you will be able to:

Learning objectives	Syllabus link
1 Explain the different methods used for measuring the success of marketing activities	3.12
2 Explain the concept of developing a coordinated approach to the marketing mix, as a means to satisfying customers' requirements and competing effectively	3.14

1 Designing a co-ordinated mix

"When considering tactical options it is useful to remember that marketers talk about mixes: the marketing mix, the promotional mix and so forth. This implies that each area of marketing impinges on every other area, and that decisions about (say) advertising tactics cannot be taken independently of decisions about pricing". Blythe, J. (2008) ■

The planning of a compatible and co-ordinated mix depends upon factors such as push-pull, the product life cycle, product/market type and buyer readiness – as well as strengths and weaknesses of the various promotional tools. Tools may be used separately, but they are often integrated.

Choosing the correct tools for a particular marketing task is not easy – although new technology is making it somewhat more scientific: computers can match databases of consumer and media profiles to formulate an optimal mix for the target market, and promotional budgets can be modelled on spreadsheets for a variety of different mixes.

At a basic level, however, **promotion planning** can be seen as a typical decision sequence.

Figure 10.1: The promotion planning process

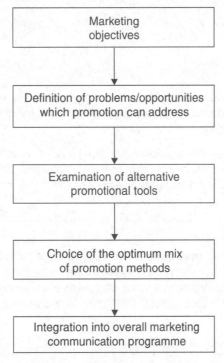

The relative emphasis placed on different promotion tools will differ according to:

- Push or pull strategy
- Type of product/market
- Product life cycle stage
- Buyer readiness stage

  EXAM TIP

Application

It is important to remember all the time that 'measuring marketing effectiveness' is really about 'achieving objectives'. Keep this in mind as you read this chapter, as it is easy to get bogged down in details and techniques.

We looked at objectives early on in the text in the context of marketing planning. A question in Section B of the specimen paper asks about the importance of the marketing planning process in helping to achieve company objectives.

1.1 Push or pull?

'Push' and 'pull' are two basic promotion strategies, according to whether the target audience is primarily **channel members** (such as distributors and retail outlets) or **consumers**.

Figure 10.2: Push and pull techniques

Push strategy involves 'pushing' the product into distribution channels. Marketing activities aim to encourage distribution and/or retail outlets to stock, promote and sell the product. Push techniques include personal selling, trade advertising and promotion, and trade exhibitions.

Pull strategy involves 'pulling' the product through distribution channels towards consumers. Marketing activities aim to arouse consumer awareness, interest and desire so that they approach distributors and/or retail outlets to make enquiries and purchases. Pull techniques include television and press advertising, sales promotions, customer loyalty programmes and point of sale display.

In practice, most marketers will use a combination of push and pull techniques. Distributors are more likely to stock a product if they can see that their own promotion/sale efforts will be supported by 'pull' promotions for the brand, sending consumers to them. Trade advertising and selling often involves demonstrating how aggressively the product will be promoted to consumers, and what benefits this will create for the distributor (as well as the supplier).

1.2 Type of product/market

Consumer and business markets behave differently. In most business markets, there are fewer, higher-value customers, who require a more complex total offering: as professional buyers, they are generally less susceptible to mass communications and prefer to negotiate and develop on-going business terms and relationships with suppliers. While **consumer markets** favour advertising (supported by sales promotion), **industrial/business markets** favour personal selling (supported by sales promotion).

Online shopping is booming despite the tough retail climate. The trend is expected to continue as internet access grows, and consumers buy more things online more often. Online retail is forecast to be worth £33.9bn by 2012.

Certain product types lend themselves to online purchasing. Electrical goods account for the majority of online retail spend at 25.1%, although online grocery shopping is now growing faster. The music and DVD category has the highest online penetration with 30.8% of all sales being made on the internet. It is forecast that by 2012, online sales will account for over two thirds of the music and DVD market. More than half of 4,059 adults surveyed said the convenience of online shopping is the main reason for its continuing success.

www.mad.co.uk – accessed 4 June 2008

1.3 Product life cycle stage

As we saw in Chapter 5, different promotion tools will be most effective at different stages of the product life cycle, depending on whether the aim is to increase awareness, maximise branding, recall and sales, or secure last available sales at low cost.

1.4 Buyer readiness

Buyers move through different stages from awareness of the product to knowledge about it, to liking, preference and conviction, and finally to readiness to buy. Different promotional tools will be effective at each stage.

- **Awareness/knowledge**: advertising, PR

- **Liking, preference, conviction**: sales promotion, sampling, exhibitions, demonstrations, personal selling, on-going advertising/PR

- **Readiness to purchase**: sales promotion, personal selling, POS display, direct marketing

Note that more labour intensive (and therefore costly) techniques such as personal selling will generally be brought into play where consumers are approaching readiness to buy, and used to 'close' the sale. (In business markets, the high value of orders makes personal selling cost-effective for more general use.)

2 Segmentation and targeting

KEY CONCEPT

Concept

Segmentation is the process of categorising consumers into groups with similar needs. It is often related to targeting and positioning: two strategies by which the marketer can tailor the marketing mix to the specific needs and characteristics of a market segment.

We will cover segmentation, targeting and positioning all here as an important part of the design of a co-ordinated mix for maximum effectiveness. These topics are essential to good marketing practice.

2.1 Market segmentation

To be effective at marketing, the organisation needs to tailor its marketing efforts closely to the needs of potential customers. Market segmentation recognises that, although buyers have diverse needs, sets of needs may be grouped together and a different marketing approach may be used for each group. This also requires information about the external environment, in order to identify targetable sections of the customer population and their characteristics, which we looked at in Chapter 4.

A total market may occasionally be 100% homogeneous (all customers are alike) but this is rare. A segmentation approach to marketing succeeds when there are identifiable 'clusters' of consumer wants in the market.

Figure 10.3: Segmented market

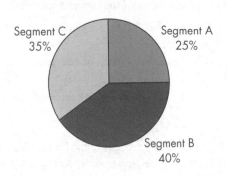

Market for Product X

- Each segment is made up of buyers with common needs and preferences, who may react to 'market stimuli' in much the same way

- Each segment can become a target market with a suitably tailored marketing mix

ACTIVITY 1

Application

What do you think are the advantages of segmentation?

MARKETING AT WORK

Application

Telecoms giant Orange is always looking for innovative ways to communicate its expanding range of services (mobile operator, broadband supplier and IPTV broadcaster) to customers. Additional to this is the winning of new customers, stemming the loss of existing subscribers and delivering a high level of customer satisfaction and loyalty across mobile and broadband. It's a wide brief in a competitive market and one that demands a variety of techniques.

Heading to where consumers are in order to talk to them might seem natural for a mobile phone operator but still requires careful segmentation, planning and ongoing investment. Understanding your community is vital when attempting to communicate with such a broad audience as Orange has.

"We identify particular sections of the market and appeal to each segment, whether it's youth or business users," says its head of digital and direct marketing. The most recent step-change has been experiments with behavioural targeting - understanding which of the 6m monthly visitors to Orange's portal are existing customers and serving them an appropriate advertisement.

The real goldmine that Orange is working towards, however, is combining customer data from the online and offline worlds. "We've worked really hard in the past year at supplementing all the great information from online to understand what the impact of it is," he says. "We do a lot of analysis, which allows us to get a more rounded picture of what people do and how they interact with our channel...we're trying to create digital experiences that are engaging, socially shareable and much more a part of the fabric of the internet."

www.mad.co.uk – accessed 4 June 2008

2.1.1 Requirements for effective market segmentation

The suitability of a market for segmentation depends on **measurability, accessibility** and **substantiality**.

The decision as to whether to target market segments may be summarised as follows.

Figure 10.4: The segmentation decision

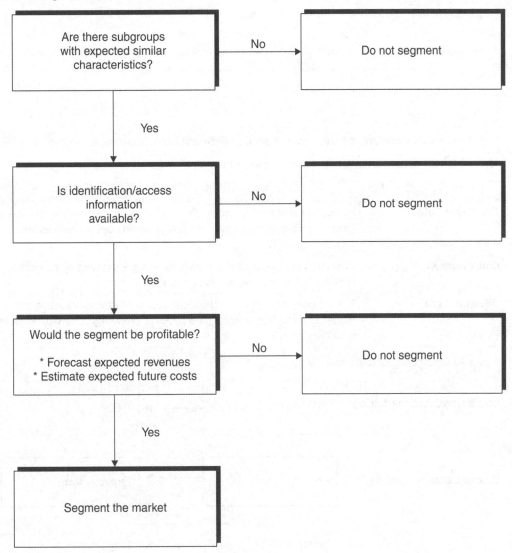

- **Measurability**

    Can information relating to the factor that the market is to be segmented on be obtained and measured cost effectively?

- **Accessibility**

    The degree to which the organisation can focus effectively on the chosen segments using marketing methods. (Educational establishments can be identified and reached easily, while individuals with income over £30,000 per annum might be more difficult to isolate effectively.)

- **Substantiality**

    Is the segment large enough to be worth considering as a separate market? Mounting marketing campaigns is expensive, and so a minimum size for a segment is required for profitability.

2.2 Targeting

Targeting involves selecting one or more customer groups (segments) and satisfying them with a tailored marketing mix. It is one way of using the marketing mix to capitalise on the potential of market segments.

Targeting is 'the use of market segmentation to select and address a key group of potential purchasers' (CIM).

2.2.1 Targeting strategies

Marketing may be **undifferentiated**, **concentrated** or **differentiated**, according to the degree of targeting used.

An organisation has several targeting options to choose from (or a combination of each).

Option	Comment
Undifferentiated	Produce a single product and hope to get as many customers as possible to buy it; that is, ignore segmentation entirely. (Not very common now. An early example was the Ford Model T car.)
Concentrated	Attempt to produce the ideal product for a *single* segment of the market (eg Rolls Royce cars, Mothercare mother and baby shops).
Differentiated	The company attempts to introduce several product versions, each aimed at a different market segment (for example, one company producing several different brands of washing powder or cereal).

Figure 10.5: Targeting strategies

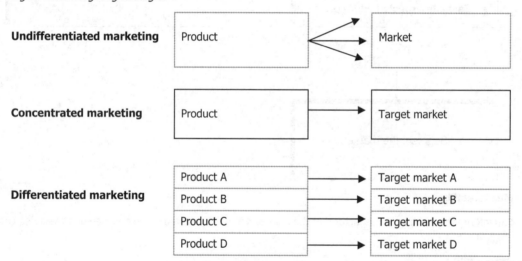

Targeting is not restricted to consumer markets: there is an opportunity for business-to-business targeting as well (for example, Rolls Royce aero engines targeting quality aircraft manufacturers).

The major disadvantage of **concentrated marketing** is reliance on a single segment of a single market, such as Barings Bank specialising in futures trading. On the other hand, specialisation in a particular market segment can give a firm a profitable, although sometimes temporary, competitive edge over rival firms, such as Aston Martin cars at the premium end of the car market.

The major disadvantage of **differentiated marketing** is the additional cost of marketing and production (more product design and development costs, the loss of economies of scale in production and storage, additional promotion costs and administrative costs). When the costs of further differentiation of the market exceed the benefits from further segmentation and target marketing, a firm is said to have 'overdifferentiated'. Some firms have tried to overcome this problem by selling the same product to two market segments. An example of differential marketing is the recent split of washing powers into general, colour, non-biological, and other categories.

2.2.2 Choice of targeting strategy

As we discussed in relation to market segmentation, targeting is not always the appropriate approach.

- Is the product and/or the market **homogeneous**? Mass marketing may be 'sufficient' if the market is largely homogeneous (eg safety matches).

- Will the company's resources be **overextended** by differentiated marketing? Small firms may succeed better by concentrating on one segment only (eg Stain Devils cleaning products).

- Is the product sufficiently **advanced in its life cycle** to have attracted a substantial total market? If not, segmentation and target marketing is unlikely to be profitable, because each segment would be too small in size.

2.2.3 Benefits of segmentation and target marketing

Market targeting, on the basis of segmentation, should result in increased total sales and profits because products/services will be more likely to appeal to the target segments and pricing policy can be more sophisticated.

Some key benefits of targeted marketing can be summarised as follows.

- **Product differentiation**: a feature of a particular product might appeal to one segment of the market in such a way that the product is thought better than its rivals.

- The seller will be more **aware** of how product design and development may stimulate further demand in a particular area of the market.

- The **resources** of the business will be used more effectively, because the organisation should be more able to make products which the customer wants and will pay for.

  ACTIVITY 2   Application

Identify one disadvantage of adopting a concentrated marketing approach and one disadvantage of adopting differentiated marketing.

3 Positioning against the competition

 KEY CONCEPT   Concept

Positioning is how a product appears (how it is perceived by the market) in relation to other products in the market.

The 'positioning' of a product or brand in relation to its competitors is defined in terms of how consumers/customers perceive key characteristics of the product. Possible positioning characteristics include:

- Specific product features, eg price, speed, ease of use

- Benefits, problems, solutions, or needs

- Specific usage occasions

- User category, such as age or gender

- Against another product, eg comparison with a market leader

- Product class disassociation ('stand-out' features from the general mass of products), eg organic food, lead-free petrol, hypo-allergenic cosmetics

- Hybrid basis: a combination of any of the above

3.1 Product maps

Market perceptions can be plotted on product maps, to suggest marketing opportunities, brand perception and competitive position. The following basic **perceptual map** is used to plot brands in perceived price and perceived quality terms.

Figure 10.6: Price/quality matrix

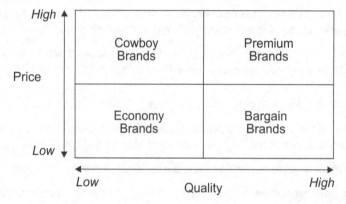

Most consumers will not see price and quality as independent variables. A 'high' price will usually be associated with high quality, and low price with low quality.

3.2 Identifying a gap in the market

Market research can determine where customers perceive competitive brands in relation to each other, and in relation to target characteristics, and any perceived gaps in the market can be identified on a perceptual map.

Figure 10.7: Perceptual map for restaurant brand

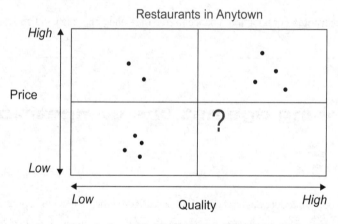

In the model above, there appears to be a gap in the market for a moderately priced, reasonable quality eating place.

3.3 Competitive positioning

KEY CONCEPT

Concept

Competitive positioning concerns implementing a general idea of what kind of offer a company should make to the target market in relation to competitors' offers.

Important considerations in competitive positioning are product quality and price. Nine different **competitive positioning strategies** have been identified.

Product quality	High price	Medium price	Low price
High	Premium strategy	Penetration strategy	Superbargain strategy
Medium	Overpricing strategy	Average quality strategy	Bargain strategy
Low	Hit and run strategy	Shoddy goods strategy	Cheap goods strategy

4 Measuring marketing success

4.1 Controlling marketing activities

  KEY CONCEPT

Concept

To **control** is to measure results against targets and take any action necessary to adjust performance.

The marketing control process can be broken down into four stages.

- Development of objectives and strategies   eg 'We want to increase our market share'

- Establishment of standards   eg 'We want to increase market share to 15% by the end of 20XX'

- Evaluation of performance   eg 'Have we increased our market share to 15%?'

- Corrective action   eg 'No, we have not. Maybe we need to reduce our prices.'

Overall marketing effectiveness can be difficult to measure. Audits, financial measures, targets and information gathering (such as customer feedback) can help. Where possible, performance should be measured in quantitative terms because these are less subjective and less liable to bias. The following are some possible techniques.

Personal selling – Sales targets

Public relations – Editorial coverage

Direct marketing – Enquiries generated

Advertising – Brand awareness

Sales promotion – Coupons redeemed

Exhibitions – Contacts made

  EXAM TIP

Application

The marketing control process is vital to the achievement of marketing objectives and the successful completion of marketing plans. Control is as important a feature of the role of the marketing manager as new product development or promotional creativity.

4.2 Methods for measuring success

Application

Examples of marketing measures

Feedback information	Standards	Control actions
Sales figures	Against budget	Simulate or dampen down demand
Complaints	Number, frequency, seriousness	Improving 'customer focus'
Competitors	Relative to us	Attack/defence strategies
Costs/profitability	Ratios	Cost cutting exercises
Corporate image	Attitude measures	Internal/external communications

The methods described in paragraphs 4.2.1 to 4.2.8 below are all specified in the syllabus.

4.2.1 Budget measurement

KEY CONCEPTS

Concept

A **budget** is a consolidated statement of the resources required to achieve desired objectives, or to implement planned activities. It is a planning and control tool relevant to all aspects of management activities.

A **forecast** is an estimate of what might happen in the future.

In terms of measuring marketing effectiveness, **budgeted** results often comprise:

(a)   Targets for the overall **financial objectives** and other strategy objectives such as productivity targets
(b)   Subsidiary **financial** targets, including the sales budget and marketing expenditure budget
(c)   Product-market strategy targets
(d)   Targets for each element of the **marketing mix**

Budgets perform a dual role.

(a)   They **incorporate forecasting** and planning information
(b)   They **incorporate control measures**, because they plan how resources are to be used to achieve the targets

The expense budgets related to marketing include those listed in the table below. **Marketing costs** analysis can be a highly detailed process and it may be difficult to allocate costs to specific marketing activities (especially staff costs, when staff may be working on several different areas at the same time).

(a) *Selling expenses budget*
- Salaries and commission
- Materials, literature, samples
- Travelling (car cost, petrol, insurance) and entertaining
- Staff recruitment and selection and training
- Telephones and telegrams, postage
- After-sales service
- Royalties/patents
- Office rent and rates, lighting, heating
- Office equipment
- Credit costs, bad debts

(b) *Advertising budget*
- Trade journal – space
- Prestige media – space
- PR space (costs of releases, entertainment
- Blocks and artwork
- Advertising agents commission
- Staff salaries, office costs
- Posters
- Cinema
- TV
- Signs

(c) *Sales promotion budget*
- Exhibitions: space, equipment, staff, transport, hotels, bar
- Literature: leaflets, catalogues
- Samples/working models
- Point of sale display, window or showroom displays
- Special offers
- Direct mail shots – enclose, postage, design costs

(d) *Research and development budget*
- Market research – design and development and analysis costs
- Packaging and product research – departmental costs, material, equipment
- Pure research – departmental costs materials, equipment
- Sales analysis and research
- Economic surveys
- Product planning
- Patents

(e) *Distribution budget*
- Warehouse/deposits – rent, rates, lighting, heating
- Transport – capital costs
- Fuel – running costs
- Warehouse/depot and transport staff wages
- Packing (as opposed to packaging)

There are several methods of setting the **marketing budget** that have been identified.

Competitive parity	Fixing promotional expenditure in relation to the expenditure incurred by competitors. (This is unsatisfactory because it presupposes that the competitor's decision must be a good one.)
The task method (or objective and task method)	The marketing task for the organisation is set and a promotional budget is prepared which will help to ensure that this objective is achieved. A problem occurs if the objective is achieved only by paying out more on promotion than the extra profits obtained would justify.
Communication stage models	These are based on the idea that the link between promotion and sales cannot be measured directly, but can be measured by means of intermediate stages (for example, increase in awareness, comprehension, and then intention to buy).
All you can afford	Crude and unscientific, but commonly used. The firm simply takes a view on what it thinks it can afford to spend on promotion, given that it would like to spend as much as it can.
Investment	The advertising and promotions budget can be designed around the amount felt necessary to maintain a certain brand value.
Rule-of-thumb, non-scientific methods	These include setting expenditure at a certain percentage of sales or profits.

4.2.2 Objectives attained

The marketing control process includes the important step of setting **objectives** and standards. Objective setting as part of the marketing planning process was discussed in detail earlier in this Text.

Figure 10.8: Marketing planning process

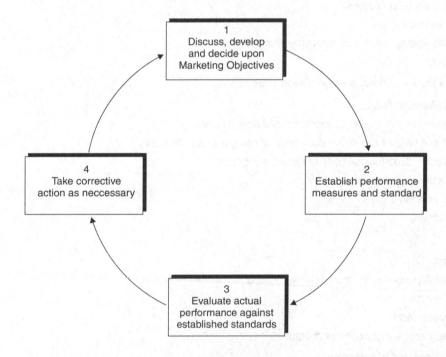

Performance standards for specific elements of the marketing mix

Activity	Performance standards
New product development	Trial rate
	Repurchase rate
Sales programmes	Contribution by region, salesperson
	Controllable margin as percentage of sales
	Number of new accounts
	Travel costs
Advertising programmes	Awareness levels
	Attitude ratings
	Cost levels
Pricing programmes	Price relative to industry average
	Price elasticity of demand
Distribution programmes	Number of distributors carrying the product

Part of the corrective action stage may well be to **adjust objectives and strategies** in the light of experience.

It is important to remember that objectives might not be mainly financial, as the following example highlights.

 MARKETING AT WORK   Application

eshopafrica.com is a website dedicated to selling the wares of African craftsmen. As well as the products themselves, the site features information about tribal traditions and personal stories about the craftsmen themselves.

Difficulties with credit card payments to Africa (the financial infrastructure being relatively underdeveloped) and the fact that the products can be obtained far more cheaply from bulk import/export businesses meant that the site struggled to break even its early days. According to the site's founder, this misses the point of the venture.

The site is aimed at improving the lot of the craftsmen, and its avowed primary goal is to create sustainable businesses for artisans. It aims to tap the snobbery market, and specifically that customer segment that is social/ego oriented and which seeks out the original and unusual at a premium price. This premium price can be seen by the customer to directly benefit an African craftsman and so the customer can feel good about him or herself.

 ACTIVITY 3    Application

Can you foresee any problems with the eshopafrica promotional strategy? Is it sustainable in the long term, even if it is effective now?

4.2.3 Sales revenue and profits

'There are two basic groups of approaches for performance analysis:

- *sales analysis, which looks at the income generated by the firm's activities; and*
- *marketing cost analysis, which looks at the costs of generating the income.'* Blythe, J. (2008)

Items of **financial information** that can be used to measure success are generally the most common measures by which marketing performance is judged.

- Total profits, sales and capital employed
- Return on capital employed
- Profit figure as a percentage of sales
- Costs as a percentage of sales
- Increase / decrease in profits and sales over the preceding period
- Sales and profits in each major business segment that the company operates in
- Dividend per share
- Levels of debt, and interest rates on that debt
- Share price, and other stock exchange information

Sales figures are often focused upon. Blythe (2005) lists some ways to analyse sales figures:

- Comparison with forecast sales
- Comparison with competitors' sales
- Comparison with sales in the industry
- Sales in terms of cash generated

- Unit sales analysis
- Sales by geographic area
- Sales by product group or band
- Sales by type of customer

Another useful measure of performance is the **market share** obtained by the organisation's product. Changes in market share have to be considered against the change in the **market as a whole**, since the product might be increasing its share simply because the market is declining, with the competition losing sales even more quickly. The reverse may also be true. The market could be expanding, and a declining market share might not represent a decline in absolute sales volume, but indicates a failure to grab more of the growing market.

 ## ACTIVITY 4

Application

What are the disadvantages of using purely financial information as a measure when collecting marketing control information?

4.2.4 Efficiency and effectiveness

Efficiency and effectiveness are generally desirable features of organisational (and hence marketing) performance.

 ## KEY CONCEPTS

Concept

Efficiency consists of attaining desired results at minimum cost. It therefore combines effectiveness with economy.

Effectiveness is achieving established objectives. There are usually several ways to achieve objectives, some more costly than others.

Some people use the word efficiency in a more restricted sense than that explained above, to mean the same thing as productivity; that is, the ratio of output to input. It is possible to be very productive in doing the wrong thing: no amount of efficiency will make a company profitable if it brings the wrong products to market.

4.2.5 Zero defects and returns

Reflecting a switch in **emphasis away from quantity towards quality**, consumers and customers have become more sophisticated and discerning in their requirements. They are no longer satisfied with accepting the late delivery of the same old unreliable products from an organisation which does not appear to care for its customers. They want new products, superior on-time delivery performance and an immediate response to their requests. Many organisations have therefore turned to quality management. By developing new products quickly and supplying them on time at a consistently high level of quality such organisations are more likely to succeed.

The management of quality is the process of:

- Establishing **standards of quality** for a product or service

- Establishing **procedures** or **production methods** which ought to ensure that these required standards of quality are met in a suitably high proportion of cases

- **Monitoring** actual quality

- Taking **control action** when actual quality falls below standard

 MARKETING AT WORK

Application

Take the postal service as an example. The postal service might establish a standard that 90% of first class letters will be delivered on the day after they are posted, and 99% will be delivered within two days of posting.

Procedures would have to be established for ensuring that these standards could be met – attending to such matters as frequency of collections, automated letter sorting, frequency of deliveries and number of staff employed.

Actual performance could be monitored, perhaps by taking samples from time to time of letters that are posted and delivered.

If the quality standard is not being achieved, management should take control action (maybe by employing more postmen!).

Quality management becomes what is known as **total quality management (TQM)** when it is applied to everything that a business does . The objective is complete satisfaction of customers through the improvement of all activities and processes, by 'getting it right first time' and removing the potential causes of any defects, because defects cost money to put right and they alienate customers. TQM aims towards an environment of **zero defects**, at minimum cost.

4.2.6 Customer service complaints

As already indicated, the most common measures by which marketing performance is judged are sales levels, costs and market share. However, responsible companies will also have ethical and social responsibility standards. The most marketing-orientated organisations will be likely to pursue relationship marketing which entails a high degree of customer care. Thus, in addition to sales measures, many companies will seek to measure customer satisfaction.

Performance standards could thus be set at sales of £X for the period, Y% market share and Z% profit, all set against a maximum number of customer complaints. Every mistake, delay and misunderstanding directly costs an organisation money through wasted time and effort, including the time taken to pacify customers.

4.2.7 Awareness and attitudes

 "Ultimately, product positioning depends on the attitudes of the particular target market, so the marketer must either take these attitudes as they are and tailor the product to fit those attitudes, or must seek to change the attitudes of the market". Blythe, J. (2008)

Ultimately, marketing communications are designed to meet three objectives.

- Awareness: increase brand awareness and establish brand recognition
- Trial: stimulate trial purchase
- Reinforcement: stimulate and reinforce brand loyalty

To succeed in achieving these goals, communications must:

- Gain attention
- Communicate a message
- Improve attitudes to the brand
- Reinforce already positive attitudes to the brand
- Obtain the readers'/listeners'/viewers' liking for the message and its execution

The usual aim of any marketing campaign is that the consumer will develop positive feelings about the product or service being advertised. The role of what is termed **likeability** becomes paramount: people need to enjoy the advertisement at the same time as finding it credible. Those advertisements that are remembered have certain characteristics. These characteristics add up to making an advertisement 'likeable'.

(a)   The product is different or new

(b)   The advertisement itself is 'different' or interesting

(c)   The message proclaims something that is personally significant and relevant to the consumer (for example, a car advertisement seen by someone who is already planning to go out and buy a car the next day)

Researchers have isolated likeability as the only meaningful indicator of the success of advertising. messages are more likely to be stored in the long term memory, and retrieved when the customer is ready to make a purchase. In an online context, the concept of likeability can also be applied to websites. Those that are enjoyable to visit and use are more likely to be remembered and revisited.

4.2.8 Repeat purchase and loyalty

Loyal customers are a prime goal of many companies. The extent to which customers are loyal can be tested by asking questions such as the following:

* First purchase date
* What is the average order size, by product?
* What is the regularity/periodicity of the order, by product?
* What is the trend in size of orders?
* What is the motive in purchasing?
* What does the customer know about the firm's and competitors' products?
* On what basis does the customer reorder?
* Were there any lost or cancelled orders? For what reasons?
* Does the customer also buy competitors' products?
* To what extent may purchases be postponed?

 MARKETING AT WORK   Application

* The CIM and *Marketing Week* run **Marketing Effectiveness Awards**. Look at the Marketing Week website: www.mad.co.uk/mw/.

* The Institute of Practitioners in Advertising (IPA) runs a bi-annual **Advertising Effectiveness Awards** competition and encourage entries from companies of all sorts and sizes. See the IPA website (www.ipa.co.uk) which gives details of the judging criteria.

* The Medinge Group, an international think-tank on branding and business, launched an annual **'Top Brands with a Conscience'** list in 2004. To see the latest news for 2010 , go to www.medinge.org.

Learning objectives	Covered
1 Explain the different methods used for measuring the success of marketing activities	☑ Budget measurement
	☑ Objectives attained
	☑ Sales/revenue, profit/loss
	☑ Efficiency/effectiveness
	☑ Zero defects/returns
	☑ Customer service complaints
	☑ Increased awareness and changing attitudes
	☑ Repeat purchase and loyalty
2 Explain the concept of developing a coordinated approach to the marketing mix, as a means to satisfying customers' requirements and competing effectively	☑ Designing a mix which is compatible and co-ordinated effectively
	☑ Being mindful of the target market, their needs and expectations
	☑ Being mindful of tactical competitive activities
	☑ Being mindful of the impact of other elements of the marketing mix

1   Who is the target audience for a 'push' strategy?

2   What does it mean when a market is 'homogeneous'?

3   Why is 'substantiality' important for segmentation?

4   Why are price and quality not necessarily to be regarded as independent variables?

5   What is the name of the strategy applied to goods of a low quality but a mid-range price?

6   How might the effectiveness of a public relations campaign be evaluated?

7   Match each cost to its budget category.

Costs: Budget categories:

After sales service   *Research and development budget*

Posters   Distribution budget
Samples and models   Sales promotion budget
Economic surveys   Advertising budget
Warehouse staff salaries   Selling expenses budget
                                                                Head office salaries budget

8   What is the most commonly used method for setting a marketing budget, and why?

9   Why is the 'likeability' of an advertisement so important?

10   A company's unit sales are increasing, but profits are down. What might it do to increase profits?

Activity debriefs

1   The following benefits can be identified.

    • The identification of new marketing opportunities as a result of better understanding of consumer needs in each of the segments.

    • Specialists can be developed and appointed to each of the company's major segments. Operating practices then benefit from the expertise of staff with specialist knowledge of the segment's business.

    • The total marketing budget can be allocated more effectively, according to needs and the likely return from each segment.

    • Precision marketing approaches can be used. The company can make finer adjustments to the product and service offerings and to the marketing appeals used for each segment.

    • Specialist knowledge and extra effort may enable the company to dominate particular segments and gain competitive advantage.

    • The product assortment can be more precisely defined to reflect differences between customer needs.

    • Improved segmentation allows more highly targeted marketing activity. For instance, the sales team develops an in-depth knowledge of the needs of a particular group of consumers and can get to know a network of potential buyers within the business and there is an increased likelihood of referrals and recommendations.

    • Feedback and customer problems are more effectively communicated. Producers develop an understanding in the needs of a target segment and expertise in helping to solve its problems.

2   Concentrated marketing runs the risk of relying on a single segment of a single market.

    The main disadvantage of differentiated marketing is the additional cost of marketing and production – extra product design and development costs, the loss of economies of scale in production and storage, extra promotion and administrative costs.

3   In theory, as more and more people buy the products and as the website becomes more and more successful, its 'snobbery' appeal will become tarnished by its own popularity. The targeted type of customer is only likely to buy from it once. Someone who is a 'snob' and who doesn't mind what they pay for an item, so long as it comes from the 'right' place, is unlikely to be loyal when the next 'in' thing comes along. The company will have to find new ways to differentiate itself from the competition. Given its product range and the fact that it is much more expensive than other distributors, this could prove extremely difficult.

4   Costs and profits may not be the best way of comparing the marketing results of different parts of a business. Some managers may prefer to quantify information in non-financial terms.

    (a) The sales manager may look at sales volume in units, size of market share, speed of delivery, volume of sales per sales representative or per call.

    (b) A stores manager might look at stock turnover periods for each item, volume of demand, the speed of materials handling, breakages, obsolescence.

    Where qualitative factors (notably human behaviour and customer attitudes) are important, financial information is less relevant.

1   The distributors – marketing strategy here aims to encourage distribution of the product

2   All customers are alike. This is rare.

3   The segment needs to be large enough to be justifiably regarded as a separate market in its own right. Marketing is expensive, and so a certain size of market is required if the expense is to pay off.

4   Consumers will usually associate a high price with high quality, and a low price with low quality.

5   A 'shoddy goods' strategy

6   By assessing the favourability (or otherwise!) of editorial coverage and other press/media comment.

7

Economic surveys – Research and development budget	**Posters** – Advertising budget
Warehouse salaries – Distribution budget	**After-sales service** – Selling expenses budget
Samples and models – Sales promotion budget	

8   'All you can afford', because it is simple to administer even if it has the disadvantage of being crude and unscientific.

9   The marketer hopes that the consumer will develop positive feelings about the product or service being advertised. Likeable messages are more likely to be stored in the long term memory, and retrieved when the customer is ready to make a purchase.

10 One of its first actions would be to investigate selling prices and costs. The price needs to rise, or alternatively if a price rise is not possible then the company will need to undertake a cost cutting exercise.

Blythe, J (2009) Principles and Practice of Marketing, 2nd edition, South-Western/Cengage Learning

Blythe, J (2008) Essentials of Marketing, 4th edition, FT Prentice Hall

Brassington, F and Pettitt, S (2006) Principles of Marketing, 4th edition, FT Prentice Hall

Dibb S, Simkin L, Pride WM, Ferrell OC (2005) Marketing: Concepts and Strategies, 5th edition, Houghton Mifflin

Key concepts

Above-the-line promotion, 140

Adoption, 97

Advertising, 140

Ansoff Product/Market matrix, 71

APIC framework, 54

Augmented product, 80

Banner advertisement, 155

BCG matrix, 85

Below-the-line promotion, 140

Brand, 82

Budget, 192

Business-to-business, 36

Channels of distribution, 122

Competitive positioning, 190

Consumer behaviour, 68

Consumer goods, 81

Consumerism, 28

Control, 50, 191

Core/generic product, 80

Corporate social responsibility, 27

Corporate strategy, 47

Cost-plus pricing, 113

Customer relationship management (CRM), 35

Demand, 109

Diffusion, 97

Direct marketing, 124, 145

Direct response advertising, 140

E-commerce, 154

Effectiveness, 196

Efficiency, 196

Ethics, 30

Fast Moving Consumer Goods (FMCG), 81

Five Ms, 69

Forecast, 192

Four Ps, 8

Franchises, 124

Frequency, 152

Industrial goods, 81

Intermediary, 123

Internal appraisal, 69

Internal environment, 62

Internet marketing, 154

Logistics, 122

Loss leader, 114

Marketing, 3

Marketing audit, 61

Marketing concept, 9

Marketing environment research, 64

Marketing orientation, 10

Marketing plan, 45

Marketing planning process, 54

Mark-up, 113

Mission statement, 48

Monitoring, 50

New product development (NPD), 93

Offline promotion, 155

Online promotion, 155

Penetration pricing, 114

Personal selling, 141

Physical distribution, 122

Place, 121

Planning, 45

Positioning, 189

Predatory pricing, 30

Press, 153

Price, 105

Price elasticity, 109

Price leaders, 108

Price sensitivity, 110

Price skimming, 113

Process, 170

Product, 79

Product life cycle, 90

Product line pricing, 114

Product orientation, 11

Product range, 84

Production orientation, 11

Promotional pricing, 115

Public relations, 144

Pull strategy, 184

Push strategy, 184

Ratings, 152

Reach, 152

Relationship marketing, 32

Sales orientation, 12

Sales promotion, 148

Segmentation, 185

Service quality, 168

Services, 88

Social responsibility, 25

Societal marketing concept, 25

Sponsorship, 143

SWOT analysis, 72

Targeting, 188

Telemarketing, 147

Web advertising, 155

Index

Accessibility, 169

Accuracy, 182
Advertising Effectiveness Awards, 198
Agents, 123
Annual targets, 182
Ansoff's Product/Market matrix, 71
APIC framework, 54
Approachability, 169
Awards, 198

Bargain price, 110

Black market, 109
Brand awareness, 81
Brand extension, 83
Brand name, 114
Brand names, 65
Branding, 81; reasons for, 83
Business analysis, 96
Business ethics, 30
Business markets, 184
Business to business communication, 145
Buyer readiness, 185
Buyer-seller relationship, 28, 34

Call centres, 147

Capital expenditure projects, 57
Catalogue marketing, 147
CIM Code of Professional Standards, 31
Commercialisation, 96
Competitive bidding, 108
Competitive positioning, 190
Competitors, 29
Computers, 66
Concentrated marketing, 188
Consumer goods, 81
Consumer markets, 184
Convenience goods, 81
Co-ordination, 15
Corporate culture, 30
Corporate identity, 145
Corporate strategic plans, 47
Cost-based pricing, 107
Cost-plus pricing, 113
CRM software, 35
Cultural changes, 65
Cultural factors, 68
Customer retention, 34
Customer satisfaction, 3
Customer service, 57

Data capture systems, 130

Data Protection Act 1998, 37
Database, 36
Database systems, 66
Dealers, 123
Demand, 109, 113
Development, 96
Differential pricing, 109
Differentiated marketing, 188
Direct mail, 146
Direct mailings, 145
Direct response advertising, 147
Direct supply, 146
Distribution strategy, 129
Distributors, 123
Diversification, 71

Early adopters, 97

Economic environment, 65
Economic influences, 65
Economic trends, 65
Effectiveness: distribution, 128
Effort required, 157
Electronic Data Interchange (EDI), 130
Electronic point of sale (EPOS), 130
Electronic point of sale information, 182
E-mail, 146
Employee newsletters, 145
Employees, 29
Environmental factors, 49
Everyday low pricing, 115
Exchange, 3
Exclusive distribution, 129
Experience curve pricing, 115

Familiarity, 157

Family branding, 83
Five Ms, 49
Ford, Henry, 11
Full cost pricing, 112
Functional quality, 168, 179

Gap in the market, 190
Geographical separation, 4
Goals, 45
Government, 111
Green concerns, 67
Green Movement, 67
Growth strategies, 70

Heterogeneity, 174

ICT, 78
Implementation, 50
Impulse buys, 81
Incentive systems, 30
Income effects, 111
Industrial goods, 81
Industrial revolution, 4
In-house magazines, 145
Initial assessment, 96
Innovators, 97
Inseparability, 173
Institute of Practitioners in Advertising (IPA), 198
Intangibility, 172
Intangible attributes, 80
Intensive distribution, 129, 135
Intermediaries' objectives, 110
Internal operations, 62

Joint products, 114
Just price, 110

Language differences, 65
Lobbying, 145
Local knowledge, 122
Loss leader, 114, 117
Loss leaders, 106
Loyalty, 33

Mail order, 147
Managing the product portfolio, 84
Market development, 71
Market level plans, 49
Market orientation, 12
Market penetration, 71
Market test, 96
Market testing, 96
Marketing audit, 49
Marketing budget, 46
Marketing characteristics of services, 89, 172
Marketing Effectiveness Awards, 198
Marketing mix, 50

Marketing objectives, 46, 53
Marketing strategies, 46
Marketing tactics, 46
Mark-up pricing, 113
Mass marketing techniques, 4
Mass production, 4
Media relations, 145
Merchandiser, 122
Mission statement, 30, 46
Monitoring and control, 46
Mothercare, 188
Multi-branding, 83
Multi-channel decisions, 129
Multiple exchanges, 35

New product pricing, 111
Non-adopters, 97
Non-consumers, 97
Non-price competition, 108

Objective and task, 194
Objective settings, 51
Objectives, 45, 148
Online auctions, 112
Online banking, 176
Online catalogues, 111
Ownership, 175

Packaging of industrial goods, 87
Perceptual ma**p**, 190
Perishability, 174
Permission marketing, 37
Personal selling, 37
Planning hierarchy, 48
Point of sale materials, 149
Political environment, 65
Poster advertising, 153
Press releases, 145
Price comparison sites, 111
Price discrimination, 109
Price elasticity of demand, 109
Price leaders, 115
Price leadership, 108
Pricing decisions, 106
Primary financial objectives, 53
Primary objective, 50
Privacy & Electronic Communications Regulations 2003, 38
Product, 79
Product characteristics, 127
Product concept, 10
Product development, 71
Product differentiation, 189
Product levels, 80

Product life cycle, 185
Product line pricing, 114
Product orientation, 11
Product portfolio, 84
Product range, 111
Production concept, 10
Profit, 51
Promotion, 122
Promotion planning, 183
Psychological factors, 69

Qualitative, 51

Quality connotations, 111
Quality control, 57
Quantitative, 50

R&D expenditure, 57

Relationships between employees, 168
Resource allocation, 49
Retailers, 123
Rolls Royce, 188

Sales promotion: objectives, 148

Sales support, 142
Satellite TV, 66
Seamless offering, 18
Segmentation, 157
Selective distribution, 129
Selling concept, 10
Service economy, 89
Service personnel, 168

Service quality, 168
Service-mindedness., 168
Shareholders and PR, 145
Shopping goods, 81
Situation analysis, 46, 49
SMART criteria, 53
Social and cultural environment, 65
Social factors, 69
Social responsibility, 111
Socio-economic classification, 66
Socio-economic groups, 66
Special event pricing, 115
Speciality goods, 81
Staple goods, 81
Sternberg, 30
Stock holding and storage, 122
Strategy, 46
Strategy development, 49
Subsidiary objectives, 52
Supplier characteristics, 128
Suppliers, 29, 111
Switching costs, 34
SWOT analysis, 46

Tangible attributes, 79

Technical quality, 168, 179
Technological environment, 66
Tele-marketing, 147
Text messaging (SMS), 147
Trade exhibitions, 145
Transport, 122

Unsought goods, 81

Review form & Free prize draw

All original review forms from the entire BPP range, completed with genuine comments, will be entered into one of two draws on 31 January 2011 and 31 July 2011. The names on the first four forms picked out on each occasion will be sent a cheque for £50.

Name: _____   **Address:** _____

_____

_____

1. How have you used this Text?
(Tick one box only)

☐ Self study (book only)

☐ On a course: college_____

☐ Other _____

3. Why did you decide to purchase this Text?
(Tick one box only)

☐ Have used companion Assessment workbook

☐ Have used BPP Texts in the past

☐ Recommendation by friend/colleague

☐ Recommendation by a lecturer at college

☐ Saw advertising in journals

☐ Saw website

☐ Other _____

2. During the past six months do you recall seeing/receiving any of the following?
(Tick as many boxes as are relevant)

☐ Our advertisement in *The Marketer*

☐ Our brochure with a letter through the post

☐ Saw website

4. Which (if any) aspects of our advertising do you find useful?
(Tick as many boxes as are relevant)

☐ Prices and publication dates of new editions

☐ Information on product content

☐ Facility to order books off-the-page

☐ None of the above

5. Have you used the companion Assessment Workbook?   Yes ☐   No ☐

6. Have you used the companion Passcards?   Yes ☐   No ☐

7. Your ratings, comments and suggestions would be appreciated on the following areas.

	Very useful	Useful	Not useful
Introductory section (How to use this text, study checklist, etc)	☐	☐	☐
Introduction	☐	☐	☐
Syllabus linked learning outcomes	☐	☐	☐
Activities and Marketing at Work examples	☐	☐	☐
Learning objective reviews	☐	☐	☐
Magic Formula references	☐	☐	☐
Content of suggested answers	☐	☐	☐
Index	☐	☐	☐
Structure and presentation	☐	☐	☐

	Excellent	Good	Adequate	Poor
Overall opinion of this Text	☐	☐	☐	☐

8. Do you intend to continue using BPP CIM Range Products?   ☐ Yes   ☐ No

9. Have you visited bpp.com/lm/cim?   ☐ Yes   ☐ No

10. If you have visited bpp.com/lm/cim, please give a score out of 10 for it's overall usefulness   /10

Please note any further comments and suggestions/errors on the reverse of this page.

Please return to: Rebecca Hart, BPP Learning Media, FREEPOST, London, W12 8BR.

If you have any additional questions, feel free to email cimrange@bpp.com

Review form & Free prize draw (continued)

Please note any further comments and suggestions/errors below.

Free prize draw rules

1 Closing date for 31 January 2011 draw is 31 December 2010. Closing date for 31 July 2011 draw is 30 June 2011.

2 Restricted to entries with UK and Eire addresses only. BPP employees, their families and business associates are excluded.

3 No purchase necessary. Entry forms are available upon request from BPP Learning Media. No more than one entry per title, per person. Draw restricted to persons aged 16 and over.

4 Winners will be notified by post and receive their cheques not later than 6 weeks after the relevant draw date. List of winners will be supplied on request.

5 The decision of the promoter in all matters is final and binding. No correspondence will be entered into.